CAMBRIDGE ECONOMIC HANDBOOKS

Edited by

C. W. GUILLEBAUD, *St. John's College, Cambridge*

and

MILTON FRIEDMAN, *University of Chicago*

Initiated by the late John Maynard Keynes and continued under the successive editorships of D. H. Robertson and C. W. Guillebaud, the Cambridge Economic Handbooks are, in Lord Keynes's words, "intended to convey to the ordinary reader and to the uninitiated student some conception of the general principles of thought which economists now apply to economic problems." The series is now edited jointly by Mr. Guillebaud and Mr. Friedman in order to bring the best American as well as British economic thinking to bear on the major problems of economics in both countries.

The Economics of Under-developed Countries
By PETER T. BAUER *and* BASIL S. YAMEY

International Economics
By ROY F. HARROD

Supply and Demand
By HUBERT HENDERSON

The Business Cycle
By R. C. O. MATTHEWS

The Economics of Trade Unions
By ALBERT REES

Money
By D. H. ROBERTSON

The Structure of Competitive Industry
By E. A. G. ROBINSON

BY R. C. O. MATTHEWS

THE BUSINESS
CYCLE

THE UNIVERSITY OF CHICAGO PRESS

Library of Congress Catalog Card Number: 59-10286

Published by The University of Chicago Press in association with
James Nisbet & Co. Ltd. and The Cambridge University Press

The University of Chicago Press, Chicago 37
James Nisbet & Co. Ltd., Digswell Place, Welwyn, England
The Macmillan Company of Canada, Ltd., Toronto 2

INTRODUCTION

TO THE CAMBRIDGE ECONOMIC HANDBOOKS
BY THE GENERAL EDITORS

SOON after the war of 1914–18 there seemed to be a place for a series of short introductory handbooks, 'intended to convey to the ordinary reader and to the uninitiated student some conception of the general principles of thought which economists now apply to economic problems'.

This Series was planned and edited by the late Lord Keynes under the title 'Cambridge Economic Handbooks' and he wrote for it a General Editorial Introduction of which the words quoted above formed part. In 1936 Keynes handed over the editorship of the Series to Mr. D. H. Robertson, who held it till 1946, when he was succeeded by Mr. C. W. Guillebaud.

It was symptomatic of the changes which had been taking place in the inter-war period in the development of economics, changes associated in a considerable measure with the work and influence of Keynes himself, that within a few years the text of part of the Editorial Introduction should have needed revision. In its original version the last paragraph of the Introduction ran as follows:

'Even on matters of principle there is not yet a complete unanimity of opinion amongst professional economists. Generally speaking, the writers of these volumes believe themselves to be orthodox members of the Cambridge School of Economics. At any rate, most of their ideas about the subject, and even their prejudices, are traceable to the contact they have enjoyed with the writings and lectures of the two economists who have chiefly influenced Cambridge thought for the past fifty years, Dr. Marshall and Professor Pigou.'

Keynes later amended this concluding paragraph to read:

'Even on matters of principle there is not yet a complete unanimity of opinion amongst professional students of the subject. Immediately after the war (of 1914–18) daily economic events were of such a startling character as to divert attention from theoretical complexities. But today, economic science has recovered its wind. Traditional treatments and traditional solutions are being questioned, improved and revised. In the end this activity of research should clear up controversy. But for the moment controversy and doubt are increased. The writers of this Series must apologize to the general reader and to the beginner if many parts of their subject have not yet reached to a degree of certainty and lucidity which would make them easy and straightforward reading.'

Many though by no means all the controversies which Keynes had in mind when he penned these words have since been resolved. The new ideas and new criticisms, which then seemed to threaten to overturn the old orthodoxy, have, in the outcome, been absorbed within it and have served rather to strengthen and deepen it, by adding needed modifications and changing emphasis, and by introducing an altered and on the whole more precise terminology. The undergrowth which for a time concealed that main stream of economic thought to which Keynes referred in his initial comment and to which he contributed so greatly has by now been largely cleared away so that there is again a large measure of agreement among economists of all countries on the fundamental theoretical aspects of their subject.

This agreement on economic analysis is accompanied by wide divergence of views on questions of economic policy. These reflect both different estimates of the quantitative importance of one or another of the conflicting forces involved in any prediction about the consequences of a policy measure and different value judgments about the desirability of the predicted outcome. It still remains as true today as it was when Keynes wrote that—to quote once more from his Introduction:

> 'The Theory of Economics does not furnish a body of settled conclusions immediately applicable to policy. It is a method rather than a doctrine, an apparatus of the mind, a technique of thinking, which helps its possessor to draw correct conclusions.'

This method, while in one sense eternally the same, is in another ever changing. It is continually being applied to new problems raised by the continual shifts in policy views. This is reflected in the wide range of topics covered by the Cambridge Economic Handbooks already published, and in the continual emergence of new topics demanding coverage. Such a series as this should accordingly itself be a living entity, growing and adapting to the changing interests of the times, rather than a fixed number of essays on a set plan.

The wide welcome given to the Series has amply justified the judgment of its founder. Apart from its circulation in the British Empire, it has been published from the start in the United States of America, and translations of the principal volumes have appeared in a number of foreign languages.

The present change to joint Anglo-American editorship is designed to increase still further the usefulness of the Series by expanding the range of potential topics, authors and readers alike. It will succeed in its aim if it enables us to bring to a wide audience on both sides of the Atlantic lucid explanations and significant applications of 'that technique of thinking' which is the hallmark of economics as a science.

April 1957

C. W. GUILLEBAUD
MILTON FRIEDMAN

ACKNOWLEDGMENTS

In writing this book I have been much indebted for what I have learnt in discussions of the subject over a period of years with economists in Cambridge, especially Dr. R. M. Goodwin, Mr. N. Kaldor, Mrs. Joan Robinson, and Professor J. S. Duesenberry when he was on a visit here. My thanks are also due to Professor W. J. Fellner, Mr. A. Silberston, Mrs. Joan Robinson, and the general editors of the series, all of whom read through the manuscript and made many valuable suggestions, and to Mr. K. E. Berrill, who performed the same service at the proof stage. None of these people is in any way responsible for my conclusions or the way I have presented them.

R. C. O. MATTHEWS

Cambridge, 1958

ACKNOWLEDGEMENTS

In writing this book I have been much indebted to many
persons for discussing with me various points raised in it,
and specially Dr. Schneider, Professor Dr. W. J. Jordan,
Mr. R. Falkner, Mr. John Thompson and Professor J. G.
Troughton. My particular thanks are also due to Mr. Clarke
who has helped me to correct the proofs, to Mr. A. Spenser
and in particular for the general subject of the matter upon
which he has taken pains to read with great care, and
specially also to Mr. K. T. Thorpe, who performed the final
work of the proofs and in book of the corrections in any
way responsible for the many errors in the way I have prepared them.

R. M. P. Morrison.

Cambridge 1957

CONTENTS

CHAPTER IV

INVESTMENT: (2) REPLACEMENT, TECHNICAL PROGRESS, AND OTHER INFLUENCES

CHAPTER V

INVENTORY INVESTMENT

CHAPTER VI

INVESTMENT IN HOUSE-BUILDING

CHAPTER VII

CONSUMPTION

CHAPTER VIII

MONEY AND FINANCE

CHAPTER IX

THE CEILING

CHAPTER X

THE LOWER TURNING POINT

CHAPTER XI

INTERNATIONAL ASPECTS

CHAPTER XII

PERIODICITY AND THE PROBLEM OF MAJOR AND MINOR CYCLES

CHAPTER XIII

THE TREND AND THE CYCLE

CHAPTER XIV

POLICY FOR THE CONTROL OF THE CYCLE

CHAPTER I

INTRODUCTORY

UNLIKE the subjects of most of the volumes in this series, the business cycle is a specific problem rather than a field of study. It is a phenomenon which calls for explanation. In almost all countries since the time they began to industrialise or to come into contact with industrial countries, the path of economic growth has been punctuated by fluctuations in income and employment.[1] Sometimes these fluctuations have been mild, sometimes they have been catastrophic. It is our business to try to understand why they have happened. Such an understanding should assist in devising policies to control fluctuations in the future.

Observation of the general course of events in actual historical fluctuations, together with deductive reasoning based on certain assumptions about economic behaviour, have between them suggested numbers of possible hypotheses as to why fluctuations occur. These hypotheses are to some extent conflicting and to some extent complementary with one another. A really comprehensive treatment of the problem of the cycle would require one to set forth the various alternative hypotheses and, after discarding any that did not stand up to the test of logical consistency, decide in the light of detailed study of observed fluctuations which of the remainder most satisfactorily accounted for the facts. In the course of such a study one would not, of course, expect to find that exactly the same conclusions held good for all countries and all periods of time; but in so far as there is a broad family

[1] An outline picture of the historical course of fluctuations in the United States and in Great Britain may be seen from Diagrams 1 (p. 5), 8 (p. 207), 9 (p. 217), and 10 (p. 219).

1

resemblance between different historical fluctuations, one
would certainly expect to find some important causal elements
in common.

The purpose of the present book is less ambitious. This
book is mainly theoretical, in the sense that most of our
space will be devoted to expounding hypotheses and considering their logical bases and implications. Our aim will be
not so much to make universally valid empirical generalisa-
tions as to provide a theoretical framework within which any
particular phase of historical experience of fluctuations, including the experience of the present day, can usefully be
studied. A certain amount of empirical material will be
included, and an attempt will be made throughout to indicate
in a summary fashion the plausibility of alternative hypotheses in relation to the facts; but the evidence will not for
the most part be analysed in any systematic way. Much of
the basic research that would be required for making such a
systematic analysis properly has yet to be done, despite the
enormous amount of literature in existence on the cycle. An
inherent difficulty in this sort of research is that the working
of the economy is so complex that the evidence usually
admits of a wide variety of interpretations. It is difficult even
with respect to a single cycle to establish or disprove a hypothesis conclusively, and generalisation is still more difficult.

Our discussion will have reference mainly to advanced or
relatively advanced countries.

Historically, fluctuations have taken place around a path
of long-run growth. The relation between the forces making
for growth and those making for fluctuations is one of the
most important issues in the theory of the cycle. Unfortunately the theory of growth is at present in an even more
unsettled and controversial state than the theory of the cycle.
As much of the theory of the cycle can be stated more or less
independently of the exact nature of the underlying growth
process, our procedure in most of this book will be to bring
in considerations relating to growth only at points where

they are an essential part of the argument. The relation between growth and fluctuations will then be discussed more systematically towards the end.

What are economic fluctuations fluctuations of? As a first approximation it does not much matter exactly how this question is answered, since as a rule roughly the same path is followed by all the chief indices of the state of prosperity in the economy—national income, production, employment, prices, profits and so on. Admittedly some of these are more volatile than others, and they are not all subject to an equally strong upward trend; thus we may find that in a year when employment falls, production merely suffers a retardation in its rate of growth. But the broad conformity is clear. However, for precision it is best to take a single yardstick, and the most obvious one is national income. Hence when we speak of economic fluctuations, we normally refer to fluctuations in national income measured at current prices.

There is general agreement that cyclical fluctuations in national income are caused by changes in the level of aggregate demand. Changes in supply conditions may play a significant part in the cycle, but it is the rise and fall in demand that constitutes its essence. The simplest demonstration of this is that in the typical boom output and prices both rise, and in the typical slump output and prices both fall. This like movement of prices and output is what is to be expected from fluctuations in *demand*. If fluctuations arose chiefly from the side of supply, we should expect instead to find output and prices moving in opposite directions.

The task then is to explain why there are fluctuations in aggregate demand, i.e. in aggregate expenditure.

Expenditure can be divided into two main components: consumers' expenditure on goods and services, referred to as consumption; and expenditure on fixed and working capital, referred to as investment. It is fluctuations in investment that are generally held to lie at the heart of the cycle.[1] The reasons for this belief are partly *a priori* and partly empirical.

On the *a priori* side, it is to be expected that the level of *consumption* spending will mainly depend on the level of the national income, since by far the greater part of consumption is paid for out of current income. If this is so, changes in consumption are to be regarded as a consequence rather than as an original cause of changes in income. Admittedly the amount of consumption expenditure that will take place at a given level of income may alter from one year to the next for various reasons, but such alterations are not likely in the normal case to be very large, and it would certainly be surprising if they followed a regular cyclical pattern. *Investment*, on the other hand, is paid for mainly out of borrowing or past savings, not out of current income. Investment will indeed be affected by the current level of national income, since investment decisions are dictated by profit expectations, and the level of national income is one of the considerations entering into these expectations. But as will be seen in the following chapters, it is by no means the only consideration. Investment is therefore more likely than consumption to vary independently and hence be an original cause of fluctuations in income.

On the empirical side, it is found that fluctuations in investment have almost always been much more violent proportionally than fluctuations in consumption. In fact in many of the less severe recessions, the fall in national income has been confined to investment, and consumption has re-

---

[1] A third component of total expenditure is expenditure by the government. It is not plausible to regard government expenditure as the main cause of past fluctuations, since the general tendency has been for government expenditure to be relatively stable, and until recent times it was only a small proportion of national income. This is not to say, of course, that government spending may not sometimes have played an important part in determining the level of demand in earlier times, as it has undoubtedly done since the war and is likely to continue to do in the future.

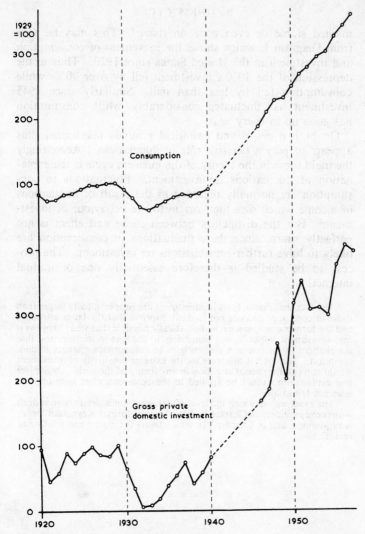

DIAGRAM 1. Consumption and gross private domestic investment at current prices in the United States, 1920–57, expressed as percentages of their values in 1929. *Source: U.S. Department of Commerce.*

mained stable or even gone on rising.[1] This may be seen from Diagram 1, which shows the movement of consumption and investment in the United States since 1920. Thus in the depression of the 1930's investment fell by over 90%, while consumption fell by less than half. Similarly since 1945 investment has fluctuated considerably, while consumption has gone up in every year.

On both *a priori* and empirical grounds investment thus appears to play a decisive rôle in fluctuations. Accordingly the main topic in the theory of the business cycle is the explanation of fluctuations in investment. Fluctuations in consumption are normally regarded as the result of fluctuations in income which owe their origin to the behaviour of investment.[2] But the distinction between cause and effect is not perfectly sharp, since these fluctuations in consumption are likely to have further repercussions on investment. The process to be studied is therefore essentially one of mutual interaction.

[1] The fact that fluctuations in investment are proportionally larger than those in consumption does not in itself disprove that the latter are cause and the former effect, since it is theoretically possible that what happens is that investment responds very sensitively to changes in income, and that the changes in income owe their origins to autonomous changes in consumption. But even if this were so, the extreme sensitivity of investment would still call for special attention in any theory of the cycle. Moreover this explanation cannot be applied to the occasions when consumption does not fall at all.

[2] The exact way in which the level of consumption is determined is dealt with more explicitly in Chapter II, § 1, where the formal Keynesian theory is expounded, and in Chapter VII, which treats the matter more fully and realistically.

CHAPTER II

SOME FORMAL MODELS OF THE CYCLE

THE hypothesis regarding investment which in one form or another is most widely held to be the explanation of fluctuations is the acceleration principle. The purpose of the present chapter is to show in formal terms the mechanism by which cyclical fluctuations can result if investment is determined by the acceleration principle and consumption is determined by the level of income. This will enable us at the same time to introduce a number of concepts that have a wide application in business cycle theory and are not confined in their use to theories based on the acceleration principle. For the moment we shall state the acceleration principle in crude and dogmatic form in order to concentrate on showing the mechanism by which it is capable of leading to cycles. Critical analysis of the economic basis of the acceleration principle and also of the factors influencing consumption is deferred to later chapters.

The corner-stone of the analysis in this chapter is the postulate of a twofold relationship between national income and investment. In the first place, the level of investment determines the level of income and consumption through the multiplier process (§ 1). In the second place, the level of national income affects the size of the capital stock that is needed and so influences the inducement to add to the stock of capital by means of investment—the acceleration principle (§ 2). The interaction of these two distinct relationships is liable to lead to fluctuations (§ 3–§ 7).[1]

[1] Parts of this chapter are unavoidably difficult, since it is necessary to treat much of the formal theory of the cycle at this stage in order to provide a rigorous background for the more realistic discussion later on. Readers who find this chapter heavy going are asked not to be discouraged and are assured that most of what follows in later chapters is less abstract and less mathematical.

§ **1. The Multiplier.** The theory of the multiplier sets out to show how the level of national income will react to changes in investment, the latter being for the moment regarded as independently determined. The theory of the multiplier is based on the doctrine that the other main component of national income, consumption, rises and falls as income rises and falls, but by less than the full amount of the change in income, the balance being devoted to saving. The proportion of an *increase* in income that is devoted to consumption is called the marginal propensity to consume, and the proportion of an increase in income that is devoted to saving is called the marginal propensity to save. The marginal propensity to consume and the marginal propensity to save are thus together equal to unity. The proportions of *total* income devoted to consumption and saving respectively are called the average propensity to consume and the average propensity to save.

Suppose investment rises to a higher level than before and stays at the new high level. Incomes earned in the investment industries rise, and their recipients increase their purchases of consumer goods. The producers from whom they make these purchases in turn enjoy increased incomes and increase their consumption. And so on, with increases in income spreading out over a wider and wider range. The consequent rise in the national income does not, however, proceed *ad infinitum*. Part of the extra incomes earned are saved rather than spent, and the amount passed on from one round to the next is therefore always diminishing. Just as the increase in investment represented an injection into the circular flow of incomes, so the increase in saving constitutes a leakage from it. When these offsetting forces are equal to each other, income will have no further tendency to change. Equilibrium will thus be reached when incomes have risen sufficiently to increase the amount that people want to save by an extent equal to the rise in investment that started the process off. This point will be reached when income has risen by an amount equal to the original increase in invest-

ment multiplied by the reciprocal of the marginal propensity
to save. Thus if the original increase in investment is £1000,
and the marginal propensity to save is $\frac{1}{10}$, equilibrium will
be reached when income has risen by £10,000, because that
is what is needed to induce extra saving of £1000. The
reciprocal of the marginal propensity to save—in this example
10—is called the multiplier.

This may be illustrated by means of a diagram (Diagram
2). Income is measured along the horizontal axis, saving
and investment along the vertical axis. The line OS shows
the amount saved at any level of income. Saving is here
assumed to be a constant proportion of income, so that the
marginal propensity to save (proportion of additional income

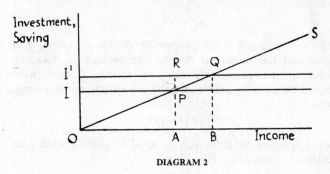

DIAGRAM 2

saved) is equal to the *average* propensity to save (the proportion of total income saved). The slope of OS (equal to AP/OA
or BQ/OB or PR/RQ) thus measures both the marginal and
the average propensity to save. Initially investment is OI
and income is at the level OA, which generates saving equal
to OI. Investment now rises to OI′. Income will rise, and
it will go on rising till it reaches the level OB, where saving
is generated equal to the new value of investment, OI′. The
multiplier is equal to the increase in income, RQ, divided by
the increase in investment, PR. This is equal to the reciprocal of the marginal propensity to save.

In principle, some period of time must always elapse between the receipt of income and its expenditure. *A fortiori*, time must elapse between a rise in investment and the establishment of income at its new equilibrium level, since this requires a number of rounds of expenditure.[1] In practice, however, changes in expenditure as a rule follow rapidly upon changes in income, and it is therefore an adequate approximation for many purposes to ignore the timelag.[2] The establishment of income at the level indicated by the multiplier can then be treated as an instantaneous process.

The foregoing can be summed up as follows, in a notation that will be much used in the rest of this chapter. The relation between saving and income for the economy is given by the equation.

$$S_t = sY_t,$$

where S is saving, s is the proportion of income saved, Y is income and the subscripts denote time-periods (S_t meaning 'saving during period t', and so forth). Consumption (denoted by C) is by definition equal to income minus saving. Hence

$$C_t = (1-s)Y_t.$$

Likewise income by definition is equal to consumption plus investment (denoted by I). Thus

$$Y_t = C_t + I_t$$
$$\therefore \ Y_t = (1-s)Y_t + I_t$$
$$sY_t = I_t$$
$$Y_t = \frac{I_t}{s}.$$

The last line is the multiplier relationship.

[1] Theoretically an infinite number of rounds, but the first few rounds will suffice to bring income near to the equilibrium level.

[2] Cf. L. A. Metzler, 'Three Lags in the Circular Flow of Income', in *Income, Employment and Public Policy, Essays in honor of Alvin Hansen* (1948), pp. 11–32.

So far we have assumed that the proportion of income saved is constant irrespective of the level of income. In practice the relation between saving and income in the course of a cycle more often resembles the pattern shown in Diagram 3. Here, as in Diagram 2, income is measured along the horizontal axis and saving along the vertical axis. The line

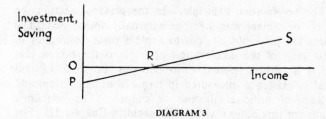

DIAGRAM 3

PS shows the amount saved at any level of income. The ratio of saving to income—the average propensity to save—rises as income rises.[1] If income is OR, saving is zero, and if income is below OR, saving is negative. The *marginal* propensity to save, as measured by the slope of PS, is constant: whatever the level of income, the proportion of an *increase* in income devoted to saving will be the same. This may be written algebraically

$$S_t = sY_t - Z,$$

where s is the marginal propensity to save and Z is a constant. (The constant, Z, is equivalent to OP in Diagram 3; it is the amount of negative saving that would take place at zero income.) In this case

$$C_t = Y_t - S_t = (1-s)Y_t + Z,$$

and the multiplier equation becomes

$$Y_t = C_t + I_t = (1-s)Y_t + Z + I_t = \frac{I_t}{s} + \frac{Z}{s};$$

[1] The reasons why this happens will be discussed more fully in Chapter VII. For the present it will suffice if consumption habits are thought of as being subject to some inertia, so that, when income changes, consumption does not change in full proportion.

income is equal to investment multiplied by the reciprocal of the marginal propensity to save plus a constant. The constant, Z/s, is equivalent to OR in Diagram 3; it is that level of income that causes saving to be zero. The presence of the constant term indicates that even if investment were zero, income would have a positive value, viz. Z/s.

§ 2. **The Acceleration Principle.** In the previous section the level of investment was taken as externally determined. The acceleration principle sets out to explain what determines it.

The basis of the acceleration principle is the notion that there is a certain normal ratio between the stock of real capital in existence (measured in terms of money value) and the level of national income or output. The economic grounds for this notion will be discussed in Chapter III. For the present it will suffice to think of it as essentially a technical matter. If in a representative industry plant and equipment costing £1000 are needed to produce an annual output of 50 units of product, each worth £10, the ratio of the value of capital to annual output will be 2. This ratio is not necessarily fixed rigidly; if the plant and equipment were worked very intensively they might be able to turn out more than 50 units a year, and on the other hand if they were left idle for part of the time they would produce less. But given the state of technique and the prices of factors of production, there will be a certain capital-output ratio that will be normal in the sense of involving neither strain nor under-utilisation of capacity.

The amount of capital that entrepreneurs will aim to have —the desired stock of capital—will therefore depend on the level of demand for final output. The latter, for the economy as a whole, is determined by national income. If we now make the further assumption that entrepreneurs are in general successful in adjusting the stock of capital to the amount desired, the stock of capital in existence at any time will be a function of the level of national income. Hence the *rate of addition* to the stock of capital will be a function of the *rate of increase* of national income. But the rate of addition to the stock of capital is the same thing as net investment (gross investment minus replacement). Hence the level of net investment is a function of the rate of increase of national income. This is the acceleration principle.

If v is the normal capital-output ratio, the acceleration principle in its simplest form may be written algebraically as,

$$I_t = v(Y_t - Y_{t-1});$$

the amount of investment done during a period will be such as to raise the capital stock by an amount equal to the increase in income since the previous period multiplied by the normal capital-output ratio. (It is convenient to divide the flow of time into discrete 'periods', but, at the present stage of the argument this is merely a matter of exposition, and the duration of the 'period' may be defined arbitrarily.[1])

§ 3. The Interaction of the Multiplier and the Acceleration Principle: Instability.

Two distinct relationships between income and investment have now been established. According to the multiplier equation, the level of income depends upon the level of investment. According to the acceleration principle, the level of investment depends upon the rate of change of income.

How can these two relationships be reconciled? At first sight they may seem irreconcilable. For example, if investment is constant over time, the multiplier will bring about a constant level of income; but in order to get a constant level of investment the acceleration principle requires not a constant level of income but a constant increase per period in the level of income. Evidently investment cannot be constant without one or other of the two relations being broken.

But a constant level of investment is not the only possibility. Let us investigate the matter more systematically by setting

---

[1] If investment projects require a certain minimum time to complete, however, the duration of the 'period' must be not less than this minimum. The concept of the 'period' is discussed further below.

the two equations against each other. We consider first the case where the proportion of income saved is constant. We then have

$$Y_t = \frac{I_t}{s} \quad \text{and} \quad I_t = v(Y_t - Y_{t-1}).$$

If both equations are satisfied, it follows by substituting the second equation in the first that

$$Y_t = \frac{v}{s}(Y_t - Y_{t-1})$$

$$= \frac{v}{v-s}Y_{t-1}.$$

The result is thus an equation of the type known as a difference equation: the variable Y is expressed as a function of its own value in a previous period. (Where, as here, Y_t is determined entirely by Y_{t-1}, the equation is called a first-order difference equation; if Y_t depended partly on Y_{t-1} and partly on Y_{t-2}, it would be called a second-order difference equation; and so on.) The requirements of the multiplier and the acceleration principle will thus both be satisfied if income in each period is a constant multiple, namely $v/(v-s)$, of income in the previous period. Since the marginal propensity to save s is likely to be well below unity and the capital-output ratio v well above unity,[1] it is safe to assume that v is greater than s. $v/(v-s)$ will then be positive and greater than unity, and the equation therefore means that income must grow at a constant proportional rate. For example if v is 3 and s is $\frac{1}{2}$, income must grow by 20% in each period. The following table illustrates the way in which the system might move in that case.

[1] The expression v measures the normal ratio between the stock of capital at a point of time and the flow of output over a period of time. In order to give a numerical value to v it is therefore necessary to specify the period over which the flow of output is to be measured. As will be explained presently, the version of the acceleration principle at present under discussion is not plausible unless the duration of the 'periods' t, $t-1$, etc., is very short. Hence the value of v appropriate in the present context will be correspondingly high. (The ratio of capital to *annual* output has usually been found to be well in excess of unity.) See also Chapter III, p. 50, n. 1.

Period	Income	Investment	Capital at start of period
1	100·0	50·0	250
2	120·0	60·0	300
3	144·0	72·0	360
4	172·8	86·4	432

If the multiplier equation is of the second type considered in § 1, namely

$$Y_t = \frac{I_t}{s} + \frac{Z}{s},$$

the equation resulting from the interaction of the multiplier and the acceleration principle becomes

$$Y_t = \frac{v}{v-s} Y_{t-1} - \frac{Z}{v-s}.$$

The result here is similar to what it was in the former case, with the difference that if Y starts off at a level below Z/s, the path it will need to follow in order to satisfy both multiplier and acceleration principle will be one of cumulative contraction rather than cumulative expansion. (This is because net investment in that case is negative, i.e. the production of capital goods is less than sufficient to provide for the replacement of those that are passing out of use through wear and obsolescence, and income must therefore be falling if the capital-income ratio is to stay constant.) There is, moreover, a possible equilibrium position where $Y = Z/s$, $I = 0$, and the stock of capital (denoted by K) $= vZ/s$. (The corresponding equilibrium point in the case where there is no constant term in the multiplier equation is when $Y = 0$.) This is an equilibrium position in the sense that if it prevails there is no inherent reason for anything to alter. But the equilibrium so represented is unstable. An accidental disturbance in either direction will lead to a cumulative movement up or down, not to the restoration of equilibrium. This is easily shown. Suppose that, as in the example above, $v = 3$, $s = \frac{1}{2}$, and that initially $Y = 100$, $K = 300$, and $I = 0$. If net investment were now accidentally to rise to some positive level, say 10, K would rise to 310 and Y would rise to 120 (by the multiplier). The ratio of capital to income would therefore fall, and the incentive to add to the stock of capital, i.e. do net investment, would increase rather than diminish. I would therefore have no tendency to revert to its original level of zero, but would diverge from it by increasing amounts. Likewise if the original accidental departure of net investment from zero were in a downward direction, income would be reduced by more than in proportion to the stock of capital, there would be excess capacity and an inducement to allow the stock of capital to fall more rapidly still. Equilibrium is bound to be unstable in this way so long as v is greater than s.

It emerges therefore that the interaction of the multiplier and the acceleration principle as so far formulated does not lead to any stable equilibrium for income. Nor, on the other hand, does it lead to cyclical fluctuations. Instead, it leads to a cumulative movement, which could be either upward or downward, away from a notional point of unstable equilibrium. If income and investment happened to be in the notional equilibrium position, there would be no inherent reason for them to depart from it; but if for any chance reason investment *were* to rise above the equilibrium level, it would raise income through the multiplier to such an extent that the required stock of capital would rise by more than the actual stock of capital had risen, and a cumulative increase in investment and income would be set in train.

Cyclical fluctuations may, however, come about if certain further assumptions are introduced. These we now consider.

§ 4. Non-linearity or 'Buffers'.

One way in which fluctuations may come about is as follows. Suppose that movements in income have cumulative tendencies of the sort just described, but that these cumulative movements are prevented from going beyond a certain point in either direction by the existence of boundaries or 'buffers'. We are not concerned at present to assess the economic plausibility of this but merely to work out its consequences. Suppose for example that an upper buffer or ceiling comes into operation when full employment of labour is reached. When this point arrives further growth of output becomes physically impossible. It might be thought that if the cumulative process carried income up to this point, equilibrium could then be maintained there. But the acceleration principle prevents this. Income can remain high only so long as investment remains high, and investment can be high only so long as income is *rising*. Once the full employment ceiling has halted the rise in income, it ceases to be necessary to add to the stock of capital, and net investment falls off to nothing. The fall in investment pulls down income through the multiplier, an inducement appears to *reduce* the stock of capital, and the cumulative expansion turns into a cumulative contraction.

A lower buffer or floor to the contraction process may operate in similar fashion. Such a buffer could appear when gross fixed investment (i.e. fixed investment including replacement) has fallen to zero. At this point investment can fall no further. Income therefore ceases to fall as well. But as soon as income ceases to fall, the desired stock of capital ceases to fall. So once the existing excess capacity has been worked off, there is no need for further negative net investment. Net investment rises from the negative level where it has been, income is pulled up with it, and the cumulative process goes into reverse.

The system therefore oscillates between its lower and upper limits; it bounces from one buffer to another, its inherent instability preventing it from coming to rest between them.

For this result to occur it is not necessary that the limits should be absolute. It is sufficient if the cumulative expansion or contraction becomes subject to some substantial retardation as soon as it passes beyond a certain point. Thus at the upper turning point a slackening in the rate of growth of output caused by the approach to full employment can operate through the acceleration principle to bring about an actual fall in investment, and this will set the cumulative process into reverse. Similarly at the lower turning point.

The essential condition for such a slowing down and hence reversal of the cumulative process to occur is that at very high or very low levels of income special forces should come into operation which are not active at other times. The relationships described by the multiplier and the acceleration principle do not then hold in the same form at all levels of income. This may be expressed in more technical language by saying that the relationships are *non-linear*. The relationship between two variables is said to be non-linear if the ratio between a change in the independent variable and the consequential change in the dependent variable is not constant but is different for different values of the variables, so that if the two are plotted respectively on the two axes of a chart, the curve expressing the relationship between them is not a straight line. Thus if investment depends on the rate of change of income but cannot go below a certain level, viz. that of zero gross investment, it follows that if the rate of fall of income is already such as to cause zero gross investment, a still more rapid rate of fall of income would not lead to any further reduction in investment, and the relationship between investment and the rate of change of income will be as shown in Diagram 4. The acceleration principle is then a non-linear relationship. The conclusion of the present section may thus be stated by saying that cyclical fluctuations may result from the interaction of the multiplier and the acceleration principle if one or both of these relationships is non-linear.

§ 5.   **Time-lags and the Concept of Overshooting.** The second way in which the instability of the unqualified multiplier-

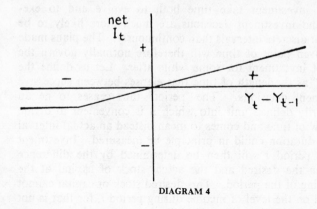

DIAGRAM 4

accelerator interaction may be modified into a cycle is quite different from that just considered. It is by the existence of a time-lag at some point in the working of the system. As will be seen shortly, the existence of any substantial time-lag might in principle cause the system to fluctuate, but one particular time-lag is probably the most important in practice, and it is it that we shall consider now.

The acceleration principle, as stated in § 2, laid down that the increase in income between period 1 and period 2 is what determines the level of investment in period 2. This is what follows from the assumption that entrepreneurs succeed all the time in adjusting the stock of capital to the level that is appropriate in the light of the current national income. But in practice it is unlikely, to say the least, that a change in national income will be matched immediately by a change in the capital stock. For this to happen it would be necessary that the process of deciding upon and carrying out investment plans should be literally a continuous one, so that the amount of investment could be altered as soon as a change of income occurred. The duration of the 'period', in other words, would have to approximate to zero. In reality plans involving capital investment take time both to evolve and to execute, and investment decisions are much more likely to be made at discrete intervals than continuously. The plans made at a given point of time will therefore normally govern the level of investment for some while after. Let us define the 'period' as the length of time that elapses between successive investment decisions.[1] The 'period' thus ceases to be an arbitrarily defined unit into which it is convenient to divide the flow of time and comes to mean instead an actual interval whose duration could in principle be measured. Investment during period t will then be determined by the difference between the desired and the actual stock of capital at the beginning of the period. This desired stock of capital cannot depend on the level of income during period t, for that is not yet known at the time when the investment decisions are made. Rather, it will depend on income during the previous period, $t-1$. Hence, writing X_t for the desired and K_t for the actual stock of capital respectively at the start of period t, we have

$$I_t = X_t - K_t$$
$$= vY_{t-1} - K_t.$$

Similarly

$$I_{t-1} = X_{t-1} - K_{t-1}$$
$$= vY_{t-2} - K_{t-1}$$

and hence

$$vY_{t-2} = K_{t-1} + I_{t-1}$$
$$= K_t.$$

Therefore substituting vY_{t-2} for K_t in the expression in the second line above, we have

$$I_t = v(Y_{t-1} - Y_{t-2}).$$

[1] We assume for the present that the length of time elapsing between successive investment decisions is not less than the length of time required to carry out investment decisions (the 'gestation period') so that investment decisions made at the beginning of one period have been fully carried into execution by the beginning of the next period. For consideration of the case where this is not so, see Chapter III, § 2, and Chapter IV, § 1.

In other words because of the time-lags involved in planning and carrying out investment, the level of investment during a period depends not on the increase in income since the previous period, but on the increase in income that occurred between the previous period and the one before that.

This *lagged* form of the acceleration principle is much more plausible than the unlagged form we have been using hitherto. We shall now go on to show that the interaction of it with the multiplier is capable of leading to fluctuations in income, even in the absence of buffers.[1]

It will be convenient to take the case where the marginal propensity to save is not equal to the average propensity to save and the multiplier equation therefore contains a constant term.   The two basic equations are then

$$Y_t = \frac{I_t}{s} + \frac{Z}{s} \quad \text{and} \quad I_t = v(Y_{t-1} - Y_{t-2}).$$

Substituting for I_t in the first equation, we get

$$Y_t = \frac{v}{s}(Y_{t-1} - Y_{t-2}) + \frac{Z}{s}.$$

This is similar to the equation derived in § 3 in that income is shown to depend on its own value in the past. In the present case, however, income depends on its value in two former periods instead of in one former period only: the equation is a second-order difference equation. Because of this, it is not nearly so obvious what path income must follow over time for it to be satisfied.

The easiest way to approach the problem is by means of an arithmetical example.   Let us assume that $v = \frac{3}{5}$ and that

[1] The following model of the cycle is similar in general type, though not in details, to the so-called 'Hansen-Samuelson model': cf. P. A. Samuelson, 'Interactions between the Multiplier Analysis and the Principle of Acceleration', *Review of Economic Statistics*, 1939, pp. 75–8.

$s = \frac{1}{2}$.[1] We suppose that initially Y is constant at a level of 100, and the capital stock K is constant at 60. This is a possible equilibrium position that has no inherent tendency to alter. The capital-output ratio is normal, and since income is constant, net investment is zero and income equals consumption. Suppose that there now occurs an autonomous rise in the propensity to consume, in the form of a once-for-all increase in the constant term Z. How does the system react to this disturbance? It will be recalled that on the assumptions of § 3, the system's reaction to a disturbance manifested complete instability. On the present assumptions, its reaction is different. The movement over time of income, consumption, net investment and the quantity of capital will be as shown in the table on p. 23.[2] To help make the arithmetic clear, the relations between the variables are recapitulated in algebraical terms in the panel at the top of the table.

What emerges is a regular cycle in each of the four magnitudes Y, C, I and K. The economic meaning of the sequence may be described in words as follows. The autonomous rise in consumption and income in period 3 increases the amount of capital needed. Because of the time-lag in reaction, the investment required to raise the stock of capital is not undertaken till period 4, and the stock of capital has not been raised to the required level till the beginning of period 5. In the meanwhile the increase in investment in period 4 has raised income further so that the stock of capital available at the beginning of period 5 is no longer adequate. Further investment is therefore undertaken during period 5. The rise in income between periods 3 and 4 having been only slightly greater than that between periods 2 and 3, the amount

[1] The value assumed for v is unrealistically low, but it simplifies the exposition at this stage by lessening the impact of certain complications that are discussed in § 6.

[2] It must be understood that investment throughout is defined as net investment, so that the negative investment shown in periods 7 to 9 means that investment falls below the replacement level by the amount indicated. Certain difficulties involved in this procedure will be discussed later.

$I_t = v(Y_{t-1} - Y_{t-2})$ by the acceleration principle.

$Y_t = \dfrac{I_t}{s} + \dfrac{Z}{s},$ by the multiplier.

$C_t = (1-s)Y_t + Z.$

$K_t = K_{t-1} + I_{t-1},$ by definition.

Putting $v = \frac{3}{5}$, $s = \frac{1}{2}$,

$I_t = \frac{3}{5}(Y_{t-1} - Y_{t-2})$

$Y_t = 2I_t + 2Z$

$C_t = \frac{1}{2}Y_t + Z.$

Initially $Y = 100$, $K = 60$, $I = 0$, $Z = 50$. In period 3, Z rises autonomously to 75 and remains at this level in subsequent periods.

Period	Z	I	Y	C	K at start of period
1	50	0	100	100	60
2	50	0	100	100	60
3	75	0	150	150	60
4	75	+30	210	180	60
5	75	+36	222	186	90
6	75	+7	164	157	126
7	75	−35	81	115	133
8	75	−50	50	100	99
9	75	−19	113	131	49
10	75	+38	225	188	30
11	75	+68	285	218	68
12	75	+36	222	186	135

(*The figures are given in each case correct to the nearest digit. This is responsible for the occasional slight discrepancies between Y and the sum of C and I and between K_t and the sum of K_{t-1} and I_{t-1}.*)

of investment needed in period 5 to raise the stock of capital to the level appropriate to income in period 4 is not much more than the amount of investment that was needed in period 4 to raise the stock of capital to the level appropriate to the income of period 3. For this reason investment and income do not rise very much in period 5. As a result the stock of capital available at the start of period 6 is nearly adequate in relation to the income of period 5, and only a small amount of net investment is undertaken in period 6. Investment in period 6 is thus lower than it was in period 5. Income therefore falls and a general contraction begins. As income falls, the stock of capital required diminishes, and net investment becomes negative. Income is thus further reduced, but the contraction ultimately comes to an end and recovery begins. The details of the contraction process and lower turning point can be worked out in terms similar to those just used for the expansion and upper turning point.

In this example the system is never in equilibrium again after period 2. However its fluctuations take place around certain central values: 150 for Y, 150 for C, 0 for I and 90 for K. If these values were once fairly established, the system would again be in equilibrium. But they never are. When the original disturbance takes place in period 3, income rises towards its new equilibrium value; but the mechanics of the system are such that it does not rest there and instead *overshoots* the mark and rises further. Presently it falls, but in its fall it again overshoots and falls too far; and so on indefinitely. The crucial feature of the system's behaviour is this persistent tendency to overshoot the mark in moving towards a possible equilibrium. The tendency to overshoot is closely related to the existence of a lag somewhere in the adjustment process.

The particular lag chosen above is not the only one capable of leading to this result. The relation between lagged adjustments and cyclical fluctuations can be illustrated by means of a celebrated mechanical analogy. Consider the case of a thermostatically controlled stove in which the input of fuel is automatically regulated by the temperature of the room that it heats. The temperature of the room in turn depends on the input of fuel. But it takes some time for the fuel fed into the fire to raise the room temperature, so this relation is subject to a lag. If now the temperature of the room falls below the desired level, the thermostatic regulator will cause more fuel to be added. Given time, this addition of fuel would be sufficient to raise the temperature to the desired extent. But at first the room temperature will scarcely be raised at all. The regulator will therefore go on adding fuel even though that already in the fire would be enough once it is fairly alight. In consequence the temperature presently rises above the desired level: equilibrium has been overshot. Fuel input will then be reduced. But now again equilibrium will be overshot, since the reduction of fuel input will not immediately lower the room temperature. The regulator will therefore reduce the input of fuel to an excessive degree, and the room, having formerly been too warm, will become too cold. And so on. Oscillations of this type and the means of avoiding them have been a good deal studied by engineers.

The economic analogy to the lagged response of the room temperature to the fuel input in the model worked out above was the lag in adjusting the stock of capital to its appropriate level in relation to income. This lag caused the system to fluctuate. The matter may be put in another way thus. In the equation

$$Y_t = \frac{v}{s}(Y_{t-1} - Y_{t-2}) + \frac{Z}{s},$$

Y_t varies directly with Y_{t-1} and inversely with Y_{t-2}. The direct dependence of Y_t on Y_{t-1} gives the system a tendency to cumulative movement up or down. In the unlagged case considered in § 3, this unstable tendency was free to operate unrestrained. In the present case, however, it is restrained by the inverse dependence of Y_t on Y_{t-2}. Cumulative movement away from the central equilibrium position is thus subject to a regulator, but the regulating mechanism works with a lag and is therefore liable to bring about fluctuations.

§ 6. Damping and Erratic Shocks.

It was shown in the previous section that a second-order difference equation is capable of leading to a cycle. It must now be explained that it will not necessarily do so, and that if it does there are two types of cycle it can produce. There are in fact four general types of possible result. These are shown in Diagram 5, which illustrates the path of income through time following upon some initial disturbance in an upward direction.

In case (1) income converges steadily to an equilibrium level. In case (2) income explodes upwards at an increasing pace. In case (3) income fluctuates in cycles of diminishing amplitude which converge upon an equilibrium level. These are called damped cycles. In case (4) the system fluctuates around the same central value as in case (3), but the fluctuations are of increasing amplitude. They are called anti-damped cycles. Cases (1) and (3) resemble each other in their stability, i.e. their tendency to move towards an equilibrium, while cases (2) and (4) are alike in their instability, i.e. their tendency to diverge by increasing amounts from equilibrium. However cases (3) and (4) are similar in that they show cyclical fluctuations, which are absent in cases (1) and (2).

Which of these four types of result is yielded by any particular second-order difference equation depends on the values of its parameters. (The term parameter is used to describe a symbol, such as v and s in the foregoing equation, which is constant in any particular case under examination but which may differ in value from one case to another.) Thus the nature of the result yielded by an equation which expresses Y_t as a function of Y_{t-1} and of Y_{t-2} will depend on the size of the coefficients of Y_{t-1} and of Y_{t-2}. If the values of these coefficients fall within a certain range, there will be explosive growth[1]; another range of values will lead to convergence to equilibrium; another to damped cycles; and another to anti-damped cycles. Finally, there is a unique value of the coefficients intermediate between the last two which will lead to cycles of constant amplitude. The values of the coefficients themselves will depend partly on the nature of the relationships postulated in the model from which the equation is derived and partly on

[1] Or explosive contraction if the initial disturbance is in a downward direction.

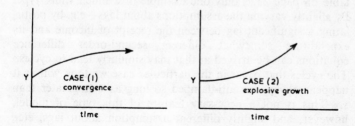

Y — CASE (1) convergence — time

Y — CASE (2) explosive growth — time

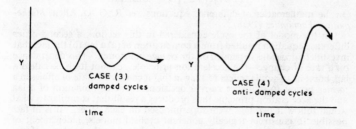

Y — CASE (3) damped cycles — time

Y — CASE (4) anti-damped cycles — time

DIAGRAM 5

the values of the marginal propensity to save, the normal capital-output ratio, and any other such magnitudes that may enter into it.[1]

The equation that was worked out arithmetically in the table on page 23 is only one example of a much wider type. By slightly varying the assumptions about lags—e.g. by postulating a significant lag between the receipt of income and its expenditure—somewhat different second-order difference equations can be arrived at that may similarly lead to cycles.[2] The cycles that occur in the particular case we took will as it happens always be anti-damped so long as v is greater than s. This is not a necessary feature of this type of model, however, and slightly different assumption about lags, etc., would make damped cycles more plausible.[3]

Because cycles of constant amplitude result from a second-order difference equation only in a special case, the hypothesis that the economic cycles of reality are due to the

---

[1] The exact conditions for getting each of the four results and the proof of them are too complicated to give here. The condition for getting cycles is, however, straightforward: cycles will result if $b^2 < 4c$, where b is the coefficient of Y_{t-1} and c is the coefficient of Y_{t-2} in the typical second-order difference equation

$$Y_t + bY_{t-1} + cY_{t-2} = \text{constant.}$$

On the mathematics of difference equations, see R. G. D. Allen, *Mathematical Economics* (1956).

[2] In the model of the cycle considered in this section, a second-order difference equation resulted from a combination of (a) a lag (b) the fact that investment decisions depended on the *change* in income. This dependence on a rate of change—the acceleration principle—cannot itself be called a lag, but it has a similar effect to a lag in that it causes the state of affairs in a *former* period to influence *current* decisions. The combination of a lag and the acceleration principle thus produces a result that is similar to what would follow if two lags were superimposed on each other. It is in fact possible to construct logically coherent cyclical models, independent of the acceleration principle or anything like it, based on the existence of two superimposed lags.

[3] There is, as a matter of fact, a certain tendency for models based on the unqualified acceleration principle to yield anti-damped rather than damped cycles, when plausible values are assigned to the parameters; but this tendency is a good deal reduced when the idea underlying the acceleration principle is reformulated in the way suggested in the next chapter (see Chapter III).

existence of a lag in the multiplier-accelerator process is subject to an objection from which the buffer or non-linearity hypothesis is immune. Since cyclical fluctuations of economic activity have persisted for more than a century without any obvious tendency to increase or diminish in amplitude, are we obliged to believe that the system's parameters have consistently maintained for all that time just those values that would yield cycles of constant amplitude? This seems barely credible in view of the fundamental changes in economic structure that have taken place over the period.

The so-called theory of erratic shocks has been brought forward to meet this difficulty.[1] According to this theory, the inherent tendency of the system is to produce damped cycles. (Damped cycles could result from a fair range of values of the parameters, so the extreme coincidence required to produce a long period of cycles of constant amplitude is avoided.) The fluctuations resulting from a single disturbance would therefore tend to disappear after a time. But further disturbances or erratic shocks will in fact occur quite frequently and at random intervals, in the shape of wars, technical innovations, political upheavals, etc. The continued occurrence of these shocks will sustain the cyclical tendency when it would otherwise disappear and will prevent the system from settling down to a steady equilibrium. The inherent tendency of the system to react cyclically to any disturbance will impart a cyclical pattern to its movement over time, even though the shocks themselves occur at random intervals. The resulting pattern will not indeed be a cycle of perfectly regular length and amplitude. But neither are the fluctuations that occur in reality. The idea may be made clearer by means of an analogy which we borrow from M. G. Kendall:

> Imagine a motor-car proceeding along a horizontal road with an irregular surface. The car is fitted with springs

[1] Cf. R. Frisch, ' Propagation Problems and Impulse Problems in Dynamic Economics ', in *Economic Essays in Honour of Gustav Cassel* (1933), pp. 171–205.

which permit it to oscillate to some extent but are designed
to damp out the oscillations as soon as the comfort of the
passengers will permit. If the car strikes a bump or pot-
hole in the road the body will oscillate up and down for a
time but will soon come to rest so far as vertical motion
is concerned. If, however, it proceeds over a continual
succession of bumps there will be continual oscillation of
varying amplitude and distance between peaks. The
oscillations are continually renewed by disturbances, though
the distribution of the latter along the road may be quite
random. The *regularity* of the motion is determined by the
internal structure of the car; but the *existence* of the motion
is determined by external impulses.[1]

§ 7. Combination of Lags and Buffers.

An alternative way
out of the damping problem is to combine the hypotheses of
§§ 4 and 5 and suppose that the interaction of the multiplier
and the acceleration principle is or may be qualified by the
existence of both lags and buffers. A very wide range of
possibilities is then covered. The existence of buffers would
cause cycles of constant amplitude to result from a system
inherently prone to anti-damped cycles in just the same way
as it does when the inherent tendency is to explosive growth
(as in the lagless case or case (2) of p. 26). Where the inherent tendency is to anti-damped cycles, however, there may
be occasional booms or slumps that terminate of their own
accord before reaching contact with ceiling or floor—a possibility absent where the inherent tendency is to explosive
growth.[2]

It is interesting to observe that where the presence of lags
causes the system to be inherently prone to cycles, a single
buffer—either floor or ceiling—may be sufficient by itself to

[1] M. G. Kendall, *Advanced Theory of Statistics*, vol. II (London:
Charles Griffin and Company, 1948), p. 423.

[2] Such a combination of buffers and a tendency to anti-damped cycles
forms the basis of the main model in J. R. Hicks, *A Contribution to the
Theory of the Trade Cycle* (1950).

ensure the continued occurrence of cycles of unchanging amplitude. This is important, because it has sometimes been argued that the notion of a floor is easier to justify empirically than the notion of a ceiling. Suppose that there is a floor, such as zero gross investment, but no ceiling, and that the inherent tendency is to anti-damped cycles, so that any upswing must eventually come to an end even in the absence of a ceiling. Now each cyclical upswing must have an identical starting point, namely the floor. There is therefore no reason why the upswing of one cycle should differ in amplitude—or anything else—from the upswing of the cycle that preceded it. Because of the inherent tendency to anti-damped cycles, the second peak would in the absence of a floor have been higher than the first peak, because the trough preceding the second peak would have been lower than the trough preceding the first peak, and the upswing would consequently have had more momentum. But if the troughs are all of the same depth because of the existence of a floor, the height of the ensuing peaks will also be uniform.[1]

§ 8. Conclusions. The interaction of the multiplier and the acceleration principle in their simplest forms leads not to fluctuations but to complete instability. Fluctuations may occur, however, if the movement of income is restrained from proceeding beyond a certain point by the existence of limits or buffers. Fluctuations may also occur if some lag or lags are present in the working of the system. The lag hypothesis by itself is not capable of explaining the recurrence of cycles of constant amplitude, except as an implausible special case. But if the system is subject to a continual series of external disturbances or shocks, continuing fluctuations may result even though the mechanism of the system is such that in the absence of these disturbances the fluctuations would die out. Alternatively, the working of the system may be influenced by both buffers and lags.

[1] Cf. J. S. Duesenberry, 'Hicks on the Trade Cycle', *Quarterly Journal of Economics*, 1950, pp. 464–76.

Within the broad framework provided by the multiplier and the acceleration principle, there are thus two main approaches to the explanation of the cycle, emphasising buffers and lags respectively. These approaches are not mutually exclusive. Moreover, both buffers and lags can be of many types and can arise from many causes. The type of theory exemplified by the models given in this chapter is therefore not an unduly narrow one, and it does not necessarily imply an unrealistic uniformity in the working of the economic system in different places and periods. None the less, as stated previously, it is based on a highly simplified theory of what determines investment. The basis of this theory and the qualifications to which it must be subjected will be considered in the next chapter.

In addition to explaining models of the business cycle based on the acceleration principle, the present chapter has served to introduce a number of concepts which are capable of being applied also in models of the cycle that do not employ the acceleration principle. (1) The concept of fluctuations resulting from a tendency to cumulative expansion or contraction being restrained by buffers is applicable whatever the causes of the tendency to cumulative movement and whatever the nature of the buffers. (2) The concept of fluctuations resulting from lags in the adjustment process is also capable of general application. This is sufficiently illustrated by the mechanical analogies quoted above. (3) The question of damping is liable to arise in any mathematically explicit theory of the cycle. (4) The rôle of erratic shocks is also something that must be taken into account in any theory of the cycle. There is no denying that erratic shocks will continually occur and that they will partially determine the level of income in any particular year. The debatable question is whether they are a necessary condition for cycles to be sustained.

CHAPTER III

INVESTMENT: (1) THE ACCELERATION PRINCIPLE AND ITS GENERALISATION

In this chapter we shall consider the economic basis of the acceleration principle. It will be shown that the original form of the acceleration principle, as presented in the last chapter—that investment is a function of the rate of change of national income—is not really tenable, but that the underlying idea can be reformulated so as to overcome the chief objections without losing the power to generate fluctuations.

§ **1. The Acceleration Principle and the Theory of Competition.** The acceleration principle lays down that the desired or appropriate stock of capital depends on the level of demand for final output, i.e. the level of national income; and that net investment, which is the *change* in the stock of capital, therefore depends on the *change* in national income. We have now to consider what is the economic basis of the idea that the desired stock of capital depends on the level of national income, or, what comes to the same thing, that there is a certain normal ratio between capital and income.

The provisional justification of this idea given in Chapter II was in terms of a *physical* relationship. It was suggested that there is a certain stock of capital which it is most convenient to have in order to produce a given output, and that investment decisions are designed to adjust the capital stock to this level. But whatever may be the underlying importance of the physical relationship, the matter does not present itself in exactly this way to the individual firm contemplating investment. Not merely is there some flexibility in the amount of capital that may be used to produce a given output, but, more important, the firm does not necessarily regard its own output as given (even if it expects the demand *schedule* for its products to remain constant).

The central consideration affecting the inducement to do investment is profitability. Investment will be done if the expected profits represent an adequate return on the sum spent. The physical relation between output and capital is important only in so far as it influences the expected rate of return on investment.[1]

The concept of the normal capital-output ratio must therefore be restated in terms of profitability. Looked at in this way, the attainment of the desired or appropriate stock of capital in an industry may be seen as substantially identical to the attainment of the state of long-period equilibrium which figures so prominently in Marshallian economics.[2] In long-period equilibrium the rate of return on capital is supposed to be exactly equal to its supply price—Marshall's 'normal profit'—and there is no tendency for the amount of capital in the industry either to increase or to diminish, so long as the level of demand remains the same. The higher the level of demand, the greater will be the stock of capital needed to give long-period equilibrium. If there is initially long-period equilibrium and there is then a rise in demand, the rise in demand will be met in the short run by more intensive use of capacity or higher prices or both. This will raise profits and so make it attractive to invest money in expanding the industry's capacity. Likewise if there is a fall in demand, profits will fall and it will cease to be worth while to renew capital when it wears out. The actual rate of profit in the industry at any time and hence the inducement to invest will depend on the extent to which the stock of capital departs

[1] On this point, and on the economic basis of the acceleration principle generally, cf. A. D. Knox, 'The Acceleration Principle and the Theory of Investment: A Survey', *Economica*, 1952, pp. 269–97.

[2] Alfred Marshall, *Principles of Economics*, Book V, Chapter V. For the relations between Marshallian long-period equilibrium and the acceleration principle, cf. N. Kaldor, 'Mr Hicks on the Trade Cycle', *Economic Journal*, 1951, pp. 833–47, especially pp. 837–41.

from the amount necessary to give long-period equilibrium at the current level of demand. It must be understood that long-period equilibrium is not a situation that is necessarily ever attained; it is a notional position that is always shifting as demand shifts, and if the general trend of demand over time is in an upward direction, the capital stock will on the average be below its current long-period equilibrium level and profits will be above their 'normal' level; but long-period equilibrium has significance as the point towards which the system is at any time tending.

All this can be extended from a single industry to the economy as a whole. Demand now depends on the level of national income. The rate of profit and the inducement to invest will depend on the extent to which the ratio of capital to national income departs from the notional normal which would make the rate of return on capital at the margin equal to its supply price. The actual size of the normal capital-output ratio in any given state of technical knowledge will depend on what the supply price of capital is, i.e. what is the minimum acceptable rate of return on capital.

It is thus possible to defend in terms of traditional Marshallian theory the underlying postulate of the acceleration principle, that there is a certain normal ratio between capital and national income and that this has a bearing on the inducement to invest. But some further steps are needed to get from here to the acceleration principle itself, viz. the doctrine that the level of net investment depends on the rate of change of national income. These will be considered in later sections of this chapter.

Before going on to that, however, it will be well to restate the theory of investment that is implied by what has just been said, since it will underlie much that follows.

The initial presupposition is that there exists an active class of entrepreneurs engaged all the time in calculating prospective returns on investment and reacting accordingly. The theory would not apply, therefore, in a country where the entrepreneurial class was weak or absent and where economic activities were conducted in an unchanging traditional pattern. Granted this presupposition, the basic postulate is that the amount of investment done is a function of the expected rate of return. If conditions are such as to promise a high rate of return, much investment will be done, and conversely. There will be a certain critical level of expected returns at which zero net investment is done; this is called the supply price of investment, or normal profit. What determines this supply price is not here specified, but the important thing is that within the cycle it does not alter significantly, or at least that any movements there may be in it are small compared with the movements that take place over the cycle in the rate of return actually expected. In other words, within the cycle *shifts* in the schedule expressing the functional relationship between investment and expected rate of profit are small compared with movements up and down the schedule.[1]

A further requirement of the theory is that in estimating likely future profits entrepreneurs are guided by the current level of demand and the rate of profit that results from it. The simplest assumption—and that which is required by the acceleration principle in its crude form—is that they suppose that the actual current level of demand will be maintained in the future. As will be seen later in this chapter, however, it is sufficient for most purposes to postulate merely that their expectations about future profits are influenced by the current level of profits and vary in the same direction as it.[2]

---

[1] The question of movements in the normal rate of profit (and hence in the normal capital-output ratio) is discussed briefly in Chapter XIII, pp. 245-8.

[2] So long as the expected level of future profits is some sort of function of the current level of profits and is not subject to arbitrary shifts, there is no difficulty in expressing investment decisions as a function of the current level of profits, provided that it is remembered that this is essentially a derived relationship and that what immediately determines investment decisions is the expected level of future profits. But unless the stricter condition is fulfilled that expected future profits are calculated on the assumption that the actual present level of demand will be maintained, certain ambiguities arise in the interpretation of the concept of normal profits and the associated concept of the normal capital-output ratio (the capital-output ratio that yields normal profits). Is normal profit to be

§ **2. The Time Factor in Investment.** In Chapter II the acceleration principle was stated in two alternative forms, one unlagged, the other lagged. As the lagged form is the more plausible, attention will in this section be confined to it.

The argument underlying this formulation of the acceleration principle runs as follows. Investment decisions made at a certain point of time determine the level of investment during the ensuing 'period'. At the end of this period the decisions have been carried into execution, and fresh decisions are made about the level of investment during the next period. The investment decisions made at the beginning of period t are dictated by the level of income prevailing during the most recent past, viz. during period $t-1$, and are designed to bring the stock of capital to the level appropriate to that income. Assuming that the investment decisions made at the beginning of period $t-1$ were similarly determined, the actual stock of capital at the beginning of period t will be appropriate to the level of income that prevailed during period $t-2$. So the net investment required during period t to bring the stock of capital to the level appropriate to the income of period $t-1$

---

defined as the level of profit which *if expected for the future* will lead to zero net investment, or is it that level of profit which *if currently experienced* will create expectations such as to lead to zero net investment? These two are not the same unless present conditions are expected to continue in the future. Thus if future expectations, while based on present experience, are usually pitched at a rather higher level (e.g. if entrepreneurs assume that demand in a year's time will be 3% higher than at present), some positive net investment will be done even though the current level of profit is not above the level which, if expected for the future, would induce zero net investment; entrepreneurs are doing investment in anticipation of the actual inducement. The second of the two definitions of normal profit suggested above will in this case imply a lower figure for normal profit than the first definition. It seems clear that the first definition is the preferable one and the one more in line with the concept of normal profit as the supply price of investment. Hence in speaking of normal profit in the remainder of this book we should be understood to mean that level of profit which if expected for the future would lead to zero net investment. Similarly, the normal capital-output ratio is to be understood as the capital-output ratio which causes the level of profit to be normal in the above sense.

will depend on the change of income between periods $t-2$ and $t-1$. Thus in symbolic terms $I_t = v(Y_{t-1} - Y_{t-2})$, v being the normal capital-income ratio at the margin.

The conclusion thus depends on two assumptions. These two assumptions are really no more than the application of the same assumption to two periods and they stand or fall together. They are first, that the stock of capital will by the end of period t have been brought up to the level appropriate to the income of period $t-1$; and second, that the stock of capital at the beginning of period t was appropriate to the income of period $t-2$. ,If the latter is not the case, and there was at the beginning of period t a deficiency or surplus of capital in relation to the income of period $t-2$, the change in income between periods $t-2$ and $t-1$ is not the only thing that decides how much investment will be needed during period t to bring the stock of capital to the appropriate level in relation to the income of period $t-1$; the initial discrepancy will also need to be taken into account.

When the normal or appropriate capital-output ratio is interpreted in the sense of Marshallian long-period equilibrium, it is plain that the assumptions referred to are not tenable. The 'appropriate' stock of capital (defined with reference to the income of the period immediately preceding the moment when the investment decisions are made) is important as affecting the inducement to invest; but it is not an operational concept from the point of view of the individual entrepreneur. In so far as there is a tendency for the stock of capital to be adjusted towards this level, it is as a result of the working of competition, not because anyone is consciously aiming at it. There is no question of firms *planning* to bring about long-period equilibrium, whether in one period or several. There is therefore no presumption that the amount of investment carried out during a period—defined in the sense of a planning period—will be exactly equal to the difference between the opening stock of capital and that indicated as appropriate by the then prevailing level of income. Much depends on how quickly and strongly firms react to a departure of the rate of profit from normal. If their reactions are sluggish, investment will fall short of the required amount. If their reactions are very prompt, it is possible that the amount of investment done will increase the stock of capital by *more* than the required amount, since the individual firms in making their investment decisions may not take sufficient account of the increase in capacity in the industry that will presently be brought about in consequence of the similar decisions of other firms in the same position. This is particularly liable to occur if the time required to carry out investment is considerable, since it will then be some while before any discouragement to further investment is afforded by the coming into operation of the newly-created capacity.[1]

The difficulty just stated arises from the working of competition. But there are other difficulties that apply equally even if the representative industry can be thought of as monopolistic, and the 'appropriate' stock of capital is therefore something that entrepreneurs do consciously try to achieve. It still does not follow that the stock of capital at the end of a planning period will have been brought up to the level appropriate to the income prevailing at the beginning of the period. For even if the investment decided upon were such as to bring this result about, it does not follow that all the work planned at the beginning of a period will have been completed by the end of it. If the time taken to carry out a project—commonly referred to as the 'gestation period' of investment—is long, it is quite possible that plans for further investment will be considered before the previous ones have been fully executed. This leads to the further complication that, if the gestation period is long, part of the investment done during a given period is likely to be the result of decisions made not at the beginning of the period but at some earlier date. In seeking to explain the level of investment, account must therefore be taken not merely of the relation between demand and capital capacity in the recent past, but

---

[1] See below, Chapter IV, § 1.

also of the corresponding relation over the whole range of past periods during which such investment decisions were taken as are still being carried into effect.

The time factor presents a similar but still more serious difficulty in the slump. So far no special distinction has been drawn between the process of adding to the capital stock and that of reducing it. In reality the two are very different. The stock of capital can be reduced only by neglecting replacement[1]—that is what negative net investment means. But even if no replacement is done at all, the stock of capital may not decline very fast, since only a certain proportion of it falls due for replacement in any year. Whereas the rate at which the stock of capital can be expanded is limited by the time taken to fulfil investment plans, the rate at which it can be reduced is limited by the life of the existing capital equipment—which may be much longer. So if there is any substantial decline in income, it is liable to be a long time before the stock of capital is reduced to the new appropriate level.

§ 3. Generalisation of the Acceleration Principle: the Capital Stock Adjustment Principle.

The conclusions that follow from the previous section are unfavourable to the acceleration principle. The stock of capital at the start of a period is not necessarily that appropriate to the level of income in the preceding period but one: there may instead be excess capacity or alternatively unfilled arrears of investment. Nor will the investment done during the period necessarily bring the stock to that appropriate to the level of income in the preceding period. Hence the level of investment during the period is not satisfactorily expressed as a function of the rate of change of income between these two preceding periods.

A very complicated reformulation would be needed to take full account of all the difficulties that have been mentioned.

---

[1] Short of actually scrapping equipment that is still capable of useful service. Whether in fact capital is more readily scrapped in the slump than at other stages of the cycle is uncertain; see below, pp. 64–6.

Most of the difficulties can be met, however, by a looser formulation. This is to say simply that investment decisions will vary directly with the level of national income and inversely with the stock of capital in existence. This incorporates the basic idea of the acceleration principle, that investment will be directed towards bringing the stock of capital into alignment with the level of income recently prevailing, without attempting any undue precision. For certain purposes it may be a legitimate approximation to suppose that the relationship in question is a linear one, and to formulate it thus :

$$I_t = aY_t - bK_t$$

or allowing for a lag

$$I_t = aY_{t-1} - bK_t,$$

where I_t and Y_t are investment and income respectively during period t, K_t is the stock of capital at the beginning of period t, and a and b are constants. This formulation will henceforward be referred to as the capital stock adjustment principle. It will be noted that it no longer contains any direct reference to the rate of change of income. However it incorporates the acceleration principle as a special case where a is equal to the normal capital-output ratio and b is equal to unity.[1]

The formulation above is cast for the sake of simplicity in aggregate terms, relating to total investment and the total stock of capital. But what is relevant to investment decisions in a particular sector of the economy is the stock of capital in that sector, not the stock of capital in the whole economy. Moreover there will be differences between sectors in the degree of sensitivity of investment decisions to changes in the national income and in the stock of capital. For any particular sector i, the capital stock adjustment principle will be of the form

$$_iI_t = {}_iaY_t - {}_ib_iK_t \quad \text{or} \quad _iI_t = {}_iaY_{t-1} - {}_ib_iK_t,$$

[1] See above p. 20, where it was shown that the acceleration principle, as expressed by the equation $I_t = v(Y_{t-1} - Y_{t-2})$, can be derived from the equation $I_t = vY_{t-1} - K_t$, where v is the normal capital-output ratio.

where $_iI$ and $_iK$ are the levels of investment and the stock of capital respectively in sector i, and $_ia$ and $_ib$ are the coefficients applicable there. The capital stock adjustment equation for the economy as a whole is properly understood as that which is obtained by *summing* the capital stock adjustment equations for the individual sectors.

The attempts that have been made to test statistically the acceleration principle proper (the doctrine that investment is a function of the rate of growth of output) have mostly been unfavourable to the hypothesis.[1] This is hardly surprising in view of the serious theoretical objections it is open to. Statistical testing of the more plausible capital stock adjustment formulation (the doctrine that investment varies positively with income and inversely with the stock of capital) has given reasonably favourable results,[2] though (in common with much work of this sort) it has been more successful in 'explaining' past data than in predicting the future. Application of the capital stock adjustment principle to individual industries has also yielded reasonably good results.[3]

For the economy as a whole, there is no doubt that the capital-output ratio is generally high in the slump when investment is low and low in the boom when investment is high. This is consistent with the basic idea of the capital stock adjustment principle as to what determines investment. But it is quite inconclusive as evidence, since it is almost equally consistent with any other theory of investment and does not in itself prove that the capital-output ratio's movements have any causal significance. Fluctuations in the stock of capital are always likely to be smaller proportionally than fluctuations in the national income, since so much of the capital stock survives in identical form from one year to the

---

[1] J. Tinbergen, 'Statistical Evidence on the Acceleration Principle', *Economica*, 1938, pp. 164–76.

[2] Cf. L. R. Klein and A. S. Goldberger, *An Econometric Model of the United States 1929–1952* (1955), which has an investment equation similar in essentials to the capital stock adjustment principle as formulated above.

[3] H. B. Chenery, 'Overcapacity and the Acceleration Principle', *Econometrica*, 1952, pp. 1–28.

next. Consequently the capital-output ratio is likely to be low in the boom and high in the slump whatever the causes of the fluctuations in investment.[1]

§ 4. The Rôle of Expectations.

The inducement to do investment depends upon the expected rate of profit. The rate of profit realised on a given piece of plant or equipment will be affected by the level of demand for the output it produces during the whole of its economic life. The level of demand at the beginning of its life is relevant, but it is not the only thing that is relevant. The acceleration principle, in postulating that investment decisions are designed to bring the stock of capital to the level appropriate to current income, is in effect assuming that entrepreneurs base their expectations about future demand on the current situation: they are assumed to act as though they believed that the level of demand in the future would be the same as at present. The capital stock adjustment principle, as stated in the previous section, does not involve such an extreme assumption, in that it merely lays down that a high current level of income will tend, *ceteris paribus*, to mean a high level of investment

---

[1] There would be firmer ground for regarding the movements in the capital-output ratio as causally significant if it could be shown that they preceded the corresponding movements in investment by some interval. In practice, however, the turning points in the two appear to come at about the same time, without either having any pronounced tendency to lag behind the other. The result is therefore indecisive. The absence of a lag may indeed be considered an objection to regarding the movement of the capital-output ratio as causally significant. Some lag is to be expected between investment decisions and investment, and moreover if the capital formation currently in progress has a significant gestation period, there will be a delay before it affects the state of the market and hence the investment decisions of other firms. Hence if the rise in the capital-output ratio at the upper turning point is the cause of the downturn in investment, it might be expected to lead it in time. This argument has less force as applied to monopolistic or oligopolistic industries than to perfectly competitive ones, since, in the former, firms are likely to be reasonably well informed of the investment projects under way in the industry before they come to fruition, and they may therefore be able to take account of them in their own investment planning at a relatively early stage. (See also p. 61, n. 1.)

decisions, without postulating that investment decisions aim to bring the stock of capital up to exactly the amount that would be appropriate to the current level of income. But the distinctive operation of the capital stock adjustment principle still applies only in as far as investment decisions are affected by the current level of income. We now have to ask to what extent it is reasonable to suppose that they are. This may be discussed under two headings: (1) the influence of the present as such, (2) the influence of the present when taken as a guide to the future.

(1) *The influence of the present as such.* Let us suppose that entrepreneurs do not necessarily expect the present state of affairs, whether boom or slump, to last for more than a short time, and that their expectations as to the more distant future are independent of present events. The present level of demand will still have some influence on investment decisions, since it will affect the level of profit expected in the immediate future.[1] The importance of this will vary inversely with the expected length of life of the capital in question. For example it will as a rule be less for buildings, which have a relatively long life, than for equipment which is expected to be worn out or obsolete in a few years. In the United States it is said that most equipment is expected to pay for itself in not more than five years—perhaps not so much because it is thought probable on balance that its useful life will actually be as short as that, but because of the large element of uncertainty attaching to all more distant projections.[2] So the state of demand for the output of a piece of equipment in the first year or so of its life is liable to be quite an important consideration, even if business men are chary about accepting the present as a guide to the more distant future. Indeed

[1] Cf. T. Wilson, 'Cyclical and Autonomous Inducements to Invest', *Oxford Economic Papers*, 1953, pp. 65–89.

[2] On this, and generally on the procedures actually adopted in the United States by businesses in making investment decisions, see Joel Dean, *Capital Budgeting* (1951); R. Eisner, *Determinants of Capital Expenditures, an Interview Study* (1956); and J. R. Meyer and E. Kuh, *The Investment Decision* (1957).

the fear that a recession is possible in a few years may even strengthen the inducement to enlarge capacity now while demand is good so as to be able to make hay while the sun shines. The influence of the present state of demand on investment decisions in the boom may be strengthened in an imperfectly competitive industry by the importance of good-will: a firm may feel that it must expand its capacity to meet the boom demand, even if it has doubts about whether it will continue, since otherwise customers may be permanently lost to rival producers.

But the influence of the present level of demand as such is unlikely to be very great in the case of investment decisions relating to very long-lived or virtually perpetual capital, like an electric power-station or a bridge. It is also likely to be relatively small in an industry where the gestation period of investment is long, since there is a danger that demand conditions will have altered before the new capital is available for use.

It may be concluded, therefore, that if the present is *not* taken as a guide to the future, it is still likely to have some influence on investment decisions, but only a limited one.

(2) *The present as a guide to the future*. The most general justification for the notion that entrepreneurs base their ideas of the future on what is happening in the present is that in a world of extreme uncertainty no better criterion is available. The present level of demand is something tangible, and unless it is patently much influenced by transitory factors, it may appear the most sensible policy to act on the assumption that it will continue.

In this connection a distinction must be drawn between the boom and the slump. We shall consider the boom first. Most economies that have been subject to cycles have also experienced long-run growth. As a result, although slumps do occur, demand does not often remain for any great length of time below its previous peak. So as a rule it is perhaps not too unreasonable if in the boom firms assume that the present level of demand will be maintained in the future. Of course if they happen to be on the eve of a major slump they will regret having based their decisions on this assumption, but that would be the exception. They will also regret it if they have failed to take sufficient account of competition that will presently be offered by capacity now under construction or about to be constructed in other firms in the industry. In some industries, e.g. agriculture, this consideration is difficult to take proper account of, and entrepreneurs after being caught once or twice may become chary of projecting present prosperity into the future. But this consideration is less important or at least less unpredictable in manufacturing industry, where monopolistic elements are stronger and information can be got more easily about the plans of rival producers.

It may be asked why entrepreneurs, if they are confident that growth is the rule, cannot base their investment decisions on the assumption that demand in the future will follow a certain trend path upwards, irrespective of the level of demand actually attained in the current year. Certain firms may be in a position to do this. But a firm may be confident that the future has promise of growth while being at the same time very uncertain as to the form the growth will take. Present experience is valuable as a guide because it provides a high-water mark not only for demand in general but for the demand for particular products. A firm may feel that if it provides capacity to meet this demand it cannot go far wrong. Moreover even if investment *is* planned on the assumption of a continuing rise in demand in the future, a firm's forecasts are likely to be affected by its recent experience: the higher the present level of demand, the more optimistic is likely to be its estimate of the level of demand in the future, especially the relatively near future.

Even in the boom, however, this will be subject to a good deal of qualification. Much will depend on the circumstances in particular industries and firms. Firms in an industry that has a past record of violent fluctuations are likely to be cautious about future projections. The temperament and experience of individual entrepreneurs will also play a part. Some of them may like to wait for some time to make sure that the boom is not merely a flash in the pan before committing themselves on the basis of it. In some industries, also, building much ahead of demand may be unavoidable, whatever the risks. It may be unavoidable, for example, if the capital is very durable and the economies of scale are such that it would be wasteful to build a small plant now and duplicate it later on when demand has risen. Railway-building is a case in point. In such cases as these, where not much return can be expected anyway from the earliest years of operation, the level of demand at the time of construction can hardly weigh very much with the promoters, unless they are extremely irrational. The violent fluctuations that have none the less been manifested by railway building and similar forms of investment are therefore a phenomenon which the capital stock adjustment principle is not well adapted to explain.

As far as periods of boom are concerned, therefore, we may conclude that over a fair range of industry the current level of demand is likely to be taken as a guide to the future, but that this will not apply universally. In periods of slump, however, the situation is quite different. Extrapolation of slump conditions implies an assumption that demand will remain indefinitely at a level below that which experience has shown it to be capable of attaining. Such a pessimistic assumption would normally be unwarranted. In looking ahead in the slump entrepreneurs are admittedly faced to some extent by the problem mentioned above, that they do not know what form the rise in demand will take when prosperity returns. But it is fair to assume that demand for most products will regain its previous peak levels once there has been a general recovery, unless there is specific reason to believe that the structure of demand has altered.

It is therefore possible that falls in national income will have less far-reaching effects on expectations and hence on investment decisions than rises in national income. But this is largely a psychological matter, and it may work out entirely differently in one slump and in another. A very long and severe slump may create fears that prosperity as it was previously known will never return. Such fears were widely felt in the United States in the 1930s, not only by business men but also by economists. Rather similar fears were also voiced in the unusually bad depression of the 1870s.

The conclusions of this section may now be summed up. Even if the present is not uncritically extrapolated into the future, the present level of demand will always exert some influence on investment decisions. Moreover there will always be a fair range of investment decisions for which the present is as good a guide to the future as any. This applies particularly in the boom. In the slump *general* extrapolation of the present is a sign of breakdown of confidence and is likely to happen only on the worst occasions. At all times, too, there will be some classes of investment decisions that have to be based on long-term expectations and will not be influenced much by the state of demand at the present. So while there is no need to reject the formulation of the capital stock adjustment principle that investment decisions vary directly with national income and inversely with the stock of capital, the degree of that variation, especially in the slump, will be less than it would be if the present were always taken without qualification as a guide to the future. The element of inertia in expectations thus serves to protect the system from the more extreme forms of cyclical instability. In some circumstances the responsiveness of investment to short-run movements in income may be too weak to lead to any sizeable fluctuations at all. In these circumstances alternative explanations must be sought for any fluctuations that do occur.

§ 5. **Restatement of the Cyclical Models.** What difference does all this make to the models of the cycle described in Chapter II? The basic idea underlying the acceleration principle, that the desired stock of capital will depend on the level of output, is a sound one and has great importance for the theory of the cycle (and for the theory of long-run economic growth). But the particular formulation of it involved by the acceleration principle, that investment is a function of the rate of growth of output, depends on too many special assumptions to be acceptable. The looser formulation, designated above as the capital stock adjustment principle, is to be preferred, viz. that investment is an increasing function of income and a diminishing function of the stock of capital: as a linear approximation

$$I_t = aY_t - bK_t,$$

or allowing for a lag

$$I_t = aY_{t-1} - bK_t.$$

This formulation itself must be understood in the light of the remarks made in the preceding section about expectations. The fact that the present is not universally taken as a guide to the future will lessen the sensitivity of investment to changes in income; it will mean that the coefficient a in the above equation will tend to be a good deal smaller than the normal marginal capital-output ratio[1] (even apart from the complications about the time-factor referred to in § 2 above). This applies particularly in periods of slump.

It will now be shown that the various cyclical and other possibilities discussed in Chapter II are capable of following from the capital stock adjustment principle in substantially the same way as they follow from the acceleration principle.

As with the acceleration principle, either lags or buffers (non-linearities) or both are necessary for the interaction of the capital stock adjustment principle and the multiplier to yield plausible cycles. If the capital stock adjustment principle works without a lag, investment will be a function of current income and the stock of capital: $I_t = aY_t - bK_t$. If there are

---

[1] For similar reasons, I_t is likely to be a function not only of Y_{t-1} and K_t but also of certain other variables, of a relatively stable nature in the short period, which affect entrepreneurs' ideas of the 'normal', e.g. the average level of income over a rather longer past period.

no buffers, this will lead either to complete instability, as in the unlagged case of the acceleration principle; or it could in some circumstances enable the system to reach stable equilibrium without fluctuations. The proof of this is along essentially the same lines as that given for the acceleration principle in Chapter II, § 3. The proof is shown in a footnote, along with an explanation of why stability without fluctuations is a possibility in this case though it was not with the acceleration principle proper.[1]

[1] The interaction of the unlagged acceleration principle with a multiplier equation involving a constant term was shown above to lead to the equation

$$Y_t = \frac{v}{v-s}Y_{t-1} - \frac{Z}{v-s}.$$

This implies instability, because so long as v exceeds s, the expression $v/(v-s)$ is positive and greater than unity and cumulative movement in Y must result. The case where s exceeds v was previously ruled out as unlikely (Chapter II, p. 14, n. 1). However if s did exceed v, $v/(v-s)$ would be negative, and Y would oscillate in alternate periods around its equilibrium level. These oscillations would not resemble the fluctuations of reality because of their short duration—twice a planning period which in this lagless case is itself *ex hypothesi* short.

With the unlagged capital stock adjustment principle, we have

$$I_t = aY_t - bK_t \quad \text{and} \quad Y_t = \frac{I_t}{s} + \frac{Z}{s}.$$

This does not directly reduce to a single equation in Y, but it can be reduced to an equation in K, and this serves equally well to show the path followed by the system as a whole.

Since

$$K_{t+1} = K_t + I_t \quad \text{and} \quad I_t = a\left(\frac{I_t}{s} + \frac{Z}{s}\right) - bK_t,$$

it follows that

$$K_{t+1} - K_t = \frac{a}{s}(K_{t+1} - K_t + Z) - bK_t$$

$$K_{t+1} = \frac{a - s(1-b)}{a-s}K_t - \frac{a}{a-s}Z.$$

If the coefficient of K_t in this equation is positive and greater than unity, the system will be unstable, as in the case of the unlagged acceleration principle proper. However there is now a possibility, the analogy of which was absent from the former case, that the coefficient of K is positive but less than unity. This will happen if a is less than s and b is sufficiently

If the system is inherently unstable, the existence of buffers will as before produce fluctuations. Once one or other buffer has halted the cumulative movement of income, any level of net investment other than zero will not be indefinitely maintainable, since presently the appropriate capital stock will have been reached. Hence income will have to come down from the boom level or go up from the slump level. The cumulative tendency will then carry it to the other extreme. To produce this result the buffers do not need to be absolute, that is, to prevent income from altering altogether; all that is needed is that they should produce a sufficient retardation of the cumulative movement. Their effect so long as they are in operation is really to transform the system from an unstable to a stable one by limiting the extent of the movements in investment and income. The unstable rise or fall in income is therefore arrested, there is a turning-point, and for a while income proceeds gradually towards the notional equilibrium that lies between boom and slump level; but as it retreats from the extreme values which brought the buffers into operation, their effect ceases to be felt and instability returns. The gradual movement is transformed into a

---

less than unity. In this case the system will tend towards a stable equilibrium.

The economic meaning of the difference between the results with the acceleration principle and the capital stock adjustment principle respectively is this. In the former case movements in investment can be kept within bounds and complete instability thereby avoided only if the normal capital-output ratio v is lower than s. Not only is this very unlikely; also, if v is as low as this, deficiencies or surpluses in the capital stock are so easily corrected by moderate movements in investment that the system repeatedly overshoots its equilibrium position in the alternate-period oscillations referred to above. With the capital stock adjustment principle, there is another different way in which instability may be avoided: by entrepreneurs reacting weakly to deficiencies or surpluses in the capital stock (e.g. because they do not take the present as a guide to the future with any confidence). This will give low values to both a and b, and keep the movements of investment within moderate limits. But in contrast to the case where the low value of the normal capital-output ratio is what keeps movements in investment down, moderate movements in investment will not now suffice to make good in a single period the initial capital deficiency or surplus, and the system will therefore not overshoot.

headlong one, the notional equilibrium is overshot, and the system does not come to rest till it reaches the opposite buffer.[1]

The time-lag explanation of the cycle likewise survives the modification of the acceleration principle. The delayed increase in the stock of capital that comes about when that stock has lately been low in relation to the level of national income can check the cumulative movement or put it into reverse. This could be shown from an arithmetical example like that in Chapter II, p. 23. Alternatively the forces at work can be seen from Diagram 6.[2]

This shows the movement over time of income, net investment, investment decisions, and the capital stock. (The scale for the four variables is not the same except for investment and investment decisions.) The verticals mark the boundaries between periods, a period being the interval that elapses on the average between investment decision and investment. The movement of investment therefore reproduces that of investment decisions one period earlier. Net investment fluctuates about the zero level indicated by the dotted line. The stock of capital rises or falls according as net investment is above or below zero. The movement of income duplicates that of investment, to which it is related by the multiplier. Peaks and troughs in each series are marked by the letters P and T respectively.

We suppose that in period 1 investment is below the replacement level but is rising. The stock of capital is therefore falling but income is rising. Investment decisions therefore rise, since they vary directly with income and inversely with the stock of capital; and this is reflected in a further rise in

[1] The type of cycle-theory described in this paragraph corresponds to the cyclical models of N. Kaldor ('A Model of the Trade Cycle', *Economic Journal*, 1940, pp. 78–92), and R. M. Goodwin ('Econometrics in Business Cycle Analysis,' in A. H. Hansen, *Business Cycles and National Income* (1951), pp. 417–68).

[2] This type of cycle theory corresponds to M. Kalecki's model. This model has been stated by its author in a number of forms. The most recent is in his *Theory of Economic Dynamics* (1954), Part 5.

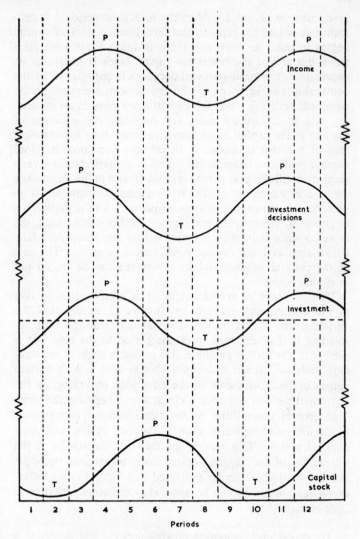

DIAGRAM 6

investment in period 2. After the middle of period 2 investment has passed the replacement level and the stock of capital begins to rise. In itself this tends to lower investment decisions, but at first the rise in the capital stock is small and its depressing effect on investment decisions is outweighed by the continuing rise in income. So investment decisions go on rising till period 3. But the capital stock rises at an increasing rate as investment rises, and presently the influence of the rise in the capital stock comes to equal, then to outweigh, that of the rise in income. Investment decisions therefore reach a peak and begin to fall. This is not reflected in investment itself till the next period (period 4), and in the meanwhile the rate at which the capital stock increases continues to go up. As income ceases to grow in period 5 and actually falls in period 6, investment decisions are further discouraged, the more so since it is not till period 6 that net investment falls below zero and the capital stock ceases to grow. The rest of the cyclical process and its recurrence can be traced out in similar terms.

This sequence of events is similar in all essentials to that in the arithmetical example in Chapter II, except that the variables are shown moving continuously through time instead of in discrete steps from one period to the next. It is similar to the former example also in that a cycle of constant amplitude will occur only as a special case. With certain values of the coefficients in the equations governing its behaviour there will not be a cycle at all. There are the same four general possibilities as described earlier: convergence to equilibrium, explosive growth, damped cycles, and anti-damped cycles. This reflects the fact that the results of the interaction of the lagged capital stock adjustment principle and the multiplier can be expressed in a second-order difference equation just as can be done when the acceleration principle is used.[1,2]

---

[1] The capital stock adjustment principle does not lead directly to a second-order difference equation in income such as we had in Chapter II.

It may be concluded therefore that the findings of Chapter II about the ways in which cyclical fluctuations may come about hold without substantial alteration when the acceleration principle is replaced by the capital stock adjustment principle. All that was said about the rôle of lags, buffers, erratic shocks, etc., still holds. Due allowance must however be made for the fact that under the capital stock adjustment principle the responsiveness of investment to changes in income will vary from time to time accordingly to the character of the investment lines which are currently most important and according to the climate of expectations, and that in certain circumstances the responsiveness may be too weak to generate cycles at all (in which case any cycles that do occur must be explained in some other way).

Further refinement in the formulation of the capital stock

It does, however, lead to a second-order difference equation involving the stock of capital, as follows:

$$I_t = aY_{t-1} - bK_t$$

$$Y_t = \frac{I_t}{s} + \frac{Z}{s}$$

$$I_t = \frac{a}{s}(I_{t-1} + Z) - bK_t$$

$$K_{t+1} - K_t = \frac{a}{s}(K_t - K_{t-1} + Z) - bK_t$$

$$K_{t+1} + \left(b - \frac{a}{s} - 1\right)K_t + \frac{a}{s}K_{t-1} = \frac{a}{s}Z.$$

The behaviour of Y can be inferred from that of K. If K converges to equilibrium or explodes or fluctuates in damped or in anti-damped cycles, corresponding behaviour will be shown by Y.

[2] It was noted above (Chapter II, p. 26, n. 2) that models based on the acceleration principle tend to yield anti-damped cycles when plausible values are assigned to the parameters. This tendency is less marked with models based on the capital stock adjustment principle, since allowance can then be made for the fact that when income rises, the induced rise in investment may (because of time-lags, insensitive expectations, etc.) fall a good deal short of the amount needed to raise the stock of capital to the level appropriate to the new income; in other words a, the coefficient of income in the capital stock adjustment equation, may be a good deal smaller than the marginal capital-output ratio. The lower the value of a, the less the likelihood of anti-damped cycles.

adjustment principle in accordance with the qualifications made earlier in this chapter about timing, etc., would for the most part alter the results in detail only. The chief exception to this is in regard to the asymmetry between positive and negative net investment (p. 40, above), which is more important. Discussion of this difficulty is postponed to Chapter X.

CHAPTER IV

INVESTMENT: (2) REPLACEMENT, TECHNICAL PROGRESS, AND OTHER INFLUENCES

THE capital stock adjustment principle does not take account of all the forces affecting investment. Hence the behaviour of investment in practice is likely to be somewhat different from that described in the models so far shown. Moreover, fluctuations in investment may in certain circumstances result from causes quite independent of the capital stock adjustment principle, and the capital stock adjustment principle may in some circumstances operate very feebly or not at all. We will now consider some of the other influences affecting investment, with special reference to those liable to cause fluctuations or to alter their pattern.

§ 1. **Overshooting Independent of Multiplier Repercussions.** In the models so far considered, part of the reason why the system tended to overshoot any possible point of equilibrium was that attempts to adjust the stock of capital to the desired level themselves altered the desired level by altering income through the multiplier, the desired stock of capital being a function of income. In certain circumstances, however, overshooting may take place even if the desired stock of capital (i.e. that which yields normal profits) remains constant; the system may fail to reach its target even though the target is standing still. Fluctuations are thus possible in industries where the desired stock of capital is not closely connected with the level of the national income or in circumstances where the multiplier effects of investment are neutralised by some other extraneous influences on income.

Overshooting of this sort may occur because of distortions introduced by competition or because of reaction lags or other lags or because of some combination of these.

The case of competitive distortion has already been briefly referred to.[1] Suppose that firms make their investment decisions in the light of the current level of profits and disregard any change that may be brought about in the profit rate in the future in consequence of additions to capacity made by other firms in competition with them. Each firm fails to take due account of the fact that the other firms are acting on the same assumption as it is, and that therefore if it is planning to do much investment other firms will be too and the profit rate will fall when all their plans come to fruition. The stock of capital in the industry as a whole will therefore be raised above that level that would yield normal profits. There will then be a reaction which will be overdone in similar fashion. And so on.

The case of reaction lags is as follows. Suppose that investment decisions react to a surplus or deficiency in the stock of capital only after a lag, because the indicators of capital surplus or deficiency take time to appear. A movement towards the equilibrium stock of capital is then liable to overshoot the mark, since if the stock of capital is deficient at the end of period 1, investment decisions taken at the beginning of period 3 will still be high, even though the investment carried out during period 2 may in the meanwhile have eliminated the deficiency.

The analysis of these forms of overshooting is set out in more formal terms in a footnote.[2] The exact nature of the

[1] Chapter III, pp. 38–9.
[2] Let I_t be investment during period t, K_{t+1}, K_t, K_{t-1} be the stock of capital at the beginning of periods $t+1$, t, $t-1$ respectively, and let K^* be the desired or equilibrium stock of capital. K^* is assumed constant.

(1) The case of competitive distortion.

$$K_{t+1} - K_t = I_t = a(K^* - K_t)$$
$$K_{t+1} = aK^* + (1-a)K_t.$$

Suppose that the working of competition causes a to be greater than unity: the independently-taken decisions of firms are then such as collectively to overshooting process depends on the character of the lags, etc., that are involved, and there will be differences in detail between different cases, but the basic source of the trouble is the same in all: namely that investment decisions are made on the basis of insufficient or faulty information on what will be the stock of capital at the time when the investment decisions come to fruition. Mistaken expectations in this regard may arise because the indicators of the state of the market used in making investment decisions are already out-of-date, or because insufficient account is taken of the current investment plans of other firms, or because insufficient account is taken of plans made by other firms at an earlier date which have not yet come to fruition in consequence of the investment concerned having a long gestation period.

It has not usually been suggested that these sources of overshooting are the *main* cause of cyclical fluctuations. In the absence of the further destabilising effect of multiplier repercussions, they will as a rule give rise only to rather heavily damped cycles. These factors have, however, sometimes been invoked as an explanation of fluctuations in particular lines of investment, such as shipbuilding and house-building, the behaviour of which appears to show some independence of fluctuations in national income and investment as a whole.

---

more than make good any initial surplus or deficiency in the stock of capital. The result is a first order difference equation involving K, where the coefficient of K_t is negative. K will therefore oscillate above and below K^* in alternate periods. The duration of the cycle will be $2t$. (This case is really the application of the cobweb theorem to the production of durable goods. On the cobweb theorem see Chapter V, § 3.)

(2) The case of reaction lags.

Investment decisions taken at the beginning of period t are based on the surplus or deficiency in the stock of capital at the beginning of period $t-1$.

$$K_{t+1} - K_t = I_t = a(K^* - K_{t-1})$$
$$K_{t+1} = aK^* + K_t - aK_{t+1}$$

This is a second-order difference equation, which will lead to cycles (as explained in Chapter II, p. 28, n.1) if $1 < 4a$. The duration of the cycle here will be greater than in the competitive distortion case, its exact value depending on the size of the parameters (where $a = 1$, the duration of the cycle will be $4t$). Cf. J. Tinbergen and J. J. Polak, *Dynamics of Business Cycles* (1950), pp. 241–5.

Moreover if the capital stock adjustment principle and the multiplier or other influences making for fluctuations are in operation, the additional sources of maladjustment named in this section will aggravate the tendency to fluctuations. This is possibly their chief importance.

§ 2. **Irrational Movements in Expectations.** Those older writers on industrial fluctuations who saw them as waves of optimism and pessimism regarded as one of the chief causes of the business cycle man's inborn tendency to be over-elated in prosperity and in adversity too much cast down. There is no doubt that in many booms there has been a widespread tendency to appraise future prospects in certain sectors of the economy more optimistically than any reasonable calculations justify. The development of such a tendency is what early nineteenth-century writers called 'mania'. In some cases, perhaps the majority, it has been the suppliers of finance rather than the entrepreneurs themselves who have been chiefly influenced by undue optimism, but the effect is much the same either way.

If a boom is receiving a substantial amount of support from irrational optimism, it is bound to be very vulnerable to any jolt to expectations. Such a jolt may be purely accidental, as where a political event starts a retreat in prices on the stock exchange; or it may be more fundamental, as where the completion of certain investment projects makes it plain that investment in that particular line has been pushed further than reasonable expectations could justify. The further such optimism has gone, the more violent will be the collapse when expectations are revised.

In emphasising the irrational element, one must not lose sight of one factor in the violent ups and downs of expectations that cannot exactly be described as irrational, even though it is unrelated to real economic forces. This is speculation. When prices are rising, speculators may buy with a view to subsequent resale and so drive up prices further, even though they understand perfectly well that the main reason why prices are rising is that other people are doing the same thing as they are. They recognise that the price-rise has gone much further than any real foundation for it would justify, but they hope to sell out before the crash comes. The only really irrational people involved are the ones who do not realise the speculative character of the market and so fail to sell out in time. Speculation of this sort depends upon the creation of favourable expectations, so it will not usually develop unless there is *some* non-speculative ground for prices to start rising in the first place. It therefore typically occurs in periods when the level of activity is already high.

Speculation can take place only in something that is readily resaleable, so it does not apply to most classes of capital goods as such. But it may well affect capital investment none the less. The chief vehicles of speculation are stocks and shares, real estate (both land and buildings), and non-perishable primary products. Speculation in the last of these is unlikely to have a great effect on fixed investment, though it may well influence inventory investment. Speculation in the other two mediums is capable of influencing fixed invest-ment more seriously. A speculative boom in share prices will lessen the cost of finance to firms and encourage invest-ment that way (cf. Chapter VIII, p. 144). Speculation in real estate will encourage building and also investment in public utilities and other services associated with land develop-ment (cf. Chapter VI, p. 108). It is probable that in both these ways speculation has contributed materially to the high level of investment in quite a large number of past booms.

A substantial proportion of the cyclical downturns of history seem to have started off with the collapse of some form of speculation or of some of the more extreme mani-festations of optimism.[1] In interpreting such events, there is always the difficulty of deciding whether the pricking of the

[1] This helps to explain the absence of a lag between the movement of the capital-output ratio and the movement of investment at the upper turning point (see p. 43, n. 1, above): on a good many occasions the proximate cause of the downturn was not an overall rise in the capital-output ratio.

bubble of expectations is to be regarded as the basic cause of the downturn and subsequent recession or whether it was merely the proximate cause of something that would presently have happened anyway. If the speculation or mania is confined to some relatively small sector of the economy, as has often been the case, its collapse should not normally lead to more than a minor contraction in activity, unless either. expectations are very volatile or else the underlying situation is such that a fall in profit rates would have occurred soon anyway. So if the contraction turns out to be a severe one, the collapse of optimism may reasonably be regarded as no more than the proximate cause of the contraction. We do in fact find quite a number of occasions when an upset of speculation took place but did *not* lead to more than a minor recession because underlying conditions were favourable. It is possible, however, that there have been some occasions when speculation really was the mainstay of the boom and its collapse was therefore in a more fundamental sense the cause of the slump. Such cases have probably been the exception rather than the rule.

§ 3. **Replacement and Scrapping in the Course of the Cycle.** The last two chapters have been concerned with the factors influencing net investment, i.e. the change in the stock of capital. But from the point of view of income determination, the significant thing is gross investment, i.e. the total output of capital goods. Capital does not last for ever, and some part of each year's gross output of capital goods is needed to replace the capital goods that are currently passing out of use because of physical deterioration or obsolescence. Net investment or the change in the stock of capital during a period is equal to the gross output of capital goods (gross investment) minus the amount of capital passing out of use.[1] The

[1] We are here defining the stock of capital and hence net investment in terms of the amount of currently useful productive capacity, without reference to its age. This is the definition that appears to be most convenient in business cycle analysis. The more usual way of reckoning net

percentage fluctuations in gross investment will normally be less than those in net investment, since only in exceptional circumstances will the amount of capital passing out of use fluctuate as much as net investment.

The general drift of the last two chapters has been that in the boom substantially all the capital passing out of use will be replaced, and new capital will be built in addition, while in the slump little new capital will be built and some of the old capital that is becoming unfit for use will not be replaced. If no new capital is built and replacement is completely neglected, gross investment will be zero. This represents the maximum possible rate of negative net investment in fixed capital. In a slump, as mentioned earlier, this may quite possibly fall short of the rate of disinvestment that would be needed to eliminate excess capacity and bring the stock of capital in an industry down into line with what is currently needed.[1] But it does not follow that in such circumstances none of the capital that is falling due for replacement will in fact be replaced. Much depends on the incidence of replacement needs. The equipment wearing out may belong to firms that for some reason are doing much better than most and have no wish to curtail operations; or it may be part of a larger installation, most of which still has some years of

investment is to deduct from gross investment not, as in the text, the value of the capital that is currently passing out of use, but rather the notional depreciation of the whole stock of capital in existence.

[1] Because of this it is not true without qualification to say as is sometimes said that the less durable is an industry's capital, the smaller proportionally will be the fluctuations in gross investment manifested by it. The idea of this is that replacement is a stable item which serves to damp down the effect of fluctuations in net investment. But as against this, the more replacement there is to be done, the more scope there is for neglecting it in the slump. Consider for example two industries in each of which the annual net investment called for half-way through the upswing, at the top of the boom, and at the bottom of the slump respectively, is 0, 10 and −10. Suppose that in Industry A the amount of capital wearing out annually is 10, and that in Industry B the capital is perpetual and never wears out. Since gross investment cannot be less than zero, its level at the three stages of the cycle will be, in Industry A, 10, 20, 0; and in Industry B, 0, 10, 0. Industry B has proportionally a more violent rise in the boom, but it does not have so far to fall in the slump.

useful life ahead of it, so that if the worn out part is not replaced the whole thing will have to be prematurely scrapped. So some replacement will probably still continue even when industry is very depressed and burdened with excess capacity.

In considering what actually happens to scrapping and replacement over the cycle, it is necessary to remember that in practice the length of life of most forms of capital is not rigidly fixed. It is unusual for capital to disintegrate catastrophically and irretrievably at a single moment of time. What normally happens is that as capital gets older it becomes progressively less economic to use, partly because it itself deteriorates physically from use[1] or from the mere passage of time and so comes to involve higher running and maintenance costs, and partly because it becomes obsolescent, that is to say, since the time when it was originally installed, technical progress has evolved new types of equipment with lower running costs in relation to value of output. As a piece of capital gets older, three choices present themselves: (1) to go on using it a bit longer; (2) to scrap it and replace it; (3) to scrap it and not replace it, i.e. permit a fall in output and capacity.[2] The relative attractiveness of these alternatives is affected by the general level of prosperity in the industry, in the following ways.

(a) In a slump scrap-and-not-replace becomes more attractive relatively to scrap-and-replace. In a boom the former hardly comes into consideration at all if the latter is possible. This is essentially the main point we have been considering in the last few chapters and does not require further discussion.

[1] In so far as deterioration is due to use, it may take place somewhat more rapidly in the boom than in the slump, because capital is used more intensively. This consideration may occasionally have a significant effect on the rate of depreciation of fixed capital, but the corresponding point with regard to inventories is much more important. See Chapter V, § 2.

[2] This does not actually exhaust the possible alternatives, but it is a simplification which serves to bring out the main points at issue. Other alternatives include demoting it to a less exacting use or holding it idle as reserve capacity, at the same time either replacing it in its former use or not as the case may be. See below, p. 66, n. 1.

(b) In a boom, go-on-using becomes less attractive relatively to scrap-and-replace; conversely in a slump. The reason for this is that in the boom capital will be used more intensively than in the slump, and the saving in running costs from having newer capital is greater, the more intensive is the utilisation of the capital. The inefficiency of the old machine will matter more if it is being used round the clock than if it is being used only one shift a day. The effect of this in the boom is that gross investment (and hence national income, via the multiplier) rises by more than might be expected if regard were had only to the factors influencing net investment, since replacement also is speeded up. The effect of the corresponding point in the slump is to weaken somewhat the conclusion stated earlier, that some replacement will go on even in depression: granted that the scrap-and-not-replace alternative may in some circumstances be out of the question, it may be possible at a pinch to postpone replacement and make do with the old capital a bit longer.

(c) Finally, in a slump scrap-and-not-replace becomes more attractive relatively to go-on-using, simply because production becomes less profitable. Conversely in the boom old equipment may be kept in service for the time being to meet the overflow demand rather than be consigned to the scrap-heap, if it cannot immediately be replaced or if the demand is thought to be only temporary. On this account, therefore, there is some tendency for old equipment to be scrapped more readily in the slump than in the boom. This counter-balances the tendency in the opposite direction resulting from the considerations mentioned in (b) above: a slump discourages scrapping if scrapping necessitates replacement, but encourages scrapping without replacement. It is therefore not clear whether in net scrapping will be higher or slower in the slump than in the boom. Unlike gross investment, scrapping does not as such have any direct influence on effective demand. It does, however, make a difference to the inducement to invest subsequently, on account of its effect on the size of the capital stock in existence.[1]

These various factors will cause the movements of gross and of net investment over the cycle to differ to a greater or less extent from what they would be if the length of life of capital equipment were rigidly fixed. As a rule, however, they will not make a major difference to the pattern of the cycle.

§ **4. Replacement: Echoes and Shocks.** We have so far been considering how fluctuations in national income may influence replacement and possibly be affected by it in turn. We turn now to another type of possibility, namely that fluctuations in replacement investment (with consequent repercussions on national income) may develop for reasons quite independent of any contemporaneous changes in national income. Such fluctuations are liable to arise if the proportion

---

[1] In addition to the three options discussed in the text, a fourth which will often be chosen in the slump is hold-idle-without-replacement. The ways in which a slump affects the relative attractiveness of this option and the other three may be summarised as follows. (In the boom everything applies in reverse.)

(1) It will become more attractive relative to go-on-using because of the fall in profits. This does not as such imply any change either in income-generating investment or in the amount of capacity in existence.

(2) *A fortiori*, it will become more attractive relatively to scrap-and-replace. This is part of the general decline in investment in the slump.

(3) Whether it becomes more or less attractive relative to scrap-and-not-replace is unclear. The advantage of holding capacity idle at any time compared with scrapping it lies in the expectation of future quasi-rents when conditions improve. In so far as a slump creates gloomy expectations about the future, scrapping will be encouraged relative to holding idle. This is analogous to the effect referred to in (c) in the text, and like it affects the subsequent inducement to invest rather than effective demand at the time. However it is less reliable than the effect referred to in (c), since the fall in expected future quasi-rents, which makes scrapping more attractive relative to holding idle, is a subjective matter, whereas the fall in current profits, which makes scrapping more attractive relative to going-on-using, is an objective fact. An influence in the opposite direction—in favour, that is to say, of holding idle—is exerted by the fall in the scrap value of old equipment in the slump.

of the capital stock falling due for replacement is subject to significant changes.

The first possible reason for such changes comes from unevenness in the age-composition of the capital stock. Suppose that all capital needs to be replaced after ten years. If net investment has been carried out at an even pace over the last ten years, 10% of the capital stock will be one year old, 10% two years old, 10% three years old and so on. 10% of the capital stock will then fall due for replacement regularly every year. But if the pace of past investment has not been smooth, the case will be different. Suppose for example that there was a great boom in year 1 to which a large part of the present capital stock owes its origin, and that after that relatively little new investment was done. Because of the uneven age distribution of the capital stock, replacement needs in year 11, ten years after the boom of year 1, will be much greater than in subsequent years. This 'hump' will repeat itself in year 21, when the capital installed in year 11 becomes due for replacement; and again in years 31, 41, etc.

The possibility of such an echo of an original boom has attracted the attention of many economists and it has sometimes even been advanced as the chief explanation of the persistence of fluctuations.[1] Karl Marx, for example, found that the average length of life of equipment in cotton textiles in his day was ten years, and he compared this with the approximately ten-year period of the cycle in Britain at that time. Others pointed similarly to the ten-year life of iron rails.

There is no doubt that a single boom will lead to unevenness in the age distribution of the capital stock and with it the possibility of echo-effects in replacement. But for the echo-effects to be other than very mild, the length of life of the capital must be very uniform. For example if the life

[1] For further treatment of the echo-effect see D. H. Robertson, *A Study of Industrial Fluctuation* (1913), pp. 36–45, and N. Kaldor, 'The Relation of Economic Growth and Cyclical Fluctuations', *Economic Journal*, 1954, pp. 53–71, especially pp. 56–61.

of different pieces of capital equipment varies between five and fifteen years, the replacement associated with a boom in year 1 will be spread over years 6 to 16, and will not make a very pronounced hump. The next hump will be even flatter. Reference to the *average* length of life of capital is irrelevant; what is needed for a real hump is that the bulk of the capital should have the *same* life. This is clearly never likely to be the case over the economy as a whole. Too much should therefore not be made of the echo possibility as an explanation of fluctuations in general. It may be of some importance, however, in the experience of particular industries, since within a single industry the length of life of capital is likely to be much more uniform than it is over the economy as a whole.

Another possible reason for year-to-year changes in the proportion of the capital stock requiring replacement is unevenness in the pace of technical progress. Here and in what follows technical progress will be understood in the broadest possible sense to cover everything that increases the value of output obtained from a given expenditure of effort.

Whatever may be its effect on net investment, technical progress will normally raise gross investment, in so far as it hastens obsolescence and shortens the life of existing capital.[1] In the long period, if entrepreneurs forsee the rate of technical progress and obsolescence correctly and adjust their depreciation allowances accordingly, any increase in gross investment that may result from a speeding up of technical progress will be offset by higher gross business saving.[2] Whether such

[1] Technical progress hastens obsolescence if it leads to the evolution of new types of machine, with lower running costs than the old, or to the development of new and preferred products, which require a different kind of machine to produce. If technical progress merely lowers the cost of producing and/or operating machines of the existing type, it will not affect the rate of obsolescence. But this will not normally be the case.

[2] This is subject to qualifications arising out of the fact that depreciation allowances based on annual depreciation in the value of the capital stock will not normally be exactly equal to current expenditure on replacement except in a stationary economy. For discussion of this point, which we

correct foresight is usual may be doubted. But in any case no offsetting movements in gross saving are to be expected in the short period. If technical advances are made at irregular intervals, gross investment will fluctuate accordingly, and in the meanwhile depreciation allowances will alter very sluggishly, if at all. Fluctuations in gross investment will therefore transmit themselves to the overall level of effective demand.

The question whether there is any systematic reason for the rate of technical progress or its exploitation to proceed otherwise than at a smooth pace will be considered in the next section. But some irregularity will be brought about in any event by the working of chance. Admittedly at any time there will be a large number of minor innovations going on, and if their timing is due to random factors, the laws of probability would make it unlikely for the number coming forward to differ a great deal from one year to the next. But there will occasionally be more important innovations, which create substantial investment opportunities, and these will be sufficiently infrequent for the law of large numbers not to operate. When such innovations occur they will be followed by a temporary investment boom. If the timing of innovations is random, some irregularity in the level of investment is therefore to be expected. This line of argument does not as such create any presumption of *cyclical* movement, but the irregular occurrence of major innovations will jolt the economy out of any equilibrium it may be in. Periodical creations of investment opportunities by technical progress are on this reckoning cast for the rôle of erratic shocks, which while not cyclical in themselves will be capable of sustaining fluctuations indefinitely if the inherent tendency of the system is to produce damped cycles (see Chapter II, § 6). In this they resemble wars and other political upheavals, and their importance is not to be underrated.

shall not deal with here, see G. Terborgh, *The Bogey of Economic Maturity* (1945), Chapter VIII, and E. D. Domar, 'Depreciation, Replacement and Growth', *Economic Journal*, 1953, pp. 1–32.

§ **5. Technical Progress as the Cause of the Cycle: The Basis of the Hypothesis.** It has been suggested, however, that technical progress has a more direct responsibility for the cycle —that it has an inherent tendency to produce periodic movements in gross investment, not merely irregularities. The idea underlying this suggestion is that investment incorporating the results of technical progress itself directly stimulates further investment in certain ways (quite independently of any multiplier effects it may have); and that a cumulative movement is thereby liable to be initiated which will continue until the stimulus is exhausted. This constitutes a possible reason for economic fluctuations distinct from any we have so far considered. It is essentially the theory of J. A. Schumpeter, and the rest of this section is based mainly on his ideas.[1]

When an industry undergoes a major technical transformation, involving extensive investment in new types of capital, it is not as a rule because of a single revolutionary invention; more often it is because the accumulation over a period of a large number of improvements have together made a major change feasible. Moreover on those occasions when a single revolutionary invention can be identified, as often as not the invention was little heeded at the time it was first made, and the resulting transformation of the industry did not take place till years later. Therefore when we find that innovatory investment has proceeded in intermittent bursts, it is not satisfactory to attribute it to the chance irregularity in the process of invention—in other words to relegate it to the category of erratic shocks—because the timing of the investment booms does not necessarily correspond to a like timing in the process of invention. There must be some mechanism which makes

---

[1] No attempt is made here to give a comprehensive account of Schumpeter's theory of the cycle. Moveover what follows differs from his treatment in arrangement and terminology and in one or two points of substance. The essence of Schumpeter's theory is contained in Chapters 3 and 4 of his *Business Cycles* (1939). Reference may also be made to his earlier *Theory of Capitalist Development* (1934), first published in a German edition in 1911.

even a smooth stream of inventions lead to intermittent bursts of innovatory investment.

The essence of the mechanism, it is suggested, is this. The initial obstacles to be overcome in making a major industrial transformation are great. And until certain first steps have been taken, other aspects of the transformation process are very difficult or impossible. But once a start has been made, the completion of the process is much easier and is done in a rush. An analogy may be drawn of a bucket into which water flows from a tap at a steady rate. The bucket has a trap-door in the bottom, normally held closed by a ball-catch, with a spring to shut it again once it has been opened. Until a certain amount of water has accumulated in the bucket, the trap-door remains shut, but presently the weight of water forces open the catch. The trap-door opens and all the water in the bucket then flows out. When it has done so, the trap-door is pulled shut by the spring and stays shut until enough water has accumulated again to force the catch open. And so on. The *regular* flow from the tap (inventions) leads to a *periodic* flow from the bucket (innovatory investment).[1]

It remains now to give more specific content to these rather general ideas. The ways in which innovatory investment facilitates further investment may be grouped under three headings: (a) imitation, (b) relative price changes, (c) increased availability of factors of production.

(a) *Imitation.* The commercial application of a new and untried idea is difficult and demands (as well as luck) special qualities of boldness, foresight, single-mindedness, salesmanship, etc., in the entrepreneur. These qualities, like any other kind of ability, are not possessed in equal measure by everyone. Therefore new methods will not be taken up equally promptly by all firms in an industry. When a new idea is first produced, in its original form it is very likely unworkable or of extremely limited application. As time passes,

[1] Cf. R. M. Goodwin, 'Innovations and the Irregularity of Economic Cycles', *Review of Economic Statistics*, 1946, pp. 95–104.

improvements are evolved, and presently one or a few firms succeed in overcoming the difficulties and apply it on a commercially significant scale. Once the way has been shown by a few such specially enterprising or lucky pioneers it will be much less difficult for others to follow suit. Moreover those who are slow to imitate will soon be driven to by competition, since those who have taken advantage of the innovation will be able to supply better or cheaper goods. Once a start has been made, there will therefore be a period of much more general investment throughout the industry. This period will go on until the whole of the sector of the economy that is affected has been adapted to the change.

The process of imitation may take a wide variety of forms apart from the mere copying of good ideas. Where the innovation consists in the development of a new type of product, fashion and the external economies and diseconomies of consumption play an important part in extending the demand for the new product. Another special case of imitation occurs when after one firm has introduced a new type of product, others follow suit not because they think it will be a particularly good idea but because they are afraid that the sales of their existing products will suffer if they cannot supply the full range of goods or services supplied by their rivals.[1]

(b) *Relative price changes.* If an industry has undergone a transformation in the way just described, the consequences will not necessarily stop there. Once the new ideas have started to be carried into effect—but not before—the prices of the products concerned will fall relatively to the prices of goods in other industries, or else their quality will rise. This will lead to shifts in demand between industries and so will alter the structure of the capital stock required to provide for

---

[1] An application of this to transport was to be seen in the investment policies of railway companies both in Great Britain and in the United States in the nineteenth century: the construction of a branch line by one company was often followed by the construction of a branch into the same territory by a rival which feared that some of its existing traffic would otherwise be diverted away from it.

the demand. Capital will in effect be made obsolescent in industries that suffer a loss of demand because they stand in a closely competitive relation to industries where technical progress has been specially rapid; and obversely investment will be stimulated in the latter industries and in those complementary with them, in order to meet the extra demand that is attracted to them. Technical progress thus stimulates gross investment not merely by causing obsolescence in the ordinary sense but also by altering the pattern of demand and so causing a different sort of obsolescence. Gross investment will remain above the normal level until this obsolescence has been made good and the capital stock has been adapted to the new pattern of demand. The stimulus to gross investment from this source is likely to be especially great if there is a wide range of goods complementary with those cheapened by technical progress. This will occur, for example, if the products concerned are raw materials or semi-manufactured goods. The greater the induced change in the pattern of demand, the greater will be the stimulus to gross investment. The indirect stimulus to investment from the change in the pattern of demand may be more important than the direct stimulus to investment in the industry where the innovation first occurred; for example metropolitan public transport improvements, in themselves no more than a moderately important source of investment expenditure, played a large part in stimulating suburban building.

(c) *Increased availability of factors of production.* If the total value of output is given, an improvement in mechanical techniques by definition reduces factor input and frees some productive resources from their existing uses. The discovery or opening up of natural resources increases the available supply of factors in an even more direct way. So if in the initial position investment is to any extent restricted by shortage of other factors (labour or natural resources) available to co-operate with the newly created capital, technical progress will stimulate investment in this way too.

The significance of this will be considered at greater length in § 7 below. However, it is not plausible to suggest that the part played by such induced increases in factor availability in causing fluctuations in investment has normally been more than permissive, at least not as far as the factor labour is concerned. This is because the condition that the total value of output is given is by no means satisfied. By its effect on productivity technical progress admittedly permits a cyclical expansion of investment and output to proceed without being brought to a halt by labour shortage, and so increases the duration of the boom. But it would be difficult to maintain that increased factor availability is an active *cause* of the expansion of investment. For after all, the proportion of the labour force unemployed normally falls, not rises, in cyclical upswings. The same may not always have been true of land and natural resources. In particular, it may well be that, in a number of those nineteenth century booms that were specially associated with expansion into virgin territory, transport improvements really did make land and mineral deposits more abundantly available in relation to demand as the cyclical upswing proceeded. Therefore although the rôle of increased factor availability has probably in most cases been only a permissive one, it cannot be entirely written off as an active cause of cyclical expansions.

§ 6. **Technical Progress as the Cause of the Cycle: Appraisal.** The hypothesis advanced in the preceding section provides the basis for an explanation of the cycle quite different from any form of the multiplier-accelerator theory. The latter attributes the concentration of investment in the boom to the fact that during the boom national income is high relatively to the stock of capital. According to the hypothesis stated in the last section, on the other hand, the concentration of investment in the boom would occur even if the national income were constant throughout the cycle; it is due to a different cause, namely the stimulus afforded by innovatory investment as such to further investment. On this interpretation the amplitude and duration of the boom depend mainly on the importance and breadth of application of the innovations carried out during it. The hypothesis as stated in § 5 falls short in a number of respects of being a complete theory of the cycle, and space does not permit inclusion here of the many refinements and elaborations with which Schumpeter sought to build it into a complete account of the cyclical process. More important now is to consider the validity of the basic idea.

The theory depends on a certain model of the innovatory process which is not necessarily of universal validity. The notion of the pioneering entrepreneurs showing the way to the herd of imitators is more applicable to a world of small competitive firms, where the personalities of business leaders count for much, than it is to a world of bureaucratic oligopolies. Schumpeter himself recognised this, and he held, quite consistently, that what he called the 'institutionalisation of innovations' might spell the end of the business cycle as hitherto known. But the social and economic characteristics of the innovatory process must have differed a good deal between industries even at the same period in history, and hence we should expect to find the Schumpeterian theory more appicable to some industries (and hence to cycles dominated by their behaviour) than to others.

It may be noted next that, as applied to particular cases, the theory under discussion is not always very clearly distinguishable from the view that the importance of technical progress is as a source of erratic shocks. No one would deny that in some booms innovatory investment in particular industries has played a conspicuous part; but if this can be attributed to a single major invention rather than to the sort of chain reaction described above, it does not stem from the inherent mechanism of the innovatory process.

Although the theory is quite unrelated to the capital stock adjustment principle, it is not in any way inconsistent with it. The cycle will almost certainly have some capital stock adjustment repercussions, even if its origin is due to the behaviour of innovations. Investment may be concentrated in the boom *both* because income is then high relatively to the stock of capital *and* because technical progress has the effects described. This would seem to be a sensible view. The room for difference of opinion is about the relative importance of the two in any particular cycle. Schumpeter's theory emphasises forces affecting individual industries or groups of industries.[1] It is therefore more plausibly applied to cycles dominated by the behaviour of particular sectors of the economy than it is to cycles that affect the whole economy fairly evenly.

The most important application of Schumpeter's theory is perhaps to those booms—which are many—in which a large or dominant part has been played by developments in the sphere of transport and territorial expansion. Here at least the theory must be considered to make an important contribution to our understanding of the cycle. As noted above (Chapter III, p. 47), the capital stock adjustment principle is not well adapted to explaining fluctuations in railway building, because of the extreme durability of the capital involved and the consequent need to build in advance of demand. The same thing applies in some degree to investment in other transport facilities. The Schumpeterian theory, on the other hand, works particularly well here, because the cumulative effects of improvements in transport are unusually extensive. Whereas many technical improvements have repercussions over only a fairly narrow range of related industries, transport improvements affect the whole economy of the area served. When railways were first built into the new lands of America, they stimulated not merely the construction of further railways to extend and serve those already built, but also all classes of investment associated with the development of the

[1] Schumpeter did attempt to show that bursts of innovation would tend to occur simultaneously even in entirely unrelated industries; but his argument to this effect is not very convincing if interpreted as anything more than a dilution of his central doctrines by extraneous elements.

region: investment in agriculture, mining, housing, etc. Nor is the significance of transport improvements in stimulating other investment confined to the case of virgin land. The effect of improvements in public transport on suburban house-building has already been mentioned, and the spread of private car ownership has had similar effects.

§ 7. **Technical Progress and the Long-run Upward Trend in Investment.** We will now consider certain effects of technical progress which may give investment a long-run upward trend. These influences do not in themselves have any tendency to cause fluctuations, but their presence may have an effect on the character of fluctuations, and they are important for an understanding of the relation between trend and cycle. The following discussion of them stands rather apart from what has been said so far in this chapter and involves some more difficult and debatable issues.

Technical progress, defined as anything that increases output per unit of input, makes possible an increase in total output and income. If this possibility of increased output is duly achieved, and if the normal capital-output ratio does not alter, a rise in the stock of capital will also be induced because of the capital stock adjustment principle. Technical progress will then have served to stimulate net investment. But it cannot simply be assumed that total output will rise when technical progress occurs. Conceivably technical progress could result in the same output being produced with less input and an increase in the amount of unemployment. The same applies to the discovery of new natural resources or to an increase in the size of the labour-force due to population growth. These make possible an increase in output, and if an increase in output does come about, investment will be stimulated; but the result *could* merely be an increased amount of productive resources idle.

The question therefore arises whether technical progress and population growth can be shown to stimulate investment

directly and so raise demand and facilitate their own absorption in the long run, even if no prior increase in output is
assumed.[1]

The effect of technical progress that has occupied most
attention so far in this chapter as a possible source of short-
run fluctuations in investment, viz. the stimulus it gives to
gross investment by speeding up replacement, does not in
itself necessarily serve to raise demand in the long run. The
reason for this is that increases in replacement investment
will tend in the long run, though not within a single cycle,
to be matched by corresponding increases in saving in the
form of depreciation allowances. But there is another way in
which technical progress may stimulate investment and hence
aggregate demand. This is through its effect in increasing
the availability of factors of production. Brief reference has
already been made to this effect on pp. 73–4, where it was
concluded that it was unlikely to have much responsibility
for the *cyclical* movement of investment. However its chief
importance is rather as a long-run factor.

The effect is in essence a simple one, and it applies to
population increases and the discovery of natural resources
as well as to technical progress. It derives from the doctrine
that the marginal physical product of one factor of production will tend to be higher, the greater is the input of other
factors relatively to the input of the factor in question. One
aspect of this is the classical doctrine of diminishing returns
—the doctrine that the extra output accruing from successive
doses of one factor will tend to diminish if the amount of
other factors used is constant. Similarly an increase in the
input of one factor will tend to raise the marginal product of
other factors (assuming constant returns to scale). In any
given state of technical knowledge, additions to the stock of
capital, if unaccompanied by an increase in the total amount

[1] Technical progress and population growth may also influence demand
and so facilitate their own absorption through their effects on *consumption*
expenditure. See Chapter VII, § 3.

of labour and natural resources available, will tend to bring diminishing additions to output, since increasing difficulty will be experienced in getting the labour and natural resources needed to co-operate with the newly-created capital. This will act as a brake on investment. But a population increase or the discovery of new natural resources will increase the supply of other factors available to co-operate with any new capital that may be created and so will increase the output obtainable from new capital. Technical progress will have the same effect of increasing the available supply of co-operating factors inasmuch as it frees resources by enabling the existing output to be produced with less input than formerly. Thus population growth and the discovery of new natural resources and technical progress will all serve to raise the rate of return on new capital and so encourage investment.

The argument as thus stated is in very broad terms. The reliability of the stimulus to investment afforded in this way and the exact manner in which it is felt will depend on various circumstances which may now be considered.

Let us first consider the case where the real wage of labour (i.e. the ratio between the money wage and the price of final output) is not flexible in response to changes in the amount of unemployment: an increase in the reserve army of unemployed does not lower real wages relatively to what they would otherwise have been. This inflexibility may result from a variety of causes: institutional obstacles may prevent movements in money wage rates; or any change in wage rates may lead to an equal proportional change in prices; or real wage rates may initially be so low as to permit of no further reduction, etc.

In these circumstances, the question whether or not an increase in labour availability due to technical progress or population growth will stimulate investment will depend on whether or not there is initially excess demand for any class of labour. If there is general unemployment and excess supply of every type of labour, a further increase in labour availability will do nothing to encourage investment. If on the other hand there is initially excess demand for labour, as might be the case if the economy were pressing against the 'ceiling' at the top of a boom, an increase in labour availability would encourage investment. In the initial situation the shortage of labour would discourage investment because of the difficulty of getting labour to man the additional capital and because it would make for difficulties and delays in the supply of the capital goods themselves. An increase in labour availability would lessen these difficulties and so would encourage investment. In order for this effect to be felt it is not necessary that there should initially be universal excess demand for labour. The effect will still be felt to some degree, notwithstanding a fair amount of unemployment, if there is, say, a shortage of labour of good quality or of labour with particular skills or of labour in a particular locality. The effect is therefore not necessarily confined in its operation to periods of violent boom, though it is then that it will be strongest.

We may now consider the case where the real wage of labour is flexible, i.e. does alter (compared with what it would otherwise have been) if the supply of labour changes relatively to the demand. Then even if there is initially no excess demand for labour, or actually excess supply of it, an increase in labour availability will raise profit margins per unit of turnover and hence will raise the rate of profit on capital and encourage investment. On the other hand the stimulus to effective demand afforded by this encouragement to investment may be offset to some extent by an adverse effect on consumption if wage-earners have a higher marginal propensity to consume than the profit-earners in whose favour the distribution of income has been shifted.

Whether in fact the real wage is flexible in response to changes in the supply of labour relatively to the demand for it is a debatable question. It is difficult to believe that it does not have some flexibility in the long run, but there are many doubts and qualifications. There is less doubt that an increase in the availability of land and natural resources will lower their prices relatively to the price of final output. Hence an innovation which lessens the input of these factors per unit of output or increases their supply can be fairly well relied upon to stimulate investment.[1]

The conclusion that emerges is that an increase in factor availability due to technical progress or population growth or the discovery of new natural resources will normally stimulate investment, but will do so to a greater or less degree or not at all according to the circumstances. The effect will be most certain if there is initially excess demand for some or all categories of labour or other resources. If there is not excess demand and if at the same time the prices of the factors in relation to the price of final output are not flexible, an increase in factor availability will not stimulate investment. If factor prices are flexible in real terms, an increase in factor availability will encourage investment, but there may be an adverse effect on consumption.

It should perhaps be emphasised that the argument throughout this section assumes that there is a class of active and energetic entrepreneurs who are ready to do investment

---

[1] If the factor which is most scarce is land, and labour is relatively abundant, a further increase in the availability of labour, brought about by population growth or labour-saving innovations, may have little or no effect in encouraging investment. However it may be noted that an innovation which directly reduces labour input rather than land input may have the effect indirectly of saving land by altering the commodity composition of output in such a way as to lessen the relative importance of commodities that require land for their production. Thus if the demand for manufactures is relatively elastic, innovations that reduce labour input and hence costs in manufacturing will increase the output of manufactures relatively to the output of the products of the soil, and so will lessen land input per unit of output averaged over the economy as a whole. The obstacle to investment presented by shortage of land will thus be partially circumvented. In the absence of the cost-reducing innovations in manufacturing, the scarcity of land would have caused diminishing returns to accrue from capital accumulation; for on the one hand it would have prevented output from increasing proportionately in agriculture, and on the other hand an increase in the output of manufactures unaccompanied by a corresponding increase in agricultural production would not have found a sufficient market on account of the relatively high cost of manufactures.

in any line where the prospective return is sufficiently attractive. If this readiness is lacking, an increase in factor availability will not, of course, have the effects described.

The significance of the encouragement given to investment by increased factor availability will be further discussed when we consider the operation of long-run forces at the upper and lower turning points in Chapters IX and X and when we consider the relation between the trend and the cycle in Chapter XIII.

§ **8. Conclusions.** In the last two chapters we have surveyed a large number of influences affecting investment. Some of these are capable of leading directly to fluctuations, others are more likely to act as trend forces or as shocks or to modify in detail merely the pattern of fluctuations. To put it in the broadest terms, the chief reason for the waves of high and low investment that are the essence of the cycle is the existence of a cumulative effect by which if investment in any period is high relatively to its long-run trend value, it encourages investment in the next period to stay high or to rise further, up to a point, while if investment is low it likewise discourages investment in the next period. This is the feature which is common to all or most cyclical fluctuations. The cumulative effect may operate, however, through a number of different channels: through the interaction of the multiplier and the capital stock adjustment principle; through the tendency of innovatory investment to encourage more innovatory investment; through the state of confidence; etc. We have given most prominence to the capital stock adjustment principle (interpreted with due regard to the working of expectations) as being probably the most fundamental, but there is no reason to suppose that one channel functions to the exclusion of all others. Moreover certain factors that do not come under the present broad heading also have some importance, notably the tendency for equilibrium to be overshot because of lags in the adjustment process or because of the working of competition.[1]

The relative importance of the various elements responsible for the cumulative expansion and contraction processes determines the exact nature of the upper and lower turning points. But there is a basic element common to most turning point situations, other than those due to shocks or to monetary or purely psychological causes. High investment, while stimulating further investment through the channels mentioned above, also has, through a different channel, the opposite tendency, in that it tends after a while to bring about a temporary exhaustion of investment opportunities, either generally (overall capital saturation) or in a particular sector or sectors of the economy (completion of a major programme of innovatory investment). Obversely, low investment tends to build up arrears of investment opportunities.[2]

The same relative importance has not necessarily attached at all periods and in all places to each of the influences on investment that have been referred to. Nor, indeed, has the tendency to fluctuations itself, from whatever cause, necessarily always been equally strong. Changes are to be expected over time according to the character of investment and according to the psychological attitudes of those responsible for investment decisions. Thus in the nineteenth century investment in transport and public utilities was a more important part of investment than it has since become. For the reasons stated above, one might therefore expect the capital stock adjustment principle to have been a less dominant factor in business fluctuations at that time than subsequently. There has also been during the last fifty years or so in the United States a substantial decline in the relative importance of construction and a rise in the relative importance of investment in machinery and equipment; this

---

[1] We defer till Chapter VIII discussion of another important category of influences on investment, namely those concerned with money and finance.

[2] Issues arising in connection with the turning points are discussed more fully in Chapters IX and X.

tendency has been marked since the war. The consequent reduction in the average length of life of capital may be expected to make considerations relating to replacement increasingly important in determining the behaviour of investment in the future.[1]

---

[1] For discussion of changes over time in the relative importance of different classes of investment, see R. A. Gordon, 'Investment Opportunities in the United States before and after World War II', in E. Lundberg (editor), *The Business Cycle in the Post-War World* (1955), pp. 283–310, and M. Hastay, 'The Cyclical Behaviour of Investment', in Universities—National Bureau Committee for Economic Research, *Regularisation of Business Investment* (1954), pp. 3–35.

CHAPTER V

INVENTORY INVESTMENT

ALL classes of investment have their own peculiarities, both in their observed behaviour and in the nature of the influences affecting them. Two classes of investment, however, are more than usually idiosyncratic in their behaviour and call for special discussion. These are investment in working capital (inventory investment), which is dealt with in this chapter, and house-building, which is dealt with in Chapter VI.

In what follows we shall adopt the American terminology and refer to stocks and work in progress jointly as inventories. 'Inventories' thus means the value of stocks and work in progress in the hands of businesses at a given point of time. 'Inventory *investment*' is the change in inventories over a given period, and may therefore be positive or negative. It is equal to the excess of output over sales, sales being partly sales to consumers and partly sales of fixed capital goods to businesses. Inventory investment is thus a component of national output, like consumption and fixed investment. A rise in inventory investment, other things being equal, involves a rise in national output and income.[1]

---

[1] It is important to avoid confusion between *inventories* and *inventory investment*, the latter being the rate of change of the former. Thus a rise in inventories betokens *positive* inventory investment, but not necessarily *rising* inventory investment. Similarly inventory investment may be rising when inventories are falling; e.g. if inventories at three successive points of time are 100, 90 and 85, inventory investment rises from a level of −10 in the period between the first two points to a level of −5 in the period between the second and third points. It is inventory *investment* that is a component of national income.

§ 1. **The Application of the Acceleration Principle.** In order to cast light on the determinants of inventory investment, let us first consider the motives for holding inventories. Inventories are held partly because they are required by the nature of the productive process (material actually in process of fabrication comes under this heading); partly because it is convenient to transfer goods from one vertical stage in production and distribution to the next in batches of a certain minimum size; partly because it may be inconvenient or impossible to raise production or acquire more purchased materials at short notice, so that it will be desirable to have a reserve of finished goods and raw materials on hand to meet unexpected increases in demand; and partly for speculative reasons, because prices are expected to rise.[1] These positive motives must be weighed against the cost in the form of interest, storage expenses, wastage, etc.

Now the desirable level of inventories suggested by these considerations (except the speculative motive, which we disregard for the moment) is one that will normally vary in the same direction as output, though not necessarily in exactly the same proportion.[2] This is equivalent to the capital stock adjustment principle. On first inspection, therefore, it appears that the behaviour of inventory investment may be not so unlike that of fixed investment.

As shown in Chapter III, the acceleration principle—that net investment is a function of the rate of growth of output—is a special case of the capital stock adjustment principle. It requires that the actual stock of capital should always be kept in line with the desired stock of capital. The accelera-

---

[1] These motives may be compared with Keynes's motives for holding cash (J. M. Keynes, *General Theory of Employment, Interest and Money* (1936), Chapter 15). The first two correspond to the transactions motive, the third to the precautionary motive, and the fourth to the speculative motive.

[2] It has been shown that on certain assumptions the desired level of stocks will vary as the square root of output. Cf. T. M. Whitin, *The Theory of Inventory Management* (1953), Chapters 3 and 4.

tion principle, in its simplest form, lays down that investment is equal to the change in output multiplied by the normal marginal capital-output ratio. This unmodified acceleration principle is open to rather less objection as applied to inventory investment than as applied to investment in fixed capital, for the following reasons.

In the first place, the time-horizon for decisions relating to inventory investment is shorter. Fixed capital is expected to last for a number of years, but inventories held now will usually have been disposed of fairly soon. Decisions about inventory investment can therefore be based on the current situation and on expectations about the immediate future, without bothering too much about the more distant prospects. The current level of income will on this account tend to have a stronger and more certain influence on inventory investment than on investment in fixed capital, since the latter is bound to be affected by long-run expectations which may not be much revised in the light of current income changes.

In the second place, a desired change in the capital stock can be brought about more quickly in the case of inventories than in the case of fixed capital, so there is less likelihood of arrears of investment building up that will destroy the connection between the level of investment and the rate of change of output. As far as one form of inventories is concerned—work in progress—the adjustment to output will be more or less automatic. The same does not apply to stocks, but so long as sales are constant (a qualification that will be taken up in the next section) all that is needed to make good a deficiency in stocks is an overall increase in the output of industry; the increase does not need to be concentrated on a single sector of the economy, the capital goods industries (in which, moreover, because of the complexity of the product the gestation period is liable to be especially long). The contrast is still more marked when a contraction in the capital stock is what is required. Given the level of sales, the rate at which inventories can be reduced will be limited only by the difficulty of cutting down production. It will surely not take as long to do this as it does for fixed capital to wear out or become obsolescent, which is what determines the maximum rate at which the stock of fixed capital can be reduced.

In so far as inventory investment is subject to the acceleration principle, it is liable, in conjunction with the multiplier, to set up fluctuations in income in one or other of the ways described in Chapter II. The special characteristics of inventory investment so far considered are such as tend to make cycles originating from it of shorter duration than cycles originating from fixed investment. The short time-horizon means that entrepreneurs will set about energetically correcting any current deficiency or surplus in inventories, without the anxieties about the more distant future that beset investment in fixed capital, so arrears of investment opportunities or excess capacity will not be allowed to develop; and the same result will tend to flow from the comparative ease with which a given increase or decrease in inventories can be achieved.

§ 2. Passive Inventory Change. But there are other considerations affecting inventory investment besides the acceleration principle. The most important of these is 'passive inventory change'. If sales rise and output for the moment does not, inventories must decline by the amount that sales have risen, even though nothing may have happened to alter entrepreneurs' ideas about the *desirable* level of inventories. Such a movement in inventories occurring as a passive response to a change in sales is referred to as passive inventory change, and it is to be distinguished from the deliberate change in inventories which firms may bring about for reasons discussed above. Passive inventory change is essentially the result of output not responding fully to changes in sales. Such inertia in output may arise from mere reaction lags; from technical obstacles to altering production quickly; or it may reflect to some extent a deliberate policy of stabilising output.[1]

The possible consequences of passive inventory change can best be seen if we abstract from the acceleration principle for the moment and assume that the desired level of inventories is fixed independently of the level of output. Temporary departures from the desired level of inventories will be permitted, but steps will presently be taken to correct them. The most natural result of inertia in output in response to a change in sales might seem to be to stabilise output; and this is what does happen if the change in sales soon reverses itself. Stocks then act as a buffer protecting output from the fluctuation in sales. But the situation is different if sales persist at the new level or even change again in the same direction. There will then come a point when inventories can no longer bear the brunt of the adjustment and output must be altered. Moreover if the new high level of sales is believed to be permanent, output will have to be raised by more than the amount of the increase in sales, to make good the recent unplanned depletion of inventories. At this point a cyclical sequence of events will tend to be set in train. The rise in output raises income and demand through the multiplier and the rise in demand leads to some further passive inventory fall. The net movement in inventories in this period will thus be influenced by two conflicting forces: the intention to increase them, and the unplanned tendency for them to fall on account of the increase in sales. In the next period there will be a further increase in output, both to meet the increase in demand and to make another effort to restore inventories to normal. Presently the passive element in the

---

[1] The analogy to passive inventory change in the case of fixed capital is a change in the rate of depreciation by wear and tear that arises from a change in the intensity of use. But the importance of this in the cycle is not comparable to that of passive inventory change, since the intensity of use is only one of many influences on the rate of depreciation of fixed capital, and its effects, moreover, will only be felt gradually, whereas there is an immediate one-for-one relation between the level of sales and the rate at which stocks are run down, assuming output fixed.

total inventory change will be overweighed and the level of inventories will actually go up. Planned inventory investment will then decline. Total inventory investment will not necessarily fall yet, because the slackening in the pace of the upswing will reduce the amount of passive inventory fall and so tend to raise the total amount of inventory investment. But the fall in planned inventory investment will continue and will ultimately prevail. As soon as total inventory investment falls, income will begin to fall and the cycle will go into reverse.

This cycle is essentially the result of a lagged reaction process of the type discussed in Chapter II, § 5, and Chapter IV, § 1. Output reacts to changes in sales with a lag; it therefore reacts to an exaggerated degree to make up for lost ground; therefore the mark is overshot and there is presently a recession. It has nothing to do with the acceleration principle, which for the moment we have assumed away by taking the desired level of inventories as a constant. It represents a possible independent source of fluctuations.

If the desired level of inventories does vary with output, and at the same time there is a lag in the response of output to sales, the combination of the two potential sources of disturbance will strengthen the tendency to fluctuations. The results are quite complicated to spell out in detail, but the general outline of the cycle will still be similar to that just described.[1] Planned inventory investment will rise through most or all of the upswing, but actual inventory investment will persistently fall short of the planned amount because of the passive inventory reduction resulting from the change in sales. As compared with a cycle in which the acceleration principle is the only source of fluctuations, the element of passive inventory change, i.e. inertia in output, will tend to

[1] Cf. L. A. Metzler, 'The Nature and Stability of Inventory Cycles', *Review of Economic Statistics*, August 1941, pp. 113–29; R. Nurkse, 'The Cyclical Pattern of Inventory Investment', *Quarterly Journal of Economics*, August 1952, pp. 385–408.

increase the duration of the cycle by making it take longer
to correct a surplus or deficiency in the level of inventories.

§ **3. The Cobweb Cycle.**   It was assumed in § 2 that sales are
given to the firm as a fixed quantity and that any divergence
between them and output is met by an adjustment in the level
of stocks. This is one type of market mechanism. A similar
one is where a rise or fall in demand relatively to output is
met by a lengthening or shortening of delivery dates. This is
what will tend to happen in industries where the practice is
to make to order. Unfilled orders may be regarded as equivalent to negative stocks. The use of variations in the amount
of unfilled orders as a buffer between demand and output is
capable of leading to cycles similar to those analysed in § 2.

An entirely different type of market mechanism is where
sales are brought into equality with current output by movements in price. There is then no question of unplanned
divergences between output and sales, and inventory cycles
of the type just analysed cannot develop. Any excess demand
on a particular day is killed off by the rise in price and is not
stored up in the form of inventory reduction or lengthened
order books. But the existence of a lag in the reaction of
output to market conditions can still cause fluctuations,
though in a different way. These are the fluctuations of the
type known as the cobweb cycle.[1] The cobweb cycle is not
essentially an inventory cycle, but it is convenient to discuss
it here, partly because like the inventory cycle of § 2 it results
from lagged adjustment of supply to demand, and partly
because it will normally *lead* to inventory fluctuations.

The cobweb cycle has commonly been advanced as a model
of fluctuations in the markets for particular agricultural commodities, and the following illustration is chosen accordingly.
Suppose that farmers' decisions as to the number of pigs to

---

[1] The name derives from the diagram that has been used to illustrate it.
Cf. M. Ezekiel, 'The Cobweb Theorem', *Quarterly Journal of Economics*,
February 1938, pp. 255–80.

raise vary directly with the current price of pigs. Suppose further that the demand for pigs is not perfectly elastic, so that their price varies inversely with the number offered for sale. Finally, suppose that a substantial period must elapse between the decision to raise a given number of pigs and the time when these pigs reach a saleable age. If in period 1 the price of pigs is low, farmers will decide not to raise more than a small number. In period 2 the number of pigs offered for sale will therefore be small and they will fetch a high price. Many pigs will now be raised, and these will come to maturity in period 3. So in period 3 the price of pigs will be low and we come back to the beginning of the cycle again.

This simple cycle is the result partly of the lag in production and partly of the distortion introduced by competition.[1] If pig production were controlled by a monopolist whose production plans were guided by the demand *schedule* for pigs rather than by their current price, the cycle would not develop. This competitive distortion is not a strategic factor in the inventory cycles described earlier in this chapter. Also unlike the latter, the cobweb cycle is independent of the multiplier. Indeed it does not necessarily involve any fluctuation in money national income at all. However, since fluctuations of the cobweb cycle kind will typically occur in industries where the gestation period (the time involved in the process of production) is substantial, the cobweb cycle in production must normally involve a corresponding cycle in investment in work in progress. The cobweb cycle will therefore affect national income through this category of inventory investment. The movement in national income may then affect demand in such a way as to amplify the cycle.

As a self-contained recurrent phenomenon, the cobweb cycle may be no more than a theoretical construction. But

---

[1] This distortion and the resulting cycle could still occur if excess demand were choked off by informal rationing by sellers instead of by price increases. The unsatisfied buyers would go round from one seller to another, and each seller would tend to get an exaggerated idea of the total amount of excess demand.

overadjustment of output of the type it portrays has on a number of occasions probably contributed to fluctuations in investment in working capital, as well as causing price fluctuations and inter-sectoral shifts of income.

§ **4. Other Influences on Inventory Investment.** Mention was made in § 1 of a speculative motive for holding inventories. The presence of such a motive in a firm's calculations does not necessarily mean that it is contemplating resale of stocks as a special operation outside its normal line of business. It may mean merely that the firm is laying in more ample stocks than usual because it suspects that prices are going to rise or is delaying buying materials because it has the opposite expectations. Such considerations are always likely to be present to some degree. They may apply in one industry only or over a large part of the economy. The withholding of stocks in order to profit by later higher prices is a well-known feature of periods of rapid inflation.

The cost of holding inventories includes an element of interest. The importance of variations in interest rates in inducing changes in inventories in normal times is open to debate, because unless inventories are held for an unusually long time, the total cost in interest will not be very great. But if the variations in interest rates are very large or if it becomes difficult to get credit on any terms, some effect must be felt. In particular the acute credit shortage or 'crisis' that has occurred in many cycles shortly after the upper turning point (see Chapter VIII, § 3) must undoubtedly have made firms anxious to cut down their stocks, especially in view of the tendency for passive inventory accumulation to occur at that time because of declining sales.

Many other factors may also be relevant. A good harvest may lead to stocks being built up and a bad harvest to stocks being run down. In periods of suppressed inflation, when excess demand is held in check by rationing and controls, there is a strong tendency for stocks to be run down in the attempt to fulfil orders as nearly as possible. (This is to be contrasted with the tendency of *open* inflation to lead to a speculative increase in stocks.) In the post-war years, moreover, the level of inventories had been a good deal affected by deliberate government policy. The government is itself a large holder of inventories, and it is also in a position to influence private inventory holdings, notably by import controls imposed to protect the balance of payments. These have on some occasions had a direct cyclical effect (on the balance of payments rather than on national income), since if imports are cut down by drawing on stocks in one year, imports in the next year will have to be especially large to compensate.

§ 5. **Inventory Investment in Practice.** Although in most years inventory investment is not a very large part of total investment, it is an exceptionally volatile part and therefore contributes disproportionately to *fluctuations* in the total. The statistics for the United States show that inventory investment has been particularly important in fluctuations of short duration. Between 1919 and 1956 there were six occasions (apart from the post-war reconversion year 1946) when gross national product fell for one year and then recovered: 1921, 1924, 1927, 1938, 1949, 1954. On these occasions the fall in inventory investment accounted on the average for no less than 75% of the fall in total investment. In the more prolonged contraction of 1929–32, on the other hand, the fall in inventory investment was only 27% of the fall in total investment. In the seven peace-time expansion phases of gross national product (1921–23, 1924–26, 1927–29, 1932–37, 1938–41, 1949–51, 1954–56) inventory investment accounted on the average for 47% of the rise in total investment. On the other hand if cyclical expansions are measured on a broader basis, disregarding one-year contractions and so yielding three expansion phases only (1921–29, 1932–41,

1949–56), inventory investment accounts on the average for no more than 26% of the rise in total investment.

It emerges therefore that inventory investment has been of decisive importance in minor fluctuations, especially in their contraction phases.[1] In longer waves its importance has been less, but still considerable.

The general tendency has been for inventory investment to fluctuate in step with national income, without any marked tendency to lead or lag. (*Inventories* go on rising after the upper turning point in income and go on falling after the lower turning point in income.) So much is plain. But the factors at work are so many and complex that it is by no means easy to establish firmly the *causes* of inventory investment's behaviour even on any particular occasion, let alone to generalise about them. Even if we understood better than we do the normal inventory policies pursued by businesses, special factors like speculation or inter-industry shifts in demand are always liable to confuse the picture. The relative importance of planned and passive movements in inventories is especially difficult to disentangle. It is found, for example, that the ratio of inventories to output generally falls in the upswing of the cycle and rises in the downswing.[2] Is this primarily because the desired level of inventories varies less than in proportion to output, or is it largely an unplanned phenomenon, which comes about because of passive inventory reduction in the upswing and passive inventory increase in the downswing? More study is needed, especially of inventory

---

[1] The greater relative importance of inventory investment in contractions than in expansions seems to reflect no more than the fact that cyclical fluctuations in inventory investment are proportionally greater than those in total investment, without there being any significant difference between the two in trend rate of growth. Part of the rise in investment in the expansion is due to trend forces, which do not affect inventory investment more strongly than they do other forms of investment, whereas *all* of the fall in investment in the contraction is due to cyclical forces, which do affect inventory investment especially strongly.

[2] M. Abramovitz, *Inventories and Business Cycles* (1950), Chapter 6. This book is a comprehensive analysis of U.S. inventory data for the interwar period.

movements in particular industries, before such questions can be confidently answered.[1]

Some students have interpreted the observed fluctuations in inventory investment as essentially self-perpetuating cycles of the type described earlier in this chapter. This interpretation leaves room for difference of opinion about the relative importance of the acceleration principle and of passive inventory change, and some responsibility for fluctuations in investment in work in progress may also be allowed to competitive overadjustment. An alternative interpretation, not inconsistent with the quantitative predominance of inventory investment in short cycles, is that endogenous cyclical tendencies in inventory investment, though real, are very damped —so damped that the cycle would practically disappear after the first time round if left to itself. Extraneous shocks will on this interpretation play a large part in initiating most inventory cycles, and the significance of inventory investment is that it acts as a *destabiliser*, picking up some movement in national income due originally to something else and making it perhaps several times larger than it would otherwise have been before permitting a reversion to normal. The shock in question may be a movement in fixed investment, which can be regarded as extraneous from the present point of view.

The difference between the two interpretations is really one of degree, since it can hardly be maintained that the inventory cycle is something that continues on its course unruffled by anything going on elsewhere in the economy. Moreover the relative importance of shocks and of factors endogenous to

---

[1] The complexity of the factors influencing inventory investment affords unusual scope for fallacious inferences and forecasts. The sort of example often encountered in the press is: 'Inventories are not too high in relation to output, so there is no need to fear a recession.' All that actually follows from the first statement is that planned inventory investment is unlikely to be negative, not that it is unlikely to fall, which of course is what would tend to lead to a recession. Or: 'The inventory-output ratio is still rising, so recovery is not yet in prospect'. This is more reasonable, but experience shows that the ratio goes on rising as a rule right up till the turning point in income, or very nearly; so nothing can really be inferred about the nearness or otherwise of the recovery.

inventories will not necessarily always be the same. One interesting suggestion that has been made is that extraneous shocks are most often decisive at the upper turning point of cycles in inventory investment and endogenous cyclical tendencies at the lower turning point.

The distinguishing characteristic of inventory investment's behaviour compared with that of other classes of investment is its tendency to have short period contractions and recoveries of sizeable amplitude at times when fixed investment is more or less steady, while sharing in the less frequent and more prolonged contractions manifested from time to time by fixed investment itself. The chief reasons for this difference between inventory investment and fixed investment, as suggested by what has been said in this chapter, are two. In the first place, divergences between the actual and the desired capital stock arise more easily in the case of inventories than in the case of fixed capital. This is partly because of the phenomenon of passive inventory change, and partly because the short time-horizon of inventory investment makes the desired level of inventories move closely in line with changes in national income. For these reasons relatively minor erratic disturbances in national income which do not significantly upset the momentum of existing tendencies in fixed investment may set in train substantial fluctuations in inventory investment. In the second place, divergences between the actual and the desired capital stock will be more quickly corrected in the case of inventories, especially when a contraction is what is called for. This means that a cycle once started will complete its course more quickly than a cycle in fixed investment.

CHAPTER VI

INVESTMENT IN HOUSE-BUILDING

§ **1. The Cyclical Behaviour of House-building.** House-building has in general been the most unstable constituent of fixed investment. It has also been one of the most important ones, amounting in some periods to a quarter or more of total investment. Moreover the volume of house-building largely determines the level of certain other forms of investment, such as the construction of urban public utilities, and it has a significant effect on the demand for consumers' durables in the form of fittings and furnishings. House-building's share in total investment has had a long-period tendency to fall, at least in the United States, but on the other hand its fluctuations have become more violent, so that its importance in the cycle has if anything increased. The violence of its fluctuations in the United States in the inter-war period may be gauged from the fact that the number of houses built in 1933 was barely one-tenth of the number built in 1925.

However it is the peculiarity of its behaviour rather than merely its quantitative importance that makes house-building require separate discussion. The movement of house-building over the last hundred years in Great Britain and the United States is shown in Diagram 7. The distinctive feature in both countries is the long duration of each cycle, averaging about 20 years in the United States and rather longer in Great Britain. Good evidence of roughly twenty-year cycles in building exists also for Germany, Sweden, and Canada.[1] In its cyclical behaviour building thus stands at

[1] Cf. G. F. Warren and F. A. Pearson, *World Prices and the Building Industry* (1937), pp. 123–7. Fragmentary data on building in the U.S.A. in the period before that covered by Diagram 7 point to booms in the 1830's and 1850's, maintaining the roughly 20-year periodicity. (Cf. Warren and Pearson, *ibid.*, p. 99.) The evidence on building in Britain before 1856 is less clear and does not on the whole support the notion of a twenty- or thirty-year periodicity in that epoch. See below, Chapter XII, p. 222.

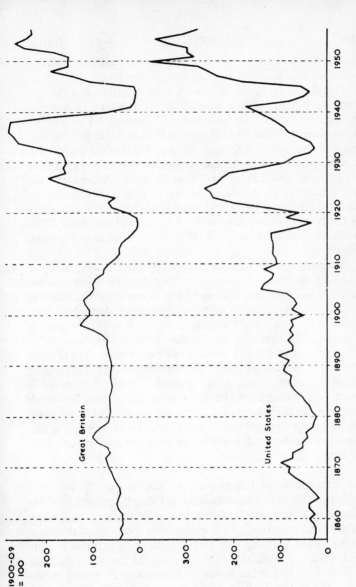

DIAGRAM 7. Number of houses built in Great Britain and in United States, 1856–1957, as percentages of average number in 1900–09. *Sources: Great Britain: 1856–1950, B. Weber, 'A New Index of Residential Construction and Long Cycles in House-Building in Great Britain, 1838–1950', Scottish Journal of Political Economy, 1955, pp. 104–32; 1951–57, Official returns. United States: 1856–88, U.S. Bureau of the Census, Historical Statistics of the United States, 1789–1945 (1949), Series H-75; 1889–1950, D. M. Blank, The Volume of Residential Construction, 1889–1950 (1954); 1951–57, Official returns.*

the opposite extreme from inventory investment, with its characteristically short fluctuations.

The corollary of the unusually long duration of cycles in building is that quite a number of fluctuations in national income leave little or no mark on building. This applies particularly to short-lived fluctuations in national income (e.g. the contractions of 1921 and 1938 in the United States) but it also applies to some longer-lasting ones (e.g. the expansions of 1886–90 and 1903–7 in Great Britain). Moreover even when building does move broadly in line with national income, there are quite often important differences in the dates of the turning points (e.g. in the American boom of the 1920s building reached a peak in 1925 and national income not till 1929).

Because of building's seemingly regular twenty-year cycle and its not infrequent divergence in behaviour from national income, some writers have been led to speak of 'the building cycle', as a phenomenon quite separate and independent from fluctuations in general business activity. It will be argued in Chapter XII that the connection between fluctuations in building and in general activity has been closer than is often supposed. But in any case to treat the two as independent is unsatisfactory on *a priori* grounds. Even if building is quite uninfluenced by the level of national income, which itself seems unlikely, national income cannot fail to be influenced by the level of building. Fluctuations in building can therefore not be treated in divorce from those in the economy at large.

§ 2. **Durability and Reaction Lags.** Let us start by assuming provisionally that house-building is basically similar to other classes of investment in that it is subject to the capital stock adjustment principle. This means that the level of decisions to undertake building will vary directly with national income and inversely with the existing stock of houses. Building will also be like other forms of investment in having multiplier effects and in being subject to erratic shocks. It may therefore be expected to play its part in any cyclical movement in investment and income that develops along the lines described in Chapter II. The question now is, how within this general framework the special characteristics of building cause it to react in a distinctive fashion.

It is natural and probably right to regard the exceptional durability of houses compared with most forms of capital as the chief reason for the long duration of fluctuations in building and its insensitivity to short-period movements in national income. Inventories are the least durable form of capital and inventory investment has particularly short fluctuations; houses are one of the most durable forms of capital and house-building has particularly long fluctuations. As far as mere physical life is concerned, houses may last for generations, given reasonable maintenance. Admittedly they fall in public esteem, i.e. become obsolescent, sooner than this, but even obsolescence takes place quite slowly.

The effect of the durability of houses in slowing down the tempo of fluctuations works most obviously in the slump. If the number of houses in existence is excessive in relation to the demand for house-room, the passage of time as such will do little to eliminate the surplus in the absence of a rise in demand. Therefore in the slump the process of wearing-out and obsolescence in other industries, where capital is less durable, may succeed in eliminating excess capacity and initiating a recovery of investment there, while there is still a burdensome excess supply of houses. If the rise in investment raises national income sufficiently, the demand for house-room may be raised sufficiently to get rid of the excess supply. But the recovery of building will at best be sluggish, and if the initial surplus of houses was very great, the new upswing in national income may run its entire course without stimulating much recovery in building.

The durability of houses also serves rather less directly to lengthen building booms. Because houses are so durable, an average year's building adds only a few per cent to the total number of houses in existence. The industry will therefore not be geared to a level of output that would substantially raise the stock of houses within a short time. So if there is a marked shortage of houses, whether because of some exogenous cause like a recent war or because a strong general boom has greatly raised the demand for house-room, this shortage will be difficult to make good quickly. The building boom will last a correspondingly long time, and may go on after other classes of investment have started to turn down.

Another possible cause contributing to the length of booms and slumps in building springs from the structure of the building industry. Since most builders employ relatively little capital equipment, excess productive capacity in the industry does not hang on during the slump the way it does in manufacturing. During the slump many small building and subcontracting firms go out of business and the flow of new apprentices to the building crafts dwindles, so that, when ultimately demand revives, the industry is for some time not in a position to handle a large amount of work. Likewise when a building boom has been in progress and demand then begins to slacken, the existence of many firms which sprang up during the boom and the attachment of a large labour force to the industry will enable favourable terms to be offered for new building, and output will therefore be kept up for longer after demand has begun to turn down than would otherwise be the case. This inertia in supply conditions in the industry not only tends to make each boom or slump in building last longer, but also tends to make the fluctuations more violent; for the longer building continues at its low (or high) level after demand conditions have begun to alter, the greater the deficiency (or surplus) of houses that will presently be felt, and the more violent the reversal will be.

A similar effect in prolonging and in amplifying building fluctuations is exerted by a rather different sort of inertia: namely the slowness of the process by which a surplus or deficiency of houses makes itself felt to builders. There are several reasons for this. House-rents have always had considerable rigidity, even before the days of rent control. The extreme imperfection of the house market makes general trends difficult to diagnose. The small size of firms in the industry does not make for well-informed reactions. Building may therefore continue at a high or low level, as the case may be, for some time after underlying conditions have begun to call for a change. There is in fact good evidence that turning points in building lag very appreciably after turning points in indices measuring the adequacy of the supply of houses—e.g. the proportion of houses vacant.[1]

Some authors have sought to explain fluctuations in building entirely in terms of lags of the type discussed in the last two paragraphs, without any reference to changes in the ultimate demand for house-room due to movements in national income or anything else. On this interpretation the required number of houses can be regarded as constant or smoothly rising, and the building cycle comes about from the building industry's persistent tendency to overshoot the mark because of lags, in the manner indicated in Chapter IV, § 1. But it is difficult to believe that if this were the only cause of instability in building, fluctuations would have been so violent or so persistent as they have actually been.[2] Moreover it would not be easy to explain on this reckoning why fluctuations in building in different parts of a country have broadly synchronised with each other, since houses in different regions form largely separate markets. It seems better therefore to conclude that while reaction lags have a significant effect on the

[1] Such statistics must, however, be interpreted with caution in view of the imperfection of the house market. What is relevant to the inducement to build is the proportion of *new* houses vacant, rather than the vacancy ratio for all houses, and the two may not necessarily move in the same direction. On this point, and also on other considerations affecting the inducement to build, cf. C. E. V. Leser, 'Building Activity and Housing Demand', *Yorkshire Bulletin of Economic and Social Research*, 1951, pp. 131–49.

[2] Analysis of data relating to the United States in the inter-war period has suggested that reaction lags by themselves would have produced only very damped fluctuations in building. See J. B. D. Derksen, 'Long Cycles in Residential Construction', *Econometrica*, 1940, pp. 99–116.

behaviour of building, they are only part of the explanation of its fluctuations.

The conclusion so far is that even if the main ultimate influences on the level of building are the national income and the stock of houses, as postulated by the capital stock adjustment principle, the unusual durability of houses and the presence of certain reaction lags in the building industry will be liable to pull movements in building out of conformity with those in other kinds of investment and into a shape more like that actually observed. But we must now go back and consider more critically what are the ultimate influences on the level of building.

§ 3. The Responsiveness of Building to Changes in National Income. The first question is how a change in national income is in fact likely to influence the demand for house-room and the inducement to build, in view of the great and obvious differences between houses and the type of industrial capital equipment to which the capital stock adjustment principle is primarily intended to apply.

An increase in income, if it is thought to be fairly permanent, may encourage some people to move from their existing houses to bigger or better ones. The net result of the ensuing general post of families between houses will be to increase the overall demand for house-room and raise house-prices and rents. Building will therefore be stimulated. This is the effect most nearly analogous to the capital stock adjustment principle as it applies to manufacturing industry. Moreover, 'better' is largely synonymous with 'newer' where houses are concerned, and a rise in income will therefore also tend to encourage building by strengthening people's preferences for newer houses and hastening the obsolescence of the existing housing stock. An important special form of increased demand for house-room that may result from a rise in national income is reduction in the amount of 'doubling-up' (two or more married couples sharing one dwelling). There may also be an increase in the number of single people seeking to occupy separate establishments rather than live as lodgers or with relations.

But an increase in national income also tends to have indirect demographic effects on housing demand that are probably at least as important as the direct effects just mentioned.

In the first place, it is well-attested that the marriage rate varies directly with the level of economic activity.[1] In a boom there will therefore be an increase in the number of young couples setting up house for the first time.

In the second place, it is a regular feature of the process of industrial development that in the boom the increased opportunities for urban employment lead to an increase in the rate of migration of rural dwellers to the towns. In the slump the movement to the towns dwindles or even reverses itself. Townward migration may or may not increase the *total* demand for house-room, but it means in any case that the existing stock of houses is no longer appropriately located in relation to the demand. The rate of obsolescence of houses is increased because houses in rural districts become obsolescent by virtue of their location. Building is therefore stimulated. The importance of this factor is underlined by the finding that, at least in Britain, fluctuations in building have been almost exclusively an urban phenomenon.[2]

In the third place, in countries and periods when immigration from abroad has been important, its volume has been found to vary strongly with the level of economic activity.[3] Admittedly even in the heyday of international migration, the number of immigrants in any one year was small in relation to the total population, but variations in the rate of immigration had a substantial effect on the rate of growth of the population and hence on the need for *additions* to the stock of houses. Moreover immigrants tended to consist chiefly of young adults, the age-group mainly responsible for the formation of new households.

[1] D. S. Thomas, *Social Aspects of the Business Cycle* (1925).
[2] B. Weber, *loc. cit.*, pp. 119–22.
[3] H. Jerome, *Migration and Business Cycles* (1926).

The needs of the newly arrived immigrants or country dwellers and the newly married couples will in some cases lead directly to the erection of new dwellings to accommodate them. More usually, however, these people will not themselves occupy new-built dwellings, since the latter mostly cater for families higher in the income scale. But these people's need for accommodation will strengthen the demand for the older and poorer quality dwellings, and so indirectly will encourage those who are better off to move into new ones. This 'filtering-up' process may take some time, so here we have a further reason why short-lived fluctuations in national income may not have much impact on building.

It may be concluded that changes in the national income *will* have an effect on building, but that the channels through which building will be affected differ somewhat from those applicable to other classes of investment and are such that it may take some time for the effect to be felt.

§ 4. Innovation in Building and its Cumulative Effects.

When building booms involve the construction of new types of houses or the development of new towns or suburbs, as they usually do, they have certain internal cumulative tendencies over and above any previously mentioned. These cumulative tendencies, by which building as such encourages more building, are essentially of the Schumpeterian type discussed in Chapter IV, § 5. Their effect may be to amplify or prolong fluctuations in building arising from other causes, or they may themselves in some circumstances be the chief motive force in a building boom.

A high level of new building hastens the obsolescence of older houses by calling attention to their lack of amenities compared with the new ones. When, because of the cyclical time-pattern of past building, a large number of existing houses are of about the same age, there may here be a significant echo-effect, with many houses sinking in the public esteem at about the same time. A similar cumulative effect arises inasmuch as the movement of better-off people away from older districts towards newly developing ones causes the older districts (typically the central regions of towns) to deteriorate socially, with the result that the remaining occupants become more anxious to move out too. Moreover, as the new suburb or new town develops, the growth of population will lead to the establishment of better transport facilities, shops, places of entertainment, etc., so that the attractions of living there will be increased.

The cumulative effect of improvements in transport is especially important. The causation works two ways: building developments stimulate transport improvements, and transport improvements stimulate building. Reference was made in Chapter IV, § 6, to the importance of cumulative effects of the Schumpeterian type in connection with investment in transport. Transport improvements create a demand for houses in new areas both by enabling people to live at a greater distance from their work and by shifting the location of production itself. The former is exemplified by movement from towns to their suburbs; the latter by the long-distance shifts made possible by the construction of railroads across the American continent. The significance of transport improvements in relation to the building cycle is twofold. In the first place, in so far as the transport improvements which stimulate building are themselves stimulated by earlier building developments, the nexus between building and transport is part of the mechanism by which building fluctuations acquire cumulative force. (It is also part of the mechanism by which fluctuations in investment in transport acquire cumulative force, the two phenomena being closely related.) In the second place, in so far as transport improvements are autonomous—due, that is to say, to innovations in the sphere of transportation itself—they act as a shock capable of setting a building cycle in motion.[1]

A rather different sort of cumulative force arises from speculation in land values. As a new urban district develops,

[1] Cf. W. Isard, 'Transport Development and Building Cycles', *Quarterly Journal of Economics*, November 1942, pp. 90–112.

streets are laid out and houses erected in areas that are
thought likely to rise in value as further development proceeds. This speculative element has played a large part in
some building booms in the United States.[1]

Forces such as these are capable of endowing building
booms with considerable momentum of their own, independent of what is happening to investment in other sectors or to
national income. What determines the duration of building
booms in which such forces play the chief part is difficult to
state exactly. Broadly speaking the boom will presumably
go on until the number of new houses available has become
large in relation to the number of people willing to contem-
plate moving to them. But the latter category is an elastic
one, depending amongst other things on the relative prices of
old and new property. One would not in any case expect
such a boom to be over very quickly once under way, since the
cumulative forces in question take some time to work out,
and in addition the factors of inertia, etc., discussed in § 2
will operate as in any other circumstances.

§ 5. Other Influences on Building. Like other forms of investment, building is subject to a variety of influences acting
as shocks, some of which have already been referred to. This
would not require special mention were it not for the fact that
the long duration of fluctuations in building means that the
repercussions of a single major shock may go on being felt
for a generation or more and may in fact dominate the movement of building during that time. One possible source of
major shocks—transport innovations—has already been referred to. But it is by no means the only one.

The most obvious form of shock is war. As a rule house-
building virtually ceases during major wars, and the resulting
shortage of houses when the war is over is increased if there
has been substantial destruction of property in the course of

[1] Cf. N. J. Silberling, *The Dynamics of Business* (1943), pp. 178–82.

hostilities. Wars also set up demographic disturbances. The birth rate tends to fall during wars and rise in their aftermath. This is reflected in the rate of formation of new households a generation later. There can be no doubt that wars have contributed very substantially to the violence of fluctuations in housebuilding both in Europe and in the United States during the last hundred years and have had a major effect on their timing.[1]

Reference may next be made to shocks arising from demographic movements more generally. Really long-term movements in population are not likely to have much effect on fluctuations in building, though they may affect building's place in the economy. But more short-term movements also occur in the size of the population and in its age-composition, due to such causes as epidemics, and also to the effect of past business fluctuations on marriage rates and birth rates. The effect of these movements on building comes into the category of erratic shocks, but in this context the term is liable to be a little misleading, inasmuch as the movements may persist over quite a number of years and be capable by themselves of causing substantial fluctuations in building. Moreover the possibility of echo-effects from one generation to the next cannot be ruled out, though the various other forces at work are likely to prevent them from emerging very clearly.

Immigration was mentioned above as one of the channels through which a rise in a country's income might stimulate building there. But migration is a two-sided affair, and building in the country from which the migrants come will by the same token be discouraged.[2] If there is a boom in country

---

[1] For a discussion of United States building cycles in which the rôle of wars is emphasised see L. Grebler, D. M. Blank, and L. Winnick, *Capital Formation in Residential Real Estate* (1956), Chapters III and XIX.

[2] In nineteenth century Britain there was a very pronounced inverse relation between the rate of emigration and the rate of townwards migration within the country. Emigrating and moving to a town evidently presented themselves as alternatives to those contemplating leaving rural areas. Since townward migration was an important source of building demand, a high rate of emigration thus served to discourage building by more than the absolute number of those migrating might suggest.

A which attracts immigrants from country B, the boom in A
will appear to country B as an external force acting to depress
building. Migration thus creates the possibility of building
fluctuating in opposite directions in the two countries.[1] This
applies whatever the cause of the fluctuations in migration.
In the case just mentioned, the volume of migration depended
on the level of activity in the country of destination A ('pull').
But the argument can be applied in reverse if the level of
activity in B is the determining factor—if what makes people
migrate is not so much good prospects abroad as bad prospects at home ('push'). A slump in B will encourage emigration, discourage building and so intensify itself; but it will
encourage building in A. Even if the stimulus to migration
comes from causes unrelated to business cycles (famines,
political upheavals, etc.) and migration therefore plays only
the part of a shock in the cyclical process, it will still have
inverse effects in A and B.

There has in fact been a marked tendency for inversion in
timing between fluctuations in building in Britain and in the
United States up till the end of World War II. This appears
in Diagram 7. There has no doubt been some element of coincidence in this inversion, and the fact that the American
building boom was in the 1920s and the British one in the
1930s can hardly have been due to the same causes as led to
inversion before 1914. But in the period 1870–1914 at least
it does appear that a systematic element was present, and the
effect of migration is the most plausible explanation.

Other influences on building include the supply and cost
of finance, and intervention by the government. In theory
building should be particularly sensitive to the rate of interest,
on account of the durability of houses, since the proportion
of interest cost to total cost of a capital good is greater the

[1] It also creates the possibility of divergent movements in building and
in other industries within B, since B's export industries, in contrast
to its building industry, will benefit by the boom in A. See Chapter
XI, § 4.

longer its life. It is possible in recent times to trace a connection between the terms on which mortgage finance has
been available and year-to-year fluctuations in the level of
building, notably in the United States, and the same was no
doubt true in former periods. But the major swings in building do not on the whole lend themselves well to explanation
in these terms, except regarded as an auxiliary factor.[1] The
same may be said of the effects of government intervention in
the housing market. Despite its great importance in recent
times it is not easy to regard this as one of the major causes
of the fluctuations in building that have occurred in the past.
In the future the case may well be different.

§ **6. Conclusions.** In trying to explain fluctuations in house-
building, there is the same room for difference of emphasis
as there is with other classes of investment regarding the relative importance of such factors as (1) the interaction of the
capital stock adjustment principle and the multiplier, (2) overshooting due to lags, (3) speculation, (4) the cumulative effects
of innovation, (5) shocks, especially wars and demographic
disturbances. The peculiarities in the behaviour of building
compared with other classes of investment are probably due
largely to the qualifications affecting the application of the
capital stock adjustment principle to building, on account of
the durability of houses, the operation of certain lags and the
indirectness of some of the channels through which changes

[1] The relative timing of recorded movements in interest rates and in the
level of building makes it more plausible to stress interest rates as a
strategic factor in building fluctuations in Britain than in the United
States. The fall in interest rates in Great Britain after 1932 from the
unusually high level that had prevailed in the 1920s suggests itself as the obvious explanation of why the main inter-war building boom took place in
the 1930s and not, as might have been expected from the very low level of
building before and during the first World War, in the 1920s. In this
case, however, the easier terms of mortgage credit made available because
of the rapid growth of the Building Society movement should probably
be regarded as an additional factor—a financial innovation—separate
from the purely monetary fall in interest rates.

in national income influence the demand for new houses. But the peculiarities in the behaviour of building are probably also partly due to the rôle played in the causation of building cycles by factors such as (2) and (4) in the list above, which are in principle independent of the level of the national income and are possibly more important in their application to building than to most other classes of investment.

CHAPTER VII

CONSUMPTION

§ 1. The Keynesian Doctrine and the Evidence. The doctrine that consumption expenditure depends principally on the level of national income is one of the foundations of Keynesian economics. It is because of this doctrine that the other main component of national income, investment, is regarded as the prime mover in fluctuations in national income, the rôle of consumption being a passive one.

Keynes postulated a 'fundamental psychological law . . . that men are disposed, as a rule and on the average, to increase their consumption as their income increases, but not by as much as the increase in their income.'[1] The application of this to the economy as a whole underlies the theory of the multiplier, as shown above in Chapter 2, § 1. We there distinguished two possible forms of the relationship between consumption and income (this relationship is commonly referred to as the consumption function: the relation between saving and income is likewise called the saving function). According to the first, the proportions of income consumed and saved respectively are simply constant. According to the second, the *marginal* propensities to consume and to save (the proportion of an *increase* in income consumed and saved) are constant, but the proportion of total income consumed (the *average* propensity to consume) falls with an increase in income, on account of the presence of a constant term in the equations relating consumption and saving to income. The two alternative forms of the relationship were shown in Diagrams 2 and 3 (pp. 9 and 11). In each case the curve relating saving to income is a straight line, but in the first case it

[1] *General Theory of Employment Interest and Money* (1936), p. 96.

passes through the origin and in the second case it does not.
One feature of the second case is that if income falls below
a certain level, saving will be negative, and consumption will
exceed income.

Developments since the publication of Keynes's *General
Theory* have not undermined the basic doctrine that income is
the main influence on consumption. But they have shown
that the shape of the consumption function—or the saving
function, it being a matter of indifference from which side the
matter is approached—is more complicated than was at first
realised.

The first attempt to test the Keynesian doctrine statistically
was with reference to the United States in the period between
1929 and the second World War. It was found that the
relation between disposable personal income (i.e. personal
income after direct tax) and saving in that period was such
that if disposable personal income were plotted on one axis
of a diagram and saving on the other, the observations for
the various years all came very near to falling on a single
straight line. This was naturally taken as a most satisfactory
confirmation of the Keynesian theory. The saving function
implied was of the type shown in Diagram 3 rather than that
of Diagram 2: while the data indicated a constant marginal
propensity to save (with a value of about one-fifth), the
average propensity to save was much higher in the boom
than in the slump, when saving was in fact negative for several
years. Some confirmation that this was the shape of the
saving function came from a different kind of evidence,
namely family budgets. It was found that in a given year
high-income families saved a larger proportion of their incomes than low-income families.

The data just mentioned relate to personal saving. Account
must also be taken of business saving (undistributed profits),
which is an important part of total saving. Data on saving
by business corporations in the United States in the inter-war
period revealed a pattern similar in general outline to that of
personal saving. Corporate saving was found to vary closely

with corporate profits. The marginal propensity to save implied by the figures was much higher than for personal saving —in the region of four-fifths. Dividends were much more stable than profits, so that corporate saving was a high proportion of profits in the boom but heavily negative in the depression of the 1930s. In this case too, therefore, it seemed plausible to postulate a more or less constant marginal propensity to save, but an average propensity to save that rose steeply with income.

However, it soon became apparent that these data (when appropriately amalgamated to show total saving out of total national income) could not be taken to have established *the* saving function. In the first place, evidence became available of the ratio of total net saving to national income in the United States per decade since 1870, and it was found that despite the great rise in national income during the period, the ratio showed no clear tendency to rise but stayed roughly constant until 1929. In the second place, forecasts of post-war saving based on extrapolation of the pre-war relationships turned out to be too high by an embarrassingly large margin. Both of these findings pointed in the same direction. The marginal propensity to save derived from the data for the period between 1929 and the war was much too high when applied over longer periods. (This remains true even if income and consumption are expressed in per head terms so as to eliminate that part of the long period increase in national income that is associated with population growth.) The rise in income after the war did not cause such a large increase in saving as expected, and in earlier periods the lower level of the national income was not accompanied by a particularly low average propensity to save.

As a result of these findings, it is now generally recognised that a distinction must be drawn between the short-run saving function and the long-run saving function. A given change in income leads to a larger change in saving and a smaller change in consumption in the short run than in the long run. The average propensity to consume appears to be fairly

constant in the long run, but in the short run it varies directly
with income.   Another way of saying the same thing is to say
that the short-run saving function shifts over time in such a
way as to cause less to be saved out of a given income as time
goes on.   The nature and causes of this divorce between
short-run and long-run behaviour will be considered in the
next section.

§ 2. **Reasons for the Cyclical Movement in the Saving-Income
Ratio.** The question is why movement of national income over
the cycle—movement, that is to say, in the level of activity—
causes changes in the ratio of saving to income, whereas the
increase in income that occurs as the result of secular growth
—movement in the levels of productivity and population—
appears not to.

There is not yet complete agreement about whether the
saving-income ratio has been constant in the long run because
the secular growth in income simply has had no tendency to
increase it or because such a tendency, though present, has
been offset by some other forces.   But the *a priori* reasons to
expect an upward trend in the saving-income ratio are not
very strong.   It might be thought that, when people become
better off, the immediate pressure to make ends meet will be
relieved and they will accordingly find it easier to save.   But
saving is essentially the postponement of consumption from
the present to the future.   Granted that a general rise in the
standard of living will make it easier for people to spare the
money to save in the present, it will also lessen their need for
money in the future; so it is not obvious that the inducement
to save will be increased.   There may, it is true, be other
rather less fundamental reasons why the saving-income ratio
should rise when the standard of living rises[1]; but to assume

---

[1] E.g. because an improved standard of living makes people less prone
to overrate present satisfactions at the expense of the future; or because it
makes them feel less helpless in the grip of economic forces and so more
able to plan ahead on a rational basis; or because the possession of
accumulated wealth is a pleasure in itself which can only be indulged
when other more basic needs have been met.

that the ratio will tend to be roughly constant in the long run is not unreasonable on *a priori* grounds.

For what reasons, then, do the consequences of short-run movements in income differ from those of long-run movements so as to produce the observed variability of the saving-income ratio over the cycle? A number of reasons may be suggested: (a) the inertia of consumption habits; (b) the belief that cyclical movements in income are only transitory; (c) the tendency for cyclical movements in income to be associated with shifts in the distribution of income; (d) the influence on saving of investment opportunities. Some of these reasons are closely related to one another and the distinction between them is not hard and fast.[1]

(a) The first reason was clearly recognised by Keynes himself. "A man's habitual standard of life usually has the first claim on his income, and he is apt to save the difference which discovers itself between his actual income and the expense of his habitual standard; or, if he does adjust his expenditure to changes in his income, he will over short periods do so imperfectly. Thus a rising income will often be accompanied by increased saving, and a falling income by decreased saving, on a greater scale at first than subsequently."[2] This probably applies particularly to falls in income, since people are reluctant to abandon their accustomed standard of living and may actually be unable in the short period to cut down some items of expenditure that are contractually fixed.

(b) The short-run inflexibility of consumption may be the result not merely of inertia but of a belief—well founded in the case of cyclical movements—that the change in income

---

[1] The short-run and long-run behaviour of the consumption function is a subject with a voluminous literature. See in particular J. S. Duesenberry, *Income, Saving, and the Theory of Consumer Behavior* (1949), and M. Friedman, *A Theory of the Consumption Function* (1957). On corporate saving, see S. P. Dobrovolsky, *Corporate Income Retention* (1951). On the British data, see L. R. Klein, 'The British Propensity to Save', *Journal of the Royal Statistical Society*, Series A, Part I, 1958, pp. 60–96.

[2] *Op. cit.*, p. 97.

is only transitory. It is reasonable to maintain a nearly steady level of consumption in face of fluctuating income if the fluctuations are expected to cancel out in the long run. No doubt it will often be difficult for an individual to distinguish between transitory changes in income and permanent ones. But in an economy with experience of fairly rapid growth, many people will be unwilling to regard any contraction of income as permanent; and they will be justified in this. When their incomes fall in the slump, they will reduce their rate of saving sharply or actually dis-save by running down assets or borrowing in order to maintain their existing level of consumption. When income recovers, this will be regarded as no more than a return to normal, and consumption will not be much raised until income has regained and passed its previous peak. To wage-earners the distinction between a permanent change in income (to which consumption standards will be adjusted fairly readily) and a transitory one (which will be met to a large extent by changes in saving) corresponds largely to the distinction between a change in the level of real wages on the one hand and a change between having a job and not having one on the other. Changes in income within a cycle are largely due to changes in the degree of unemployment, and are therefore accompanied by large changes in saving[1]; longer-period changes in income are chiefly due to changes in the general level of real earnings, and consumption is therefore more fully adjusted to them.

(c) The fall in income that takes place during a slump does not affect all members of the community equally. Among

---

[1] If the unemployed were already spending nearly all their income when they were still in employment and have little borrowing power or accumulated assets, they will not be able to maintain their previous level of consumption, or anything near to it, out of their own resources; but the same result from the national point of view is produced if they draw unemployment benefit from trade union funds or the state, since funds taken from these sources will not normally lead to a reduction in anyone else's consumption.

wage-earners, it is the unemployed who are most affected.
The real wages of those who remain in employment more
often rise than fall. The fall in income of those who lose
their jobs may therefore exceed the total fall in the wage-bill.
Since those whose incomes have risen are more likely to treat
the change in income as permanent and adjust their consumption accordingly than are those whose incomes have
fallen, aggregate consumption is on this account likely to
keep up better than it would do if the fall in national income
affected everyone equally.[1]

Those who become unemployed are not the only class who
suffer a fall in their share of the national income in the slump.
The same is true of profits. The proportion of the national
income going to profits rises and falls over the cycle, primarily
at the expense of salaries and other relatively fixed incomes,
the proportion going to wages remaining roughly constant.[2]
Since the short-run marginal propensity to save out of profits
is especially high, this tends to make the proportion of total
national income devoted to saving rise and fall with the level
of activity.

The reasons for the high short-run marginal propensity to
save out of corporate profits are themselves no doubt largely
connected with the great cyclical variability of profits.[3]

[1] Thus suppose that the marginal propensity to consume in response to
changes in income that are regarded as permanent is 0.9, and the marginal
propensity to consume in response to changes in income that are considered
transitory is 0.5. Suppose that in the slump the total wage-bill falls by
100. If all wage-earners were equally affected and all believed that the fall
in income was transitory, consumption would fall by 50. If on the other
hand the incomes of those who lost their jobs fell by 120, and they regarded
this fall as transitory, while the incomes of those who kept their jobs rose
by 20, and they regarded this rise as permanent, the consumption of the
unemployed would fall by 60 and that of the employed would rise by 18,
making a net fall of 42 only.

[2] M. Kalecki, *Theory of Economic Dynamics* (1954), pp. 28–41; E. H.
Phelps Brown and P. E. Hart, 'The Share of Wages in National Income',
Economic Journal, 1952, pp. 253–77, especially pp. 264–6.

[3] It is not suggested that this is necessarily the only reason. It is probable
that even in the long run the marginal propensity to save out of profits is
higher than out of other classes of income.

Company directors know by experience that the large cyclical fluctuations in profits are transitory, and they dislike ever having to make a reduction in dividends. Dividends are accordingly kept much more stable than earnings. As with other classes of income, the distinction between permanent and transitory changes in profits will commonly be a difficult one to make. Whereas with wage income, unemployment may give a criterion, with profits some guide may be provided by the distinction between a change in profits due to a change in the profit rate per unit of capital invested—a typically cyclical and transitory phenomenon—and one due to an increase in the total amount of invested capital, which can reasonably be regarded as permanent.

(d) Much business saving is done specifically in order to finance new investment within the enterprise. Since the inducement to do investment is higher in the boom than in the slump, this also will tend to cause cyclical movements in the saving-income ratio. The stronger the boom, the higher will the proportion of profits saved tend to be on this account.

These reasons serve to explain why the saving-income ratio changes in response to changes in the level of activity within the cycle. They are all essentially short-run factors and do not create any presumption that the saving-income ratio will alter in response to long-run growth in income. They thus serve to explain why the marginal propensity to consume is lower in the short run than in the long run.

§ 3. Consequences of Movements in the Saving-Income Ratio.

The high value of the marginal propensity to save within the cycle is important in limiting the amplitude of fluctuations in national income. The greater the extent to which saving, rather than consumption, is altered in response to changes in income, the less will be the cumulative effect on expenditure and on income itself. It is because the saving-income ratio rises in the boom and falls in the slump that fluctuations in consumption are proportionally smaller than fluctuations in investment.[1]

The behaviour of saving is also capable of providing a link between cyclical fluctuations in demand and long-run growth in demand. We have seen that the saving-income ratio depends not so much on the level of income as such, as on the level of activity, in so far as the latter causes incomes—or rather some people's or businesses' incomes—to depart from that which they are accustomed to and regard as normal or else causes changes in the distribution of income or in the prospective rate of return on investment or in the asset-income ratio. It follows from this that, if productivity and/or population are subject to a long-run upward trend, any given level of income will as time goes on be accompanied by a lower level of saving; for comparing a later date with an earlier one, a given absolute level of income will represent a lower level of activity (higher unemployment, lower profit rate, etc.) and a lower level of income in relation to the normal. Thus if saving is to be expressed as a function of income alone, the function will shift downwards over time. This downward shift, equivalent to an upward shift in the consumption function, is capable of imparting an upward trend to the level of effective demand.

The exact nature of this upward shift in the consumption function, and hence the nature of the long-run effect on

[1] The stabilising effect on income of the responsiveness of the saving-income ratio to changes in activity is seen in its most extreme form when, as may happen in some circumstances, it causes the marginal propensity to save for the economy as a whole to exceed unity or causes saving to fall without there being a fall in income. This may occur if there is a slight fall in the level of activity and employment, involving only a small fall in national income or even merely a slackening in its rate of growth. Consumption may then go on rising while saving falls. In such years many people's income will continue to go up with the trend rise in productivity, and their consumption will be raised accordingly. Those who become unemployed and some profit-earners will suffer a fall in income, but since they will regard this as transitory they will allow their saving to take most of the strain, and their consumption may fall less than the consumption of other people rises. The total fall in national income will then be less than the fall in investment. This is what happened in the United States in the minor recessions of 1949 and 1954.

demand, depends on which of the factors enumerated in § 2 is the most important. If the most important thing is the tendency for any fall in income below its previous peak to be regarded as transitory, the shift of the consumption function will tend to be a discontinuous process. Throughout the duration of a slump people will continue to view the level of income reached in the previous boom as their standard of normality and to adjust their incomes with reference to it. So long as income remains below its previous peak, the standard of normality will therefore remain the same and there will be no upward drift in the consumption function. Consequently the consumption function will not assist in bringing about the recovery of income at the lower turning point. Nor will it by itself be sufficient to cause income in one boom to rise above the level reached at the top of the previous one, for as soon as income regains its previous peak, the saving-income ratio reverts to its former level. What it will do, however, is ensure that *if* successive booms carry income to ever higher levels, income will not fall as low in one slump as it did in the preceding one. For in the preceding slump (slump 1) the standard of normality will have been set by the income attained in the boom preceding it; and this may be assumed to have been lower than the income attained in the most recent boom, which is what sets the standard of normality in the current slump (slump 2). Therefore in slump 2 saving at any given level of income will be lower than it was in slump 1, and likewise the income required to generate a given amount of saving will be higher in slump 2 than in slump 1. So even if investment (and hence saving) falls to as low a level in slump 2 as it did in slump 1, income will not fall so far. This is sometimes referred to as the ratchet effect. The mere fact that income has once gone up prevents it from slipping the whole way back.

On somewhat different assumptions the upward trend in the consumption function may be continuous and hence a factor tending to raise the level of effective demand at all stages of the cycle. It will then contribute to the explanation of the lower turning point and of the upward trend in income between successive booms as well as of the upward trend in income between successive slumps. This is what follows if, for example, short-run movements in the saving-income ratio are related to the amount of unemployment, this being taken as the measure of the divergence between the actual level of income and that which would be normal for the economy at its current level of population and productivity. If between two periods the overall level of real income remains the same but productivity rises and employment therefore falls and unemployment rises, saving may be expected to fall for the reasons indicated in § 2. The real incomes of those in employment will rise and they will treat this as permanent and adjust their consumption accordingly. Those who have lost employment will suffer a fall in income, but they will regard this as transitory and will try to maintain their consumption. They will be less ready to alter their consumption in response to the change in their incomes than will be those who have kept their jobs and have enjoyed a rise in real wages. Hence consumption in total will rise and saving will fall. Applying this now to the process of long-run growth, the secular rise in productivity and population will cause a given level of national income and output to be accompanied by a smaller amount of employment as time goes on. Therefore there will be a steady tendency for the amount saved at any absolute level of income to fall and the amount consumed to rise. This will impart an upward trend to the level of effective demand.[1]

§ 4. **Expenditure on Consumers' Durables.** While the considerations already described account for the general pattern of consumption's behaviour over the cycle and between cycles, there are many other factors that are liable to affect

[1] The effect of the behaviour of consumption and saving on the long-run growth in demand will be further discussed in Chapter XIII. See also R. C. O. Matthews, 'The Saving Function and the Problem of Trend and Cycle', *Review of Economic Studies*, 1954–55, pp. 75–95.

consumption in any particular year. These include both temporary influences which act as erratic shocks and long-term influences which affect the average value of the consumption-income ratio without having any distinctively cyclical effects. These influences include: the distribution of income after tax; the amount of liquid and other assets owned; the age-composition and family structure of the population; the standard of education as influencing the amount of consideration given to future needs; the institutional facilities for borrowing and lending; and capital gains or losses resulting from movements in stock exchange prices. The many influences at work make it difficult to explain why exactly such-and-such a proportion of income was consumed in any particular year. They make it still more difficult to forecast the consumption-income ratio in a future year. It is not clear, for example, precisely why the proportion of disposable personal income saved in the United States since 1950 has apparently been somewhat higher than it was in the boom years of the 1920s (about 7% as against about 5%). Still less clear are the reasons for the great rise in personal saving since 1952 in Great Britain.

In addition to the various factors named above, there is one that is or may be more systematically related to cyclical fluctuations and therefore requires further discussion. That is expenditure of consumers' durables—consumers' goods that yield utility without being immediately used up in the process. Such goods range in durability from motor-cars, household equipment and furniture to such semi-durables as clothing.

From the consumer's point of view the purchase of such goods is the acquisition of an asset. In this it resembles saving, which is the acquisition of a financial asset. Consumers may for this reason regard expenditure on durables as an alternative to saving rather than as an alternative to expenditure on non-durables. Purchases of durables will therefore be affected to some degree by the same considerations as affect saving. They will tend to rise and fall strongly with short-run changes in income, just as saving tends to rise and fall over the cycle more than in proportion to income. Strong cyclical variation in expenditure on durables will of course tend to lessen cyclical movements in saving and will increase the amplitude of fluctuations in consumption as a whole compared with what it would be if all consumption consisted of non-durables. Expenditure on consumer durables in this way acts as a destabiliser.

However this is not its only distinctive feature. Such expenditure has affinities with investment as well as with saving. In particular the demand for consumer durables is affected not only by the level of income but also by the amount of them already owned by consumers and by the extent to which those at present in consumers' possession are considered inferior by reason of deterioration or obsolescence to those currently offered for sale. Thus the demand for motor-cars at any level of national income will be lower after a period of heavy buying of new cars than it will be if the cars at present on the roads are few or old, as after a slump or a war. This is similar to the influence exerted on the inducement to invest by the size of the existing stock of capital, as postulated by the capital stock adjustment principle. In some circumstances the demand for durables may therefore fall off in the boom before income has reached its peak, if the stock in the possession of consumers has approached the point of satiety. Moreover it is possible for purchases of durables to develop replacement cycles or other such fluctuations that are at least partly independent of what is happening to national income. Movements in car sales in the United States in recent years have been such as to suggest the operation of some cycle of this sort.[1]

If consumers' expenditure on durables were entirely at the expense of their consumption of other things, the considerations

---

[1] For a fully elaborated model of the demand for consumer durables based on their affinities to producers' capital goods, see J. R. N. Stone and D. A. Rowe, 'Aggregate Consumption and Investment Functions for the Household Sector Considered in the Light of British Experience', *National-økonomisk Tidsskrift*, 1956, pp. 1–32.

just mentioned would affect only the composition of aggregate demand and not its amount, since a change in expenditure
on durables would be accompanied by an opposite change in
expenditure on non-durables. But, as stated above, saving,
rather than expenditure on non-durables, is likely in many
cases to be the effective alternative to the purchase of
durables. Fluctuations in the purchases of durables will
therefore affect the level of aggregate demand as well as its
composition.

So far we have been speaking as if durables were paid for
entirely out of current income. In fact they are not, and this
introduces further complications. Consumers' durables are
commonly paid for wholly or largely out of past savings
(which may or may not have been saved up expressly for the
purpose) or else by a credit that has to be repaid in instalments over a relatively short period (hire purchase). Consequently if circumstances favour the purchase of durables,
the total sum spent on them is capable of being considerably
larger than the sum that consumers have to disburse for the
purpose out of their current income. This enables fluctuations in expenditure on durables to be much larger than
would otherwise be the case. A further result is that an
impact on saving and spending is felt in periods other than
the one in which purchases are made. The obligation to pay
hire purchase instalments on past purchases will diminish
consumers' capacity to enter into new hire purchase commit-
ments. Likewise the desire to save up for future purchases
(if hire purchase facilities are not available or if a large
initial deposit is required) will curtail current spending power.
Quite complicated overall effects on saving are thus possible.
The fact that durables are largely not paid for out of current
income also means that the terms and availability of hire
purchase facilities and the amount of liquid assets owned by
consumers may have an important effect on the level of their
expenditure.

For all these reasons the functional relationship between
total consumption expenditure and income is liable to be less

regular than the functional relationship between non-durable consumption expenditure and income.

The importance of the part that has actually been played by the demand for consumers' durables in business fluctuations is difficult to assess. At the least it has acted as a de-stabilising factor, in whose absence aggregate consumption expenditure would have responded less to movements in income. More than this, it may itself have been to some extent a positive source of disturbance through its liability to develop fluctuations like those of investment, though it is difficult to believe that up to now this has been more than a minor factor in business fluctuations as a whole. On a few occasions its influence on aggregate demand has been fairly clearly identifiable.[1] Since a rising standard of living tends to increase the proportion of consumers' spending that is devoted to durables, this class of expenditure is capable of developing into an increasingly important source of disturbance in aggregate demand in the future.

[1] A good example was in the United States in 1955, when despite a substantial rise in disposable personal income there was a fall in personal saving, apparently attributable to an increase in purchases of automobiles.

CHAPTER VIII

MONEY AND FINANCE

IT was at one time thought that the causes of fluctuations lay wholly or largely in the sphere of money and finance. The trend of opinion has now swung in the opposite direction. Most modern theoretical treatments of the cycle are based on an analysis of real forces, and it is implicitly assumed that secondary importance, at most, attaches to any effects that may be brought about by changes in the cost and availability of finance.

But even if this approach is broadly correct, monetary factors must have at least a permissive significance in the cycle: even if fluctuations originate from real forces, monetary conditions must be such as to allow the real forces scope to work themselves out. One task of the present chapter is therefore to consider the reactions on the monetary side to a tendency for fluctuations to arise from real causes. If it is the case that monetary factors do not have more than a permissive significance in the cycle, this subject is less basic to the theory of the cycle than the matters we have been dealing with in earlier chapters; but it is none the less of some importance.

Moreover it would generally be agreed that on some occasions at least the significance of the monetary factor has been more than merely permissive. Attention will therefore also be given in the following pages to the ways in which developments in the sphere of money and finance may aggravate fluctuations or otherwise alter their character or act as an independent cause of them.[1]

---

[1] Throughout this chapter we disregard as a rule developments in the monetary sphere that are due to a country's international transactions. These will be dealt with in Chapter XI.

§ 1. Responsiveness of Supply of Money to Demand: (1) Through Changes in Interest Rates.

Let us first consider in what way the supply of money needs to behave in order to permit cyclical movements in national income to take place, assuming that a tendency to such cyclical movements arises from real causes.

The problem may be put in terms of Irving Fisher's 'equation of exchange' or else it may be put in Keynesian terms.

Fisher's equation of exchange, $MV = PT$, states that the total value of transactions in the economy over a period (expressed as PT, where P is the price-level and T is the physical volume of transactions) is identically equal to the volume of money, denoted by M, multiplied by its velocity of circulation, i.e. the number of times it changes hands on the average during the period, denoted by V. During a cyclical upswing the value of transactions rises, and there must therefore be a rise in M or V or both. Likewise in a downswing, M or V must fall. The present question is by what means the requisite movements in M or V are procured.

The question comes to the same thing if stated in Keynesian terms. The amount of active money (called M_1) that is needed in the economy varies directly with national income. We have to ask what are the means that bring about the rise and fall in M_1 that are made necessary by fluctuations in income.[1]

---

[1] One possible answer to the questions is that the monetary authorities simply vary the supply of cash in such a way as to enable the banks to 'meet the needs of trade'. In some countries and periods this is more or less what has happened, either as a result of conscious policy or because the central bank was following some rule of thumb that had this effect, e.g. keeping its discount rate constant. But such a policy runs counter to the general trend of thought about central banking that developed in the nineteenth century. According to this doctrine the duty of the central bank was to try to keep the quantity of money stable unless gold was flowing in or out of the country. Strict adherence to the rules of the international gold standard tied the amount of money in the country to its holding of gold, and so made it impossible for all countries simultaneously to expand their money supply, though a single country would be able to if

The most usually accepted answer to this question is that suggested by the Keynesian theory of the rate of interest. If the total quantity of money (M) is constant, an increase in active money (M_1) can occur only if there is a fall in idle money (M_2), M_1 and M_2 being together equal to M.[1] Now the reason why some people hold idle money, which does not yield any interest, instead of securities, which do, is that they are afraid that if the price of securities falls, holding securities may involve them in capital losses larger than the interest foregone by holding money instead. This is what Keynes calls the speculative motive for holding money. People will be induced to give up holding idle money if they can be made less apprehensive about the risk of capital loss. This result, according to Keynes, will be achieved by a fall in the price of securities, i.e. a rise in the rate of interest[2]; for people's views about the future price of securities are fairly sticky, and an absolute fall in the current price will therefore entail also a fall in it relatively to the expected future price. The likelihood of capital loss is thus felt to be reduced and that of capital gain increased when the rate of interest rises. Furthermore the rise in the rate of interest will increase the sacrifice of immediate income involved by holding idle money. For these two reasons a reduction in M_2 can be brought about by a rise in the rate of interest, and this is the way in which the extra M_1 that is needed in an upswing is made available.

The precise process by which the increased demand for M_1 leads to a fall in security prices may take various forms with-

it happened to be gaining gold from other countries. In view of the widespread adoption of this doctrine, at least in principle, by central banking authorities until fairly recent times, mere passive adjustment of the quantity of money by the central bank in response to demand cannot provide a general answer to the question asked in the text, though it may provide a partial one. For simplicity we shall assume in the rest of this section that the amount of cash made available by the monetary authorities is held constant.

[1] A rise in M_1 at the expense of M_2 is equivalent to an increase in the velocity of circulation of money.

[2] A fall in the market price of fixed-interest securities is tantamount to a rise in the rate of interest received on the sum invested.

out altering the final upshot; firms may themselves sell securities to provide themselves with extra working capital and so drive down their prices; or they may for the same purpose obtain advances from banks which then sell securities to avoid increasing their total asset holdings; or an increase in the amount of cash needed for hand-to-hand circulation may reduce the amount of cash held by banks and so force them to sell securities so as to keep constant their ratio of cash reserves to total assets. The extent of the rise in the rate of interest in each case depends upon the responsiveness of M_2-holders to interest rate changes. In the limiting case where the slightest change in the rate of interest causes large changes in the opposite direction in the demand for M_2, the extra M_1 can be procured with only a minimal rise in the rate. All this applies in reverse in a cyclical downswing when the need for M_1 is diminishing.

The rate of interest does in fact have a clear tendency to rise in the upswing and fall in the downswing, as the above line of argument requires. (The relationship is, however, subject to lags, which will be discussed presently.) But as a rule interest rate movements have probably not been the only agent at work in adjusting the supply of active money to the demand for it, and their extent has therefore been less than it would have had to be if they had been. The nature of the other forces contributing to the adjustment will now be considered.

§ 2. Responsiveness of Supply of Money to Demand: (2) Other Channels.

In the course of a general business expansion, manufacturing and other non-financial concerns may reduce their own accumulated balances of idle money in order to meet their needs for extra working capital or to finance fixed investment. During the slump they held the money idle because they thought it would be needed for their own internal purposes when business improved, and they preferred not to hold securities because of the risk of capital loss on selling out when the money should come to be needed. When business improves they may distrust securities as much as ever, but they think that the opportunity they have been waiting for to use the money in their own concerns has now arrived.[1] It is difficult to measure the importance of this as a way of making more money active during the upswing, but it may be considerable.

Another possibility is that banks may allow their reserve ratios—the proportion of their total assets held in cash or its equivalent—to fall in the upswing of the cycle and rise in the downswing, and thereby bring about cyclical movements in the quantity of bank deposits without any action on the part of the central bank. The motives for holding cash that have been discussed so far may apply to banks as well as to others. Keynes's 'speculative motive'—the expectation that security prices will fall—is capable of affecting banks no less than other investors, and a rise in interest rates during the upswing may therefore induce banks to lower their reserve ratios as well as inducing the public to lower its holding of idle money. Moreover even in the absence of interest rate movements bank reserve ratios may vary over the course of the cycle for a reason similar to that considered in relation to non-financial businesses in the last paragraph above. The most profitable use of a bank's resources is in advances to its customers. Advances are repayable at a set date (usually not a very distant one) and so they do not involve the bank in any risk of capital loss through market fluctuations. The risk is a different one, namely that the borrower will not be able to meet his obligations. What limits the amount of

---

[1] In Keynesian terms this may be described as a reduction in the amount of cash held for the precautionary motive, one part of the precautionary motive being the expectation that at some uncertain future date there will be an opportunity to make advantageous purchases. The reason why the firms hold idle money rather than securities in the slump is not that capital loss on securities is necessarily thought by them to be on balance more likely than capital gain, but merely that there is *some* risk of capital loss. This is what distinguishes the precautionary motive for holding cash from the speculative motive proper. Cf. R. F. Kahn, 'Some Notes on Liquidity Preference', *Manchester School*, September 1954.

advances at any time is therefore the number of credit-worthy applicants. In a slump this will be small. In such circumstances the bank can invest its surplus resources in securities, but if it does this it will have to sell out later on when business improves in order to be able to expand its advances, and selling out involves a risk of capital loss. It may therefore prefer to hold idle cash in the meanwhile and get rid of the excess liquidity when the opportunities for making advances improve.

In Britain bank reserve ratios have now come to be very stable and changes in them are not important. But the maintenance of a constant reserve ratio did not become an article of faith to British banks before the present century, and even in the inter-war period it was not always rigorously observed. In most other countries bank reserve ratios have been a good deal more variable. In some countries minimum reserve ratios are laid down by law, but the banks still can and do vary the amount of reserves held in excess of the minimum. The experience of the United States affords a good example of the way in which variations in bank reserve ratios may help to make the money supply fluctuate with the state of trade. Before the first world war reserve ratios showed a clear tendency to fall in the upswing of the cycle and rise in the downswing. With the institution of the Federal Reserve System, minimum reserve ratios were prescribed for member banks, and in the 1920s reserve ratios varied much less, though still tending to be above average in years of poor trade. Then in the 1930s a much larger rise in reserve ratios took place under the combined influence of a major depression and a large influx of gold from abroad.[1]

In an economy where confidence in the soundness of the banks is less than complete, the volume of money in the form of bank deposits is liable to fluctuate over the cycle for a

[1] See W. C. Mitchell, *What Happens during Business Cycles* (1951), Chart 1, Figs. 41 and 43, on pp. 45–6; also N. J. Silberling, *The Dynamics of Business* (1943), pp. 370–85.

reason additional to those already mentioned. The likelihood of banks failing or becoming temporarily unable to pay cash on demand because of the illiquidity of their assets will naturally seem greater in the slump than in the boom. Some people will therefore wish to hold cash rather than bank deposits, and moreover the banks will try to increase their reserve ratios as a precautionary measure and will therefore cut down their lending. This point is further considered below (pp. 138–41).

The various ways that have now been described in which changes in the level of business activity as such are capable of inducing the requisite changes in the supply of active money even in the absence of any change in interest rates serve to reduce the extent to which interest rates need to rise in the upswing and fall in the downswing. In principle a change in the level of business activity could even raise the supply of active money by more than the demand for it, thus making the rate of interest vary in the opposite direction to the level of activity, instead of in the same direction, for all or part of the cycle.[1]

---

[1] We have been concerned in this section with the means by which idle money is made active. The question may be asked why anyone should ever hold idle money at all if there is the alternative of holding interest-bearing short-dated securities or making some other form of short-term loan; for the risk of capital loss, which has been put forward as the main objection to holding securities, is virtually absent if repayment at par is due at an early date or possibly even on demand. This is a question of some theoretical importance, because money lent on short term is *prima facie* not idle and does not therefore provide a reserve capable of being drawn on to meet an increasing demand for active money. This question needs to be answered rather differently for banks and for members of the general public. (a) *Banks* may prefer to increase their cash holdings rather than acquire bills (short-term securities) if the rate of interest on bills falls so low that it is no longer enough to compensate for the costs of acquiring the bills (stamp duties, etc.) and for their slight illiquidity compared with cash and for any element of risk they may possess. Alternatively there may be collusion between banks to avoid bidding the return on bills down to this low level. (This is what happened during the 1930s.) (b) For *investors other than banks* it will not usually be convenient to buy bills. What they will do instead is to hold their money on deposit account at a bank, where

It is sometimes suggested that the increase in M_1 resulting from the increase in national income is not the only reason why the rate of interest will tend to rise during the upswing: for does not the whole of the increase in investment need to be financed and does not this constitute an increase in the demand for loanable funds?   The fallacy of this is shown up by the opposite and equally fallacious contention that the rate of interest must tend to fall during the upswing because of the increase in saving.   In a closed economy saving (income minus consumption) is equal to investment (output minus sales of consumer goods).   Therefore in the simplest case an increased demand for finance, resulting from an increase in investment, will be exactly matched by an increased supply of finance, resulting from purchases of securities by savers. So an increase in investment will not as such create either excess demand or excess supply of finance.

This is subject to some qualification on account of time-lags, however.   If firms seek finance for investment in advance of its execution, or if savers make their savings available on the capital market only after some delay, a rise in investment will tend to make finance more scarce: for the process of investment or saving will then involve some temporary locking up of cash over and above that required for normal

---

it earns interest and is repayable at short notice.   Now the point is that although deposit-account deposits earn interest, they are in effect idle, or partially so.   This is because banks keep a cash reserve against them, and therefore do not reduce their earning assets (or not to a fully corresponding extent) when customers want to make their money active and therefore transfer their deposits from deposit account to current account.   If banks keep the same reserve ratio against current-account deposits and against deposit-account deposits, as British banks do, the transfer of £1000 from a customer's deposit account to his (active) current account will not require the bank to reduce its earning assets at all, and the total amount of active deposits will therefore rise by the full £1000.   If the banks follow the American practice of keeping a lower reserve ratio against deposit-account deposits than against current-account deposits, they will have to reduce their earning assets to some extent, but by less than £1000, so the total amount of active deposits will still rise; more specifically, total current-account deposits will rise by a fraction of £1000 equal to the deposit-account reserve ratio divided by the current-account reserve ratio.   (I am indebted to Mr. Kaldor for illumination on this point.)

transactions purposes.[1] This will strengthen any tendency
that may be present for the rate of interest to fluctuate
cyclically for other reasons.

§ 3. The Rôle of Monetary Factors in the Cycle. In so far as
the rate of interest tends to rise and fall with the state of
business activity, the effect of the monetary factor on the cycle
would appear to be a stabilising one: high rates of interest
discourage investment in the boom and low rates of
interest encourage it in the slump.[2] If the relation between
the interest rate and the level of activity is linear and not
subject to any lags, interest rate movements will lessen the
amplitude of the cycle in this way without altering its fundamental character.

But the relation may not be linear: a rise in national income may affect the rate of interest particularly strongly if
the level of national income is high to start with and the more
easily available sources of idle money have already been
drawn on. In this case the shortage of money is capable not
merely of damping down the upswing but also of putting it
into reverse. It acts as a 'ceiling' in the manner analysed in
Chapter 2, § 4. The monetary factor limits or prevents further increase in income, and this leads to an actual contraction
because real forces do not permit investment to stay at its
present level unless income goes on rising. The evidence does
not suggest that shortage of money has normally been the

[1] Moreover when there is an increase in income some of the resulting
increase in saving will be of the 'unplanned' variety that arises from people
holding money temporarily until it is convenient to spend it on consumption. Such saving is unlikely to be made available on the capital market.
Since unplanned saving is essentially the result of an *increase* in national
income, it follows that the supply of finance in relation to the demand may
depend partly on the rate of change of investment and income as well as
on their absolute level.

[2] The movement in the rate of interest may exert a stabilising influence on
aggregate demand not only by affecting investment but also by affecting
saving in the opposite direction. While the direct effect of changes in the
rate of interest on the inducement to save is unlikely to be important,
difficulty in securing external finance for investment because of high rates
of interest may induce firms to increase their own saving so as to provide
finance, if they are determined to proceed with the investment.

decisive factor at the upper turning point.[1] But it is possible that some recessions have been triggered off in this way.

Monetary factors may also play an active part in the cycle if their working is subject to lags. At a turning point in activity it will usually take some time for it to become plain that the reversal is more than another of the temporary and irregular movements that are always going on. So long as it is thought to be temporary, individuals and banks will probably be content passively to allow their cash holdings to alter. Only when they are satisfied that the change in circumstances is permanent will they take steps to adjust their cash holdings and so bring about movements in the rate of interest. Moreover, in addition to this source of lag, it is the short-term rate of interest that is most directly affected by changes in the demand for cash, and the long-term rate of interest usually follows the short-term rate only after some further lag. These considerations help to explain the well-attested fact that turning points in interest rates, especially in the long-term rate, normally occur later than turning points in general activity. Now this lag means that over part of the cycle interest rates are moving in a way calculated to increase the amplitude of fluctuations, rising when income is falling and falling when income is rising. The cyclical upswing and downswing in income may therefore in their earlier stages owe some of their strength to monetary factors, and when after a time the movement of the interest rate changes direction, this lessens the force of the cumulative movement and so contributes to its ultimate termination. The existence of a lag in the monetary adjustment process thus creates a tendency to overshoot in the same way as any lag in the working of the system is liable to do (see Chapter 2, § 5). In this way it introduces cyclical potentialities additional to any that may be arising from real forces.[2] It is possible to construct a

[1] For a classic statement to this effect see Allyn A. Young, *An Analysis of Bank Statistics for the United States* (1928), p. 28.
[2] For a more explicit treatment of this see J. R. Hicks, *A Contribution to the Theory of the Trade Cycle* (1950), pp. 145–63.

model of the business cycle in entirely monetary terms along these lines.

Independently of any lags, the monetary factor may also act as a destabiliser in a more straightforward manner. As was suggested on p. 134 above, a change in the level of business activity may in some circumstances alter the supply of active money by more than it alters the demand for it. If this happens the rate of interest will fall in the upswing of the cycle and rise in the downswing, thus aggravating the cyclical movement of investment. Or if the rate of interest does not behave in this way over the whole of the cycle, it may at certain phases of it. Thus the reason why interest rates are observed to go on falling during the earlier phases of the upswing may be not merely that there is a lag of the type referred to in the previous paragraph, but also that the means analysed in § 2 above by which a rise in the level of activity directly increases the supply of active money operate more forcibly in the earlier phases of the upswing, when there is still much slack in the monetary system, than they do in its later phases.

The observed lag at the *other* end of the cycle—the fact that the rate of interest goes on rising for some time after the peak—undoubtedly owes much to a factor that comes under the same broad heading. This is the contraction in the supply of active money that takes place during the so-called 'crisis'. The nature and significance of crises calls for further discussion.

The term crisis is used to denote a pathological breakdown of confidence and scarcity of credit experienced at some point during or at the beginning of the cyclical contraction. Most major cyclical contractions in Britain in the earlier part of the nineteenth century were accompanied by crises, the last serious one being in 1866. Crises have fairly regularly accompanied major contractions in the United States until our own times, the most recent being in 1933. Crises arise essentially out of a pathological increase in the desire for liquidity, stemming from the fear that debtors, especially banks, will not be able to meet their obligations. They usually take their starting point from some prominent business failures. As a rule the first failures to attract attention are not of banks, though on some occasions bank failures or suspensions have occurred out of a more or less clear sky. But banks known to be creditors of the failed concerns become suspect, and those holding the deposits or notes of the banks in question demand payment in cash and so precipitate their downfall. Cash is probably also withdrawn from other banks as well, in consequence of the loss of confidence, and the drain of cash forces the banks to make a multiple contraction of deposits in order to avoid a fall in their reserve ratios. Moreover in such circumstances the banks will probably be trying to *increase* their reserve ratios as a precaution. The acute shortage of credit that results leads to further business failures and further destruction of confidence. Banks are obliged to suspend payments because their debtors default or because their assets cannot be turned into cash fast enough to meet the increasing withdrawals of deposits. These withdrawals are motivated by the fear that banks will become insolvent or by the belief that other people entertain such a fear. The fear contributes largely to bringing about its own realisation. Banks that are fundamentally quite sound are forced to suspend payments. No one who has cash will be willing to part with it for fear of not being able to get it back. The situation may end in wholesale closing of banks and complete paralysis of all business dependent on bank credit.

Crises have most often occurred shortly after the upper turning point of the cycle and so contributed to raising interest rates at that stage, but this has not been a universal rule. The business failures that start off the trouble may be due to a contraction which has already begun in some sectors of the economy or to the increasing credit stringency associated with the later stages of the boom or to mere mismanagement in the firms concerned or to some combination of all three. Very often they arise as a result of a decline in the prices of securities or commodities that have been the object of speculation during the boom. Since such price declines occasionally precede the turning point in activity as a whole, crises have sometimes occurred before any general contraction is clearly apparent. They then start it off. On other occasions the crisis has not come till the very end of the contraction process, as in the United States in 1933.

Whether a recession is or is not accompanied by a crisis, and if so how serious a one, depends on many things besides the severity of the recession itself. Some of these may be enumerated. (1) The overall strength of banks, and the extent of public confidence in them. The unitary banking system of the United States has been a disadvantage in this respect by limiting the extent to which risks can be spread within the assets of any one bank. (2) The policies followed by banks during the previous boom. The situation is worst, obviously, if they have allowed their reserves to fall or have acquired a large proportion of very illiquid or risky assets. (3) The extent to which investment during the boom was financed by loans, especially loans that can be withdrawn at short notice or loans from intermediaries (banks) which are themselves liable to repay their creditors at short notice, rather than by an expansion of equity capital. (4) The ability and willingness of the central bank to act as lender of last resort, i.e. to lend freely in the crisis in order to help restore confidence. The absence of any central bank in the United States before 1914 undoubtedly had much to do with the tendency to banking crises at that time.[1] (5) The state of the balance of payments. Most crises in nineteenth-century Britain occurred at times when a drain of gold out of the country had already brought about some degree of credit shortage.

If a crisis does develop, it will obviously strengthen very powerfully the contraction already arising from the operation

[1] The banks in New York and other large cities served some of the functions of a central bank and held large deposits belonging to other banks, but so far from lending freely when the crisis came they commonly suspended payments themselves and so made matters very much worse.

of real forces. On some occasions—the crisis of 1907 in the United States was probably one—weaknesses in monetary institutions have led to a crisis and hence to a severe contraction in activity when the real forces at work would by themselves have brought about no more than a mild or sectoral recession. On the other occasions, the crisis, while certainly making matters worse, was more or less inevitable in view of the gravity of the depression arising from the real forces.

§ 4. The Cost of Finance to the Firm.

So far in this chapter we have been concerned with the supply and demand for money. But the availability of finance to a firm depends not only on the general monetary situation but also on the view taken by those with funds to lend of the firm's individual position and prospects. This is commonly expressed by saying that the rate of interest a firm has to pay on a loan will exceed the 'pure' rate of interest (i.e. that payable on a perfectly safe government security of the same period) by an amount that depends on the credit rating of the firm, the excess being of the nature of a premium to compensate the lender for the risk of default.[1] It is the rate of interest including the risk premium that is relevant to the firm. Moreover the lender's assessment of the borrower's credit-worthiness will be reflected not only in the rate of interest charged but also, and perhaps more important, in a limitation of the absolute amount that can be borrowed at any rate of interest. Consequently factors governing the pure rate of interest are not the only ones affecting the availability of finance. Attention must therefore be paid to the possibility of systematic cyclical movements in lenders' risk assessments.

If lenders adopt a less cautious attitude in assessing risk

---

[1] The rate of interest paid by a firm on funds raised by the sale of its securities in the open market will also be affected by the marketability of its securities, and hence will tend to be higher for small firms than for large ones.

in the boom than in the slump, this will to some degree coun-
teract the stabilising influence exerted by whatever tendency
there may be for the pure rate of interest to be higher in the
boom than in the slump. On *a priori* grounds it seems inevitable that at least some lenders will behave in this way.
There is also empirical evidence that they do. The prices of
low grade corporate bonds have been found to vary *directly*
with the level of activity, instead of inversely as high grade
bond prices do.[1] It has also been shown that agencies whose
business it is to advise the public on the quality of bonds have
followed less strict standards in the boom than in the slump.[2]
It does seem therefore that lenders' attitudes towards risk are
significantly influenced by the level of activity. In earlier
times, when financing through the stock exchange was relatively a novelty, the scope for a destabilising effect on the
level of activity arising from this source was particularly
great, because of the high risk premiums normally required
on account of the untried nature and high ratio of debt to
total capital of many of the companies concerned—notably
American railroad companies.

Firms can raise finance by selling ordinary shares as well
as by borrowing. The income derived from a share is more
uncertain than that derived from a loan, so it might be thought
that cyclical variations in capital-owners' risk assessments
would be even more likely to make the availability of finance
move with the level of activity in the case of shares than in
the case of borrowing. But it is not quite so simple as this.
Certainly the prices of ordinary shares rise and fall with the
level of activity to a very marked degree. But the real cost
of raising funds by share-issue—what may be thought of as
the rate of interest paid by the company to the new share-
holders—depends not only on the price at which the new
shares are sold but also on the future earnings of the company, since the new shareholders will be entitled to participate

[1] W. C. Mitchell, *What Happens during Business Cycles* (1951), p. 170.
[2] W. B. Hickman, *Corporate Bond Quality and Investor Experience*
(1958), Chapter 3.

in these. The amount payable in the future to the new share-holders will be equal to the number of new shares issued multiplied by the earnings of the company per share. The number of new shares is equal to the total sum of money raised by selling them divided by their price per share. The amount payable in the future to the new shareholders, ex-pressed as a proportion of the sum raised by selling the shares, will thus be equal to the future earnings per share divided by price per share at the time the new shares were issued. This is the cost to the company of raising the new funds. The company's directors do not know the future earnings, but their estimate of them, taken in conjunction with the price per share, determines their assessment of the real cost of issuing new shares. If in the course of the upswing of the cycle the directors' expectations of future earnings rise to the same extent as the market price of the shares (or more), the real cost of share finance to the company will be constant (or rise). Now share prices are largely determined by the *market*'s expectations of the firm's future earnings. If they are entirely so determined, the rise and fall of share prices over the cycle will reflect the rise and fall in market expecta-tions of future earnings. In this case the real cost of share finance will vary over the cycle only in so far as the market's expectations of future earnings are more or less volatile than those of the management. It is not clear which way the difference will be if there is one. A *general* improvement of expectations will not as such reduce the cost of share finance.

Share prices will also be influenced, of course, by the 'pure' rate of interest; if the price of risk-free bonds falls when the level of activity rises, one would *ceteris paribus* expect ordinary share prices to rise by rather less than in pro-portion to the rise in the market's expectations of future earnings. There is, however, one reason why the cost of share finance may not rise in the boom by as much as the pure rate of interest, or may even fall. The prices of shares are influ-enced not only by expectations of firms' future profits but also by expectations of capital gains or losses. If share prices are rising and have been rising for some time, this may generate an expectation of continued rise and so drive up the price to more than would be justified by profit expectations alone. In so far as the rise and fall of share prices over the cycle is due to this speculative element, it will affect the cost of finance to the firm. The extent of speculative movements in share prices will vary much from one cycle to another. On some occasions it is blatant, as in 1929, when the stock market boom in the U.S. undoubtedly reduced the real cost of share finance and even led firms to seek out pretexts for issuing new shares. On other occasions it is much less prominent.

As the cost of share finance depends on a psychological factor—future earnings expected by management—it is not susceptible to direct measurement. There is some evidence, however, that share finance as a rule becomes more attractive relatively to bond finance when trade improves. In the U.S. the amount of new *shares* put on the market has varied positively and strongly with the cycle, but the amount of new *bonds* offered has most often varied inversely with the cycle, at least until about 1930: bonds are replaced by shares in the boom and replace them again in the slump.[1] Since it appears that risk premiums on bonds are less in the boom than in the slump it follows *a fortiori* that the real cost of share finance also falls in the boom relatively to the pure rate of interest.[2]

Another very important source from which firms can finance investment is their own accumulated funds. For

[1] W. B. Hickman, *The Volume of Corporate Bond Financing since 1900* (1953).

[2] Changes in capital-owners' expectations over the cycle may influence the cost of finance not merely by affecting the extent to which the rate of interest that has to be paid by the representative firm exceeds the pure rate of interest, but also by affecting the pure rate of interest itself. If there are some people who regard the holding of idle money and the holding of risky securities as direct alternatives, the increased attractiveness of risky securities in the boom will reduce the amount of idle money held and so lessen the extent to which the pure rate of interest needs to rise to elicit the extra supplies of active money required to support the higher level of the national income.

various reasons that need not be gone into here, firms often have a marked preference for such internal finance, and a good deal of the investment financed in this way would probably not be done at all if finance had to be raised externally.[1] If firms have such funds in their possession and they are not earmarked for some other purpose, the opportunity cost of using them for investment will be comparatively low, since it is customary to hold reserves in gilt-edged securities or even in cash. What matters is therefore the amount of such resources at firms' disposal at any time. Whether the supply of internal finance does normally become more or less abundant relatively to demand at the several stages of the cycle is not clear. Much will depend on how the development of the cycle affects the distribution of financial resources between firms that are anxious to do investment and have difficulty in securing external finance and firms that are in the opposite position in one or both of these respects. The more imperfect is the capital market, the more important is this liable to be on any particular occasion, but there seems to be no general presumption as to the direction in which it will work.

There is some reason to suppose that the proportion of investment financed externally is higher in the boom than in the slump,[2] and if this is so it would appear that on balance movements in the supply of internal finance over the cycle are less of a destabiliser than movements in the supply of external finance.

To an individual firm the amount of saving (undistributed profits) which it sets aside or is able to set aside is a major factor determining the availability of finance for investment. Hence it has sometimes been suggested that the effect of the

[1] See M. Kalecki, *The Theory of Economic Dynamics* (1954), pp. 91–95; Brian Tew, 'The Finance of Investment', *Oxford Economic Papers*, 1952, pp. 108–20; L. Tarshis, 'The Flow of Business Funds, Consumption and Investment', in *Post-Keynesian Economics* (1954), edited by K. K. Kurihara, pp. 365–87.

[2] Some evidence on this, which is admittedly far from clear, may be found in S. P. Dobrovolsky, *Corporate Income Retention* (1951), Chapter 6.

level of profits on the supply of finance is an important element in the cumulative expansion and contraction processes of the cycle: an initial rise in investment raises national income and profits, therefore businesses are able to save more, therefore investment is further stimulated. This argument, however, appears to be fallacious, at least in its simple form; it is an example of a proposition which is valid for an individual firm but cannot be applied in the same way to the economy as a whole. It is akin to the fallacy mentioned above (pp. 135–6) that the increase in *total* saving during the upswing must lead to easier terms of finance. What it overlooks is that, since saving equals investment, a rise in business saving (assuming business saving is a constant proportion of total saving) implies an equal proportional rise in investment, and this investment must be financed somehow. If it is financed currently, the saving is absorbed by it and does not facilitate the financing of investment planned for the future. If present investment was financed in advance, so that current saving is uncommitted, the investment must still have used up financial resources that would otherwise be available now, and the increase in saving merely serves to replenish these resources and ease the relative scarcity of finance that their absorption must have created. What this means in an imperfect capital market is that if firm A increases its investment, the diffused multiplier effects on income and profits will make it easier for other firms to finance their investment plans, but firm A itself will be in a *less* good position to finance further investment plans, because it will have used up that much more of its financial resources. The *overall* availability of finance for new investment plans will in the most general case be the same as it was before the original rise in investment.[1] (Of course if the original rise in invest-

---

[1] It should be noted that we are not here passing judgment one way or the other on the controversial question whether a rise in the corporate (or other) *propensity* to save will increase the availability of finance. We are concerned only with the effect on finance of the increase in saving due to the rise in investment and income in the boom.

ment was due to some externally originating increase in the supply of finance, for instance an increase in the quantity of money, things will be different: this extra finance is not permanently used up by the original increase in investment, and the consequential rise in profits and savings of other firms is the way in which the extra finance gets passed on in successive rounds.)

A better case can be made for saying that finance will be made easier if there is a rise in the *proportion* of business net saving to total net saving in the upswing. Such a rise is in fact likely, on account of the exceptional volatility of business net saving. If it comes about, it will tend to make finance easier to procure, inasmuch as an increase in businesses' own capital relatively to their outside borrowing will involve a reduction in risk.[1] As against this, however, businesses whose savings are not currently required to finance their own investment may be more prone than personal savers are to hold their savings in the form of idle balances.

§ 5. Conclusions.

In the simplest case limitations on the money supply must be expected to make the rate of interest move in such a way as to exert a moderating influence on the cycle. But if there are lags in the working of the monetary mechanism its influence may be more equivocal. Moreover the moderating influence will certainly be weakened and may even be reversed for part or all of the cycle by the direct response of the supply of money and money-substitutes to changes in the level of activity. A destabilising effect is also introduced by the tendency for capital-owners' risk

[1] Loans at fixed interest involve a risk in the event of a fall in the firm's earnings. For the lender the risk is that earnings will be inadequate to pay the interest due; for the borrower the risk is that the fixed interest payments will take up all the earnings. The higher the ratio of a firm's own capital to its borrowing, the less are these risks, since the firm's own capital acts as a shock-absorber. An increase in the firm's own capital achieved through ploughing back profits will therefore increase both lenders' willingness to lend to it and its own willingness to borrow. (This is the 'principle of increasing risk'; cf. Kalecki, *loc. cit.*)

assessments to be more optimistic when trade is good than when trade is bad; this financial channel is, indeed, probably one of the most important ways in which variations in the state of confidence make themselves felt. Finally, pathological situations such as financial crises and speculative stock exchange booms have often (though not always) developed in the course of the cycle and have then aggravated it to a serious extent. In one or other of these ways, monetary and financial factors are capable of strengthening rather than weakening the tendency to fluctuations, and this has in fact probably been their most common effect. On some occasions they may actually have been the main cause responsible for magnifying the effect of a relatively minor disturbance (itself either in the monetary sphere or not as the case may be) into a major movement in income and activity.

CHAPTER IX

THE CEILING

§ 1. The Ceiling: The Questions at Issue. Most of the issues about the upper turning point of the cycle are part and parcel of the problem of what causes the cycle generally—the relative importance of the capital stock adjustment principle, of time-lags, of innovatory investment, of changes in expectations, of monetary factors, etc. Models of the cycle that do not postulate a 'ceiling' do not need to offer any *special* explanation of the upper turning point; the same basic mechanism as causes the cumulative expansion and contraction is responsible for the downturn, and any special features that phase may have are merely incidental. The ceiling hypothesis, however, is something specific to the upper turning point, and requires separate discussion.

The essence of the ceiling hypothesis is that when income has risen above a certain level, there will develop scarcities or bottlenecks of some sort, which were not previously felt because of the presence of slack in the system, and that these scarcities play a decisive part in obstructing the rate of growth of income and preparing the way for an ultimate downturn. The formal theory of models based on the ceiling concept was outlined in Chapter II, § 4 and § 7. It remains now to consider more closely the economics of the matter.

Before considering the possible modes of operation and plausibility of different types of ceiling, we must be clear on what exactly is involved by acceptance or rejection of the ceiling hypothesis.

The following propositions would be accepted by both supporters and opponents of the ceiling hypothesis:

(a) at all times except possibly in severe depressions there will be supply inelasticities or bottlenecks somewhere

149

in the economy, and these may tend in some degree to lessen the force of a cumulative expansion in income;

(b) such bottlenecks will become more widespread as the level of activity and employment rises;

(c) at the upper turning point the force of the cumulative expansion process is by definition exhausted and the system is not subject to upward instability.

According to the ceiling hypothesis, the upswing is initially of an explosive character, or at least of such a character as to lead to anti-damped fluctuations, and the reduction in the elasticity of supply of factors of production as the expansion proceeds acts as a brake and transforms the unstable expansion into a weaker movement which cannot avoid presently going into reverse. According to the opposite view, there is no potential instability in the upswing even in its initial stages, and the increased scarcity of factors of production which will admittedly occur later in the boom is not a necessary condition of the downturn, though it may possibly hasten it. An intermediate view is that some upswings are potentially unstable and require to be halted by bottlenecks, while other upswings—the weaker ones—are not potentially unstable and come to an end of their own accord. Denial of the ceiling doctrine does not involve denying that factor scarcities tend to act as a brake on expansion; all that is denied is that there is a decisive difference between the significance of this brake in the earlier and later stages of the expansion respectively. Acceptance of the ceiling doctrine does not imply that factor scarcities set an absolute bar to further growth of income; all that is required is that they should restrain the expansion process sufficiently to eliminate the tendency to instability.

When the ceiling hypothesis is looked at in this way, it can be seen that the difference between models of the cycle that do involve a ceiling and models that do not is not necessarily a very radical one.

Supposing that the ceiling hypothesis is correct, further questions arise. In the first place, what exactly is it that acts as a ceiling, and how does it do so? In the second place, for how large a proportion of the upswing are the supply inelasticities that constitute the ceiling felt? Does the encounter with them bring the boom to an end almost at once, or are they in operation for the greater part of the upswing, so that there is only a comparatively short period at the beginning of the upswing when the system's inherent instability is manifested?[1]

In the next three sections we shall consider a number of different types of ceiling and their possible manner of operation.

§ 2. The General Full Employment Ceiling.

The most general kind of ceiling possible is that of overall full employment of labour. The first question to ask is, therefore, what are the theoretical grounds on which it may be expected that the advent of full employment will tend to bring the boom to an end?[2]

[1] One of the main advantages claimed for the inherent-instability-plus-ceiling hypothesis by its exponents is that it explains the persistence of cycles without having to invoke erratic shocks. If the hypothesis is to succeed in doing this, it is necessary that the instability of the upswing should continue until at least above the level of investment that would leave the rate of profit constant. In a trendless system this equilibrium level of investment will be zero net investment; if demand is subject to an upward trend, it will be a level of net investment sufficient to provide for that upward trend. If the instability of the upswing has already been checked by the time that the equilibrium level of investment is reached, the persistence of fluctuations in the absence of erratic shocks will not be explained. The short phase of instability will then be merely an incidental feature of the cycle, not an inherent part of its mechanism.

[2] Full employment is, of course, not a clearly defined concept. In practice more labour can almost always be squeezed out by such means as increasing the ratio of economically active to total population. Moreover full employment will not be achieved simultaneously in all parts of the economy. The full employment ceiling should not therefore be thought of as a rigid barrier that it met abruptly at some point of the expansion process; rather, its operation is manifested in gradually increasing shortage of labour as the boom progresses. For simplicity's sake the case considered in the text is that where the supply of labour at some point in the boom becomes completely inexpansible, but quite similar reasoning can be applied to the more realistic case where the increase in income merely causes the overall supply of labour to become *more* inelastic than it has previously been, without necessarily making it completely inelastic.

On the face of it the advent of full employment might seem likely to strengthen rather than weaken the upward instability of the system. If at the point when full employment is reached there is an 'inflationary gap'—investment tending to exceed saving—this gap will be more difficult to eliminate than it was when there were still unemployed resources, since it will no longer be so easy to raise real income and hence real saving.[1] But this holds only if the inducement to invest is assumed constant. The advent of full employment will tend to lower the inducement to invest for the following reason. In the boom the level of investment is high and the stock of capital is increasing. If the labour supply cannot be increased, this increase in the stock of capital must be accompanied by a rise in the ratio of capital to labour. According to the principle of diminishing returns, the addition to output procured by an addition to the stock of capital will therefore fall in a way that it did not do earlier in the boom when extra labour could be drawn in without difficulty to co-operate with the newly created capital. Real output and income will rise less rapidly than the stock of capital. Individual firms may try to avoid this by bidding labour away from other firms, but for the economy as a whole it is unavoidable. The fall in the marginal physical product of capital must tend *ceteris paribus* to lower the inducement to invest.[2] This will ultimately lead to a general downturn.

As so far stated, the argument neglects technical progress and population growth. Population growth means that the supply of labour will be increasing even though the present labour force is fully employed. Technical progress has a similar effect by reducing the amount of labour required to

---

[1] Comparison may be made with Wicksell's concept of the cumulative process. Cf. K. Wicksell, *Interest and Prices* (English edition, translated by R. F. Kahn, 1936), pp. 102–21, and J. R. Hicks, *Value and Capital* (1939), Chapters XX and XXI.

[2] The argument here is the obverse of that advanced in Chapter IV, § 7, with regard to the encouragement afforded to investment by the effect of technical progress in increasing the availability of factors of production at any given level of output.

produce a given output. The rise in population and productivity increases the available supply of labour at a certain pace, and it is only if capital is accumulating faster than this that its marginal physical product will tend to fall. If the rate of accumulation of capital is less fast, its marginal productivity will be *increasing*, and *ceteris paribus* the inducement to invest will therefore be increasing also. Finally there is one unique rate of capital accumulation that will leave the marginal product of capital constant. Thus a positive level of net investment with full employment of labour, such as is found in the boom, will not necessarily be accompanied by a fall in the marginal physical product of capital. It depends on the rate of increase in the capital stock relatively to the rates of increase of productivity and population. This raises some interesting issues which will be discussed further in Chapter XIII. For the moment we will merely say that if the rate of capital accumulation in the boom is sufficiently high relatively to the rates of population growth and technical progress, the advent of full employment must ultimately tend to lower the marginal physical product of capital.

In itself this will not necessarily reduce investment, for the inducement to invest depends not only on the marginal physical product of capital but also on the rate of profit per unit of turnover.[1] The latter will have some tendency to rise in the situation envisaged. Prices and wages will both be rising, but prices tend to rise faster, since the excess demand for labour is derived from the excess demand for goods, the latter being the prime mover in the process. But the rise in the profit margin per unit of turnover will have to be a cumulative one if it is to succeed in offsetting the discouragement to investment that results from the fall in capital's marginal physical product, since the latter will be cumulative so long as the stock of capital goes on increasing faster than the available labour supply.

---

[1] The inducement to invest is governed by the rate of profit per unit of capital; and the rate of profit per unit of capital is equal to profit per unit of output multiplied by output per unit of capital.

If the inflationary gap in existence at the moment when full employment is reached is a considerable one, it may be some time before the accumulation of capital has proceeded to the point that spells a general contraction. In the meanwhile prices will rise. If this creates expectations of further rises in prices, people will become anxious to acquire real assets (both producers' and consumers' durables) and to get rid of money and assets valued in terms of money. The stage is then set for a runaway inflation, and considerations about the marginal physical productivity of capital will get pushed into the background. In this case the advent of full employment may fail to bring about a downturn.

The conclusion of this section may be summarised by saying that there is a good theoretical reason for supposing that the advent of general full employment will lower the inducement to invest and so precipitate a downturn, but that this result is not inevitable and that in some circumstances an unstable expansion in money income might continue notwithstanding full employment or might even be fostered by it.

§ 3. **Supply Inelasticities in the Investment Industries.** Bottlenecks due to the inelastic supplies of factors are likely to be met at different stages of the upswing in different sectors of the economy. A hypothesis based on a particular application of this is that the ceiling that halts the boom is not general full employment but full employment of the labour attached to the investment industries. Since investment fluctuates more violently than consumption, the pressure on resources may be expected to be felt in the investment industries at an earlier stage of the upswing than elsewhere in the economy. The possibility of transferring labour from other industries is limited, especially in the short period. This bottleneck will slow down or halt the expansion of investment. This will lead through the multiplier to a corresponding slowing down in the expansion of national income, and this in turn, if it is sufficiently pronounced, will lead through the capital

stock adjustment principle to an actual contraction of investment, since the rate of growth of income will be reduced
below the rate of growth of the capital stock and the profit
rate will therefore fall.[1]

For a downturn to result in this way, it is not enough that
the rate of growth of investment in real terms should be reduced, since if the supply inelasticities in the investment industries raise the unit cost of investment goods to a sufficient
extent, the rate of growth of investment in money terms may
actually be raised, and this will strengthen the boom rather
than weaken it. Arrival at an investment ceiling may therefore not precipitate a downturn if the volume of investment is
relatively inelastic in response to changes in its unit cost.[2] On
the other hand a decline in the rate of growth of investment
in money terms will be more likely if the bottlenecks in the
investment industries lead, as they may well do, to lengthened
delivery dates or refusal of orders rather than to increased
prices.

A hypothesis logically distinct from that just considered,
though similar in its implications, is that what checks the pace
of the expansion is not the advent of full *employment of
labour* in the investment industries, but the advent of the
point at which full *use of capital capacity* is being made in
those industries. So long as there is excess capacity in the
investment industries, it is suggested, the upward tendency of

[1] The way in which the boom may be halted by full employment in the
investment industries is thus slightly different from the way in which it
would be halted by general full employment. Full employment in the
investment industries obstructs the *expansion* of investment and thereby
indirectly through the multiplier-accelerator interaction prevents even the
maintenance of investment at its present level. General full employment
directly discourages the maintenance of investment at its present level by
making it difficult to get labour to man the newly created capital. The
distinction, however, is not a perfectly sharp one, since full employment in
the investment industries will discourage even the maintenance of investment at its present level if part of the new capital is for installation in the
investment industries themselves.

[2] As it will be, for example, if a substantial proportion of the investment
projects under consideration are expected to yield a good deal more than
the minimum acceptable rate of return.

income has an explosive or unstable character; but when this point has been passed, the rise is slowed down in such a way that there is presently a reversal.   There is a distinct element of paradox about this: for surely pressure against capital capacity is normally a stimulus to investment, not an obstacle to it?   So long as there was excess capacity in the investment industries, there cannot have been much inducement to expand capacity in them; when the excess capacity is absorbed, will not investment be encouraged rather than the reverse? What the hypothesis really suggests is that the admitted encouragement to add to the capacity of the capital goods industries themselves will be more than offset by the discouragement to add to the capacity of the consumer goods industries.[1]   The duration of the boom will on this hypothesis depend very much on past history, since that is what will determine how much excess capacity there is in the investment industries at the beginning of the upswing.

§ 4. The Monetary Ceiling.   A ceiling of a quite different type from those so far considered is one due to shortage of money.   If the supply of money for transactions purposes becomes increasingly inelastic as the level of activity rises, the upward instability of the system may be checked and a downturn brought about.   Reasons why the supply of money might behave in this way have been mentioned above (p. 136). Under the gold standard or similar arrangements, where the supply of money for domestic use is tied to the level of the country's reserves of foreign exchange, similar results may follow from the progressive depletion of the country's reserves that will occur if the boom gives it an adverse balance of payments (see below, p. 184).

---

[1] This can be supported on the grounds that entrepreneurs in the capital goods industries are likely to be less ready to expand capacity in response to an increase in demand than entrepreneurs in the consumer goods industries, because the greater violence of past fluctuations in the capital goods industries will make them especially hesitant to believe that an increase in demand is going to be permanent.

Shortage of money is not a *real* scarcity like those previously considered, but it may have the same effect as a real scarcity would have. Moreover under the gold standard what appears as a monetary ceiling may in fact be due to real causes, in the following way. When the economy reaches or approaches full employment, the difficulty of increasing domestic output is liable to lead to an increased proportion of the national income being spent on imports. This will strengthen the tendency to an adverse balance of payments and to a resultant contraction in the supply of money for internal transactions.

§ 5. The Rôle of Supply Inelasticities in Practice.

The record of past cycles is not very favourable to the view that the upswing retains its unstable character until a late stage and is then checked by the advent of general full employment. It is certainly easier to point to historical occasions when the proximate causes of the downturn had plainly nothing to do with any increased incidence of labour bottlenecks than it is to point to cases that show the opposite equally plainly. In most booms there has been a not negligible amount of unemployment even at the peak, and moreover the labour force has sufficient flexibility (through immigration, increased employment of women, overtime, and transfer of workers from low-productivity employments such as agriculture and domestic service) to prevent the impact of full employment from being very sharp. Rather more cases might perhaps be quoted where there were signs of a monetary ceiling coming into operation at a late stage of the upswing, but this can certainly not be said to have been a general rule.

The evidence is more favourable to the notion that the instability of the upswing is confined to its early stages and that some sort of ceiling is in operation for most of the upswing.[1] The term ceiling is really rather a misnomer on this

---

[1] This version of the ceiling hypothesis would appear to be implied if the capital capacity of the investment industries is the bottleneck that is mainly emphasised.

version of the hypothesis, since there is no question of anything like an absolute barrier to growth; what happens is
merely that once the recovery has got beyond a certain point
and some of the excess supply of labour and idle capacity
has been absorbed, there is a sufficient number of supply inelasticities to act as a brake and convert the upswing from an
unstable explosive one to one that will presently reverse itself.
No striking manifestations of increased scarcity of factors of
production in the vicinity of the upper turning point need
then be expected. The positive evidence in favour of this
version of the hypothesis is that there has been a fairly clear
and general tendency for the level of activity to rise more
rapidly in the earliest phase of cyclical upswings—their first
quarter or less—than in their later phases.[1] What this evidence suggests is, of course, merely that some check to expansion is felt at an early stage of the upswing on account of
lessened elasticity of supply. It does not directly help to
establish that such a check is an inherently necessary condition of the downturn, which is really the distinctive feature
of the ceiling hypothesis.

The behaviour of prices might seem a good test of the
ceiling hypothesis: increased pressure on resources as the
boom progresses should lead to rises in prices. But prices
may rise for reasons other than pressure on resources, and
when there is a pressure on resources, suppliers may prefer to
deal with it in ways other than raising prices—e.g. by lengthening delivery dates, by lessening the amount of credit
allowed, or by declining orders. The evidence yielded by the
behaviour of prices is therefore indecisive. Such as it is, it is
mainly negative. Prices do of course rise as the boom advances, but the rate of rise is by no means always greater in
the later stages of the upswing than in the earlier ones; the
reverse has quite often been the case. Nor does the proportion of the increase in national income that is due to price
increase as opposed to volume increase regularly tend to rise

[1] Cf. Wesley C. Mitchell, *What Happens During Business Cycles* (1951),
pp. 299–305.

as the boom advances. Finally the statistics do not reveal any clear tendency for the prices of investment goods to fluctuate more violently than those of other classes of goods, as might be expected if the significant bottleneck lay in the investment industries.[1]

The problem of what causes the boom to come to an end has sometimes been likened to the problem of human mortality. There are many possible causes of death, any single one of which may be avoided, but everyone dies in the end. The analogy may be pressed a little further. It is one thing to find out which diseases are liable to be fatal and which of them are in fact the commonest cause of death; it is another to ask what are the fundamental reasons that prevent people from living for ever. The emphasis in the present and previous chapters has been on the former type of question. This is the type of question that is relevant if one is trying to explain the business cycle as a historical phenomenon. From the point of view of policy, on the other hand, it is necessary to consider what, if any, are the ultimate inherent reasons why a boom cannot go on indefinitely. This aspect of the matter will be further discussed in Chapter XIII, § 3, and Chapter XIV, § 6–§ 7.

[1] The statements in this paragraph are based chiefly on evidence relating to the United States. See for example the systematic analysis (chiefly of inter-war data) in the charts on pp. 32–49 of Wesley C. Mitchell, *op. cit.*, and the statistics of output and prices over a longer period given in U.S. Bureau of the Census, *Historical Statistics of the United States, 1789–1945* (1949).

CHAPTER X

THE LOWER TURNING POINT

§ 1. Why the Lower Turning Point Presents a Problem. On the face of it the lower turning point should be easier to explain than the upper one. , Economies subject to cyclical fluctuations almost always manifest long-term growth, and the resumption of upward movement at the lower turning point might therefore be regarded as no more than a return to normal after the temporary interruption of the recession. Yet in spite of this, the end of the downswing has commonly been felt to be more difficult to explain than the end of the upswing.

The basic reason for this is the asymmetry between positive and negative net investment, which prevents the capital stock adjustment principle from working in the same way in the slump as it does in the boom. In all types of cyclical model based on the capital stock adjustment principle—both those that make use of a buffer or 'floor' to explain the lower turning point and those that do not—the notion of a declining stock of capital (negative net investment) in the slump plays a crucial part. In models which do not involve a floor, it is the favourable influence exerted by the reduction in the capital stock on profit rates and hence on the inducement to invest that both stops the contraction and initiates the recovery. In models where a floor does come in, the contraction stops or slows down because gross investment in fixed capital is approaching the floor below which it cannot fall, namely zero.[1] If gross investment is zero, net investment must be

---

[1] The concept of the floor relates only to fixed investment, not to inventory investment, since the latter is not subject to the comparatively low maximum rate of disinvestment that applies to fixed capital.

negative.   Arrival at the floor does not in itself bring about recovery.   But it checks the fall in income; and the conjunction of constant income and a declining stock of capital (negative net investment) gradually reduces the excess capacity and provides some inducement to raise the level of gross investment above zero.   When and only when the stock of capital has been reduced to the appropriate level—appropriate, that is to say, in relation to the low level of income that will be associated with negative net investment—will there be any inducement to add to it.

This dependence of the models on negative net investment lays them open to objections on both *a priori* and empirical grounds.   The *a priori* objection is that since negative net investment in fixed capital can take place only by the neglect of replacement, it is bound to be a very slow process.   The difficulty of reducing the stock of capital within a short space of time (it is argued) is attested by the excess capacity which is a well-known feature of the slump.   If the recovery could not take place till substantial amounts of capital had worn out, slumps would be much more protracted affairs than we know them to be, and they would persistently be longer than booms (since there is not the same difficulty about raising the stock of capital as there is about reducing it).   Admittedly disinvestment in inventories does not present the same difficulties as disinvestment in fixed capital, and if inventories do fall, some inducement to increase inventory investment should presently be felt.   But if the amount of excess capacity in fixed capital is great, the recovery in inventory investment may not carry income up far enough to eliminate the excess capacity.   In that case the cycle in inventory investment may turn down again without having triggered off a general boom.

This argument about the implied duration of the slump is not decisive, since just how long it takes to effect a significant reduction in the stock of capital is a matter of degree, and it must be remembered that capital may pass out of use because of obsolescence as well as physical decay.   But taken in conjunction with the empirical objection to be mentioned in a moment, it does at the very least call for some modification in the simpler capital stock adjustment models.

The empirical objection is simply this: in most slumps negative net investment does not occur. Investment certainly falls in the slump, but it appears to be very exceptional for it to fall below the replacement level over the economy as a whole. Estimates have been prepared of reproducible tangible wealth (an approximation to the concept of capital) for the United States over the period 1896 to 1939, and these do not show negative net investment in any year save in the exceptionally severe depression of 1931–35. The years in which positive net investment is recorded include such markedly depressed ones as 1897, 1908 and 1921.[1] This finding is consistent with the general impression derived from business annals relating to other periods and countries. References to reductions in the stock of fixed capital as a factor in the recovery process are not often encountered. So the trouble is not merely that the reduction in the stock of capital is likely for *a priori* reasons to be a slow process, but also that it does not in practice usually occur at all.

Of course it is possible to set about explaining the lower turning point in terms of models that make no use or only subordinate use of the capital stock adjustment principle— models, for example, that lay the chief emphasis on monetary or psychological factors. In that case the difficulty under discussion is less acute, since reduction in the capital stock is not the motive force relied upon to give recovery. But it can scarcely be denied that there *is* excess capacity in the slump, and that its presence discourages investment. Some account must be taken of this in any realistic model of the cycle. If the evidence shows that this excess capacity is not as a rule removed by net disinvestment, there is on any reckoning *some* problem in explaining the recovery in investment that occurs.

[1] Raymond W. Goldsmith, 'The Growth of Reproducible Wealth of the United States of America from 1805 to 1950', in *Income and Wealth Series II* (1952), edited by S. Kuznets, pp. 247–328. These estimates take account of obsolescence.

§ 2. Secular Growth Factors. If there are certain forces making for an upward trend in effective demand, irrespective of the phase of the cycle, then it may be that although the stock of capital does not cease to grow in most slumps, the pace at which it grows is less than that required by the upward trend in demand. Excess capacity may then be eliminated without any actual disinvestment.

The nature of these trend factors has already received some discussion (see Chapter IV, § 7, and Chapter VII, § 3). Their operation in the context of the lower turning point may now be considered.

(1) Technical progress causes capital to become obsolescent before it is physically worn out, and so encourages investment. This is important, but it is not very helpful in the present connection, since the statistics quoted earlier which fail to show negative net investment in most slumps purport to take full account of obsolescence. If in any year the level of gross investment is inadequate to provide for the replacement of equipment made obsolete by technical progress, the statistics should show it. However apart from obsolescence in the normal sense technical progress probably does cause a sort of economic obsolescence which it would be difficult to take account of statistically, when a whole industry or section of an industry finds the ground cut from under its feet by the development of a competing product. In so far as this happens, technical progress may bring about a decline in the stock of capital in an economic sense which fails to register in the statistics or to rank as obsolescence in the minds of the entrepreneurs affected.

(2) At any given level of real output, an increase in productivity or in population will increase the amount of factors of production unemployed and available for use. This, it was suggested, should serve to encourage investment. But this effect is likely to be at its least potent at the bottom of the slump, when there are plenty of unemployed resources available anyway. It might however have some significance if the trend forces manifested themselves in an innovation which

substantially increased the availability or reduced the cost of some rather specific factor of production which had previously been scarce even in the slump. The discovery of new oil deposits or other natural resources might be an example.

(3) The growth of population or productivity imparts an upward trend to the consumption function. Whether this trend is in operation throughout the cycle or whether it is in suspense during the slump depends on various considerations that were discussed above (Chapter VII, § 3). It may be noted that if the consumption function does have a tendency to shift upward even during the slump, this tendency will probably be stronger in short slumps than in prolonged ones, since in a prolonged slump the psychological obstacles to reducing consumption will be weakened and the means of dissaving will be impaired by the running down of assets.

On this showing, the trend forces do amount to something, but their operation during a slump does not seem very powerful or very reliable. They would probably be able to bring recovery if the contractionary forces they had to contend with were mild or if the contractionary tendencies had actually exhausted themselves and the economy were stabilised in low-level equilibrium at a floor. But if the contractionary forces were strong, the secular growth factors would scarcely in themselves be powerful enough to outweigh them. The real problem is, therefore, how it is possible, if the initial contraction is severe, for some floor-level stability to be established or at least for the deflationary tendencies to be slowed down sufficiently for the trend forces to be an adequate offset, so long as net investment (and *a fortiori* gross investment) remains well above zero, as we know that it normally does during the slump. To this problem we now turn.

§ 3. **Expectations and Sectoral Investment Floors.** In order to understand the forces tending to slow down or halt the contraction, it is necessary to reconsider the nature of the contraction process and in particular the reasons for which investment falls, according to the various theories so far discussed.

Some part of the fall in investment that occurs in a cyclical downswing is normally due to causes other than the decline in national income and would take place even if income did not decline. We may distinguish two types of investment to which this may apply:

(a) Investment that is not much affected at all by the level of national income but which has recently been carried on at an unusually high level and has now achieved what it was designed to achieve. The obvious example is investment needed to carry into effect a particular innovation or group of innovations.

(b) Investment that is or could be affected by the level of national income, but which has been pushed to the point where the stock of capital of the type concerned is adequate or excessive in relation even to the boom level of income. A fall in this class of investment could not be avoided by stability in income at the boom level and perhaps not even by any rise in income that is for the present within the bounds of physical possibility. It will not therefore be much affected by the extent to which income falls *below* the boom level.

The magnitude of the fall in investment that comes into the foregoing categories depends on the character of the preceding boom. If the boom was based largely on innovatory investment which has now run its course, the fall in investment will be large. The same is true if the investment boom was so violent that over large areas of the economy the stock of capital was built up to a level adequate or excessive in relation to any currently possible demand. This applies particularly if speculation or miscalculation has caused the investment boom to be concentrated unduly in particular industries.

In so far as the fall in investment is due to such causes as these—causes, that is to say, other than falling national income—it does not necessarily have cumulative tendencies. The position is simply that there are certain classes of investment that are due to come to an end whatever happens to income, and when they have all come to an end there is no scope for further contraction. In the absence of other influences on investment, the economy would then find a low-level equilibrium.

But of course part of the fall in investment in the slump *is* due to the fall in income. This is, indeed, the basis of theories of the cycle founded on the capital stock adjustment principle. Once the upper turning point is passed, the prospective rate of profit on investment falls because income is falling relatively to the stock of capital. The inducement to invest gets less and less so long as income goes on falling, and the reduction in investment *causes* income to go on falling in a vicious spiral. This *is* potentially a source of cumulative contraction in income. What is capable of stopping it so long as net investment remains positive?

To answer this it is helpful to go back to what was said in Chapter III about the psychological basis and scope of the capital stock adjustment principle. A change in the current rate of profit due to a change in national income will have only a limited effect on investment unless it is expected to continue in the future. The investment that is likely to be strongly affected by a fall in national income is therefore (a) investment which is much influenced by immediate conditions because the capital concerned is short-lived (e.g. inventory investment) and (b) investment by firms that give much weight to the present in their estimates of the future. Now whereas extrapolation of the present into the future is fairly reasonable in the boom, it is much less so in the slump because of the upward trend of the system. For many firms the long-term expectations generated by the boom are not destroyed by the advent of a recession. They will therefore carry on with their investment plans despite the currently low level of profit. Some investment projects, moreover, will be continued despite the fall in the current rate of profit because the prospective rate of return on them was initially well above the minimum acceptable level.

How many firms carry on with investment depends on the extent to which the depression damages expectations. This in turn depends partly on more or less intangible factors, but also partly on the severity and duration of the slump itself. If therefore conditions are such as to cause large falls in the classes of investment that do *not* depend much on expectations (investment that is due to fall independently of any fall in national income, and short-range investment), there is likely to be a further secondary effect through the damage done to expectations.

What light is shed by these differences in behaviour between different classes of investment on the problem of what slows down or halts the contraction?

The first point is a straightforward one. As a result of differences in conditions and entrepreneurial policies between sectors of the economy, the floor of zero gross investment is a position that will be reached in different firms and industries at different times. Long before the total of fixed investment has fallen to zero, a floor will have been reached in particular sectors. As different sectoral floors are successively reached, the contractionary forces will come to operate over a narrower and narrower front, and the impetus of the downswing will be correspondingly weakened.

But not merely does the front on which the contractionary forces operate become narrower; also, and perhaps more important, it becomes increasingly difficult to penetrate. The classes of investment that fall soonest and fastest are those that are due to decline for reasons other than the fall in national income and those that are particularly sensitive to falls in income. The most vulnerable classes of investment reach their respective floors first, and the investment that continues will come to contain an increasing proportion of investment that does not have any independent tendency to fall and is insensitive, or relatively so, to short-term falls in national income. Ultimately a situation may even be reached in which all of the investment that is continuing is of the insensitive type. When this happens the economy as a whole may be described as resting on a *subjective floor*, even though some classes of investment are continuing quite strongly and the overall level of net investment is well above zero. This subjective floor is not, of course, as secure as the real floor of overall zero gross investment would be, since if confidence is weakened the decline in investment may spread to sectors that have hitherto proved insensitive.

§ **4. The Recovery.**   The partial insensitivity of entre-preneurs' expectations to falls in income thus serves to soften the force of the downswing (just as consumers' tendency to maintain consumption in face of falling income softens it); and it may even succeed in halting the fall in investment entirely, well before the point of overall zero net investment is reached. But although the establishment of sectoral floors to investment may slow down or even halt the fall in income, it does not in itself bring about a rise in income. The fact that some investment carries on more or less unaffected by the slump does not necessarily mean that such investment is *rising*. Firms that take a long view may not be seriously discouraged by the slump, but the slump can hardly make them *more* optimistic about the future.

Possible real causes of the recovery once the contraction has been slowed down or stopped include first, the secular growth forces already discussed and secondly, disin-vestment in *particular sectors* of the economy. Although there is not net disinvestment for the economy as a whole, there will be in individual sectors. Net disinvestment in a particular sec-tor may occur either because technical progress has caused especially rapid obsolescence there or because the slump has brought about an exceptionally sharp decline in investment there. Inventory investment can be relied upon to fall into the latter category, because it is dictated by short-term con-siderations and because the reduction in stocks can be carried out more easily than the reduction in fixed capital. (The occurrence of negative investment in inventories in the slump is, of course, well attested empirically.) Net disinvestment in fixed capital, on the other hand, is more likely to take place in sectors of the economy where technical progress happens to be causing especially rapid obsolescence and the slump is preventing this from being matched by a correspondingly high level of gross investment.

It may seem paradoxical to suggest that *sectoral* disinvestment (whether in inventories or fixed capital) can cause a *general* recovery. Will not the encouragement to investment due to the fall in the stock of capital in one sector be more than offset by the discouragement to investment caused by the accumulation of capital elsewhere, since over the economy as a whole net investment is positive? If so, how can investment and income rise, let alone rise by enough to absorb the excess capacity? The answer to this is that changes in the stock of capital in one sector of the economy may have very much more influence on investment than changes in the stock of capital in another. Those areas of the economy in which net investment is still continuing in the slump are *ex hypothesi* those in which entrepreneurs are not unduly concerned about the present relation between capacity and demand, because they can afford to take a long view and do not expect the present slump to last indefinitely or because the prospective rate of profit on their investment is well above the minimum acceptable. Consequently the further accumulation of capital in these sectors may make little difference to investment there. The persistence of excess capacity there will reflect not so much inability to reduce the stock of capital as absence of any desire to do so. On the other hand those sectors of the economy where disinvestment is going on will consist largely of those that did prove very sensitive to the fall in income, and in which, therefore, entrepreneurs may be presumed to be much influenced by current conditions. Inventories are the prime example. Hence the encouragement to investment afforded by the reduction in the stock of capital in some sectors may very well outweigh the discouragement that results from the increase in the stock of capital in other sectors, notwithstanding that there is a net increase in the stock of capital over the economy as a whole.

The above are possible systematic causes of recovery. However once the contraction has been checked and some sort of floor-level stability established, the way is clear for a variety of other factors to help towards recovery. If the level of activity is at a floor, even if only a subjective one, there are by definition less obstacles to its rising than to its falling. Hence favourable shocks (harvest improvements, major innovations, etc.) are capable of bringing about recovery, whereas unfavourable shocks will do only a limited amount of damage because investment is resistant to further falls. Likewise if because of lags the rate of interest goes on falling after the fall in national income has slowed down or ceased, as experience shows that it tends to do, this will stimulate investment in at least some sectors; and so long as the floor remains firm, investment in other sectors will not fall, even though excess capacity there may be large or increasing.

§ **5. Financial Factors at the Lower Turning Point.** The downswing phase of the cycle has commonly been marked for part or all of its length by unusual disruption of the monetary and credit mechanism, amounting in some cases to a 'crisis'.[1] The extent of this disruption depends largely on the character of the preceding boom. It will tend to be most severe if the boom has been a very speculative one and banks have not taken due precautions to prevent themselves from being involved. The failures of some banks and the difficulties of others reduce the amount of accommodation that can be extended to business and cause some deposits to become temporarily frozen or even permanently lost. Investment projects that require to be financed by outside funds will be postponed if it is at all possible for them to be. Firms whose financial resources are limited may be driven to bankruptcy even though their fundamental position is sound and the

[1] Cf. Chapter VIII, § 3.

demand for their products is little affected by the recession. This in turn will cause dislocation in the operations of the firms who are accustomed to buy from or sell to them. But this state of affairs in its worst form will not normally last for very long. The firms, both in finance and in industry, that are weakest are weeded out or bought up, and as soon as some semblance of stability is restored, the lack of confidence which was largely responsible for the trouble will be remedied. This may very well occur even though the national income has not yet begun to rise again or is still falling.

When the worst pressure of the crisis has abated and the financial mechanism has reverted more or less to normal, some improvement in the general state of business is likely to follow as a consequence. But the recovery from the crisis will not bring a true recovery unless the slump was mainly *due* to the financial disturbances—as, of course, it has sometimes been. The restoration of the financial system to normal cannot do more than remedy those aspects of the situation that were due to the financial dislocation. If there are other more fundamental reasons for the slump, these will remain in force, and all the considerations discussed earlier in this chapter will continue to be relevant. In the nineteenth century, when the occurrence of a crisis shortly after the upper turning point was the rule rather than the exception, we accordingly find that quite a common sequence of events was for there to be a fairly prompt but limited recovery once the crisis was over but for trade to continue depressed with little or no further improvement for some time afterwards. In seeking to explain particular historical instances of cyclical recovery, it is useful to distinguish between this sort of limited recovery and the real recovery that carries the economy up into a boom.

§ 6. **Price-flexibility.** Prices may be said to be flexible in face of a fall in demand if producers are willing to accept a fall in receipts per unit of output rather than curtail production—in other words, if supply schedules are inelastic downwards. The consequences of such downward price-flexibility can conveniently be considered here. They are, however, relevant to the whole contraction process rather than to the lower turning point alone.

Price-flexibility may or may not involve significant changes in *relative* prices. We shall discuss first the case where it does not, and all prices, including wage-rates, fall roughly together. This is the case that would result if wage-rates were flexible and profit margins were kept a constant proportion of prime costs.

A situation in which a fall in demand is met by entirely inelastic supply schedules is highly unrealistic. But as a theoretical limiting case it may be regarded as the reverse of the situation discussed in Chapter IX, § 2—the situation where a rise in demand at the top of the boom encounters inelastic supply because of full employment. Up to a point the formal analysis of the two situations is similar. Suppose a deflationary situation has developed, with investment tending to be less than saving. Price-flexibility prevents a fall in real income and hence in real saving; so the fall in prices does nothing to narrow the deflationary gap, and as long as the inducement to invest remains unchanged, prices will go on falling. But if the level of net investment is below zero[1] the stability in real income will help in the longer run, because it ensures that the fall in the stock of capital is not outrun by a fall in income and that the ratio of capital to income will therefore fall. According to the capital stock adjustment principle a fall in the capital-income ratio encourages investment, and so in the end the inducement to invest will rise sufficiently to bring a recovery. If prices had not been flexible, not merely would real income have fallen more but also, because of this, a longer period of negative net investment would have been needed to get rid of excess capacity.[2]

---

[1] Or is below zero in the sectors of the economy where investment decisions are sensitive to changes in the stock of capital—see § 4 above.

[2] However, price-flexibility will not in itself bring about recovery or even stability so long as the capital stock goes on increasing, because then

It follows from this that general price-flexibility will mitigate the severity of the slump in real terms, though prices
may fall a long way in the process. (It is possible, indeed
probable, that *money* income will fall by more than it would
have done with inflexible prices and falling output.) But this
is all very theoretical. There are many complications that
will affect the result in practice. A protracted fall in prices
may have a bad effect on expectations. It will also increase
the real burden of debt. This will make things more difficult
for numbers of firms. On the other hand consumption by
creditors and those holding money balances may be encouraged (this is what is sometimes referred to as 'the Pigou
effect').[1]

Similar conclusions, appropriately toned down, apply if
there is a limited degree of price-flexibility, i.e. if supply
schedules are fairly inelastic but not completely so.

We have so far been concerned with the case of a uniform
proportional reduction in prices, including wage-rates. Economists at one time tended to believe that the existence of
unemployment in the slump indicated that a reduction in
wages relatively to prices was appropriate and that this was
what would happen in the absence of institutional rigidities.
It is now generally agreed, however, that the trouble in the
slump is not that there is excess supply of labour relatively
to other factors of production but there is a deficiency in the
overall demand for commodities and hence in the demand for
all factors of production. Hence a reduction in real wage
rates is not especially natural or appropriate. On the contrary, the most likely case of non-uniform reduction in prices
in practice is that wages should fall less than prices and that
profit margins should suffer. If firms decide to maintain

---

there will be nothing tending to raise the inducement to invest. A fall
in real investment from its boom level is thus a necessary condition for
ultimate recovery, in order to halt the increase in the capital stock. This
may be achieved, notwithstanding price-flexibility, if the volume of real
investment is inelastic with respect to changes in its unit cost, which seems
quite likely.

[1] Cf. A. C. Pigou, *Employment and Equilibrium* (1949), pp. 131–4.

output despite a fall in prices, the demand for labour will remain high and there will not be much pressure on wages. Such profit-flexibility is most likely to be found if fixed costs are a high proportion of total costs and competition between firms is strong. The effect of profit-flexibility is less favourable than that of uniform price-flexibility inasmuch as the reduction in the proportion of national income going to profit will lower the inducement to invest at any given ratio of the stock of capital to national income. The recovery of investment will thus be delayed longer than in the case of uniform price-flexibility. As against this, however, the marginal propensity to save out of profits is likely to be higher than the marginal propensity to save out of wages, and hence a rise in real wage rates at the expense of profits will encourage consumption.[1] So it is not clear whether profit-flexibility is more or less conducive to recovery than uniform price-flexibility.

It has often been suggested that prices have become less flexible than they used to be, and that in earlier times the severity of cyclical contractions was therefore mitigated by price-flexibility to an extent that it has not been more recently. This appears from the evidence to be broadly true, though the behaviour of prices has varied very much from one cycle to the next and the trend towards less price-flexibility has not been a uniform one.

If we take as the criterion of price-flexibility the ratio of the percentage fall in prices to the percentage fall in manufacturing production, major contractions in the United States may be ranked in descending order of price-flexibility as follows: 1882–85, 1872–76, 1920–21, 1929–32, 1892–94, 1937–38,

[1] There is some reason to believe that the difference between the marginal propensity to save out of profits and the marginal propensity to save out of wages is especially pronounced in the short run, if only because the extremely high marginal propensity to retain corporate earnings appears to be largely a short-run phenomenon. Hence the effect on consumption of a shift in distribution that results from a slump may well be more important than is the corresponding effect on consumption of shifts in distribution that may result from the operation of long-run changes in factor availability in the manner discussed in Chapter IV, § 7.

1907–8. Data for before the Civil War are not good, but as far as they go they point to roughly the same degree of price-flexibility as in the 1870s and 1880s.[1] The break, such as it is, seems to have come around 1890, rather than at a later date. (There has not yet been a major contraction to test the possibility of a further decline in price-flexibility since 1938.) This is confirmed by the experience of minor contractions, which until about 1890 appear to have been virtually confined to prices. Since cyclical contractions in production have generally been more severe since 1890 than before, it may be tentatively concluded that price-flexibility did mitigate the severity of depressions in earlier times.

Evidence points to a similar decline in price-flexibility in the British economy. The following data on exports are interesting because they cover a very long period and are based on reliable official statistics, though of course exports are not necessarily representative of industrial production as a whole. They show the percentage decline in the price of British exports divided by the percentage decline in the values of British exports in major cyclical contractions since 1825. They thus measure the contribution of prices to the fall in values. A figure above unity means that the fall in prices exceeded the fall in values and implies that the volume of exports rose notwithstanding the fall in value.

$$\frac{\text{Percentage fall in price of British exports}}{\text{Percentage fall in value of British exports}}$$

1825–29	2·8	1866–68	2·5	1907–08	0·3
1836–42	2·7	1872–79	1·0	1920–21	0·6
1845–48	2·0	1882–86	1·4	1929–32	0·4
1857–58	2·3	1890–94	0·6		

These data point clearly to two breaks in trend, one around 1870 and the other around 1890. The interpretation of the

[1] The ranking in the text is based on the index of manufacturing production shown in Diagram 8 and the Bureau of Labour Statistics index of wholesale prices. Production data for before the Civil War are available only for a limited number of individual commodities.

data is not free from ambiguity, since a high figure may reflect not so much inelasticity in the supply curve as an upward shift in the supply curve. On the face of it, however, price-flexibility may be inferred to have declined around the two dates mentioned.

It is doubtful if reductions in wage-rates in the slump were much if at all greater in the nineteenth century than in the twentieth, in either America or Britain.[1] So it seems likely that the higher degree of price-flexibility in the nineteenth century was due largely to flexibility in profits. The extent to which the burden fell on profit-earners rather than on wage-earners was a common subject of remark in nineteenth century depressions. The reduction in profit-flexibility at the end of the nineteenth century may perhaps be related to the well-known strengthening of monopolistic tendencies about that time.

§ 7. Conclusions.   In order for there to be a recovery from the slump, investment must rise. The inducement to invest appears on the face of it unlikely to rise at all strongly unless some reduction can be brought about in the stock of capital, so as to eliminate excess capacity. But the notion that excess capacity is eliminated by negative net investment is open to serious objections on both *a priori* and empirical grounds. Hence the difficulty in explaining the lower turning point.

The resolution of this difficulty may proceed in two stages. First, why does the cumulative contraction normally come to a halt before net investment has fallen below zero? Secondly, once contraction has stopped, what promotes a recovery?

[1] The inter-war data for the United States in D. Creamer and M. Bernstein, *Behaviour of Wage-rates during Business Cycles* (National Bureau of Economic Research Occasional Paper No. 34, 1950), especially the table on p. 37, may be compared with the figures for average hourly earnings over a longer period in U.S. Bureau of the Census, *Historical Statistics of the United States, 1789–1945* (1949), pp. 66–7. For Great Britain see A. L. Bowley, *Wages and Income in the United Kingdom since 1860* (1937).

Not all the causes that contribute to the fall in investment in the downswing will necessarily have a cumulative tendency; some may rather be of a once-for-all character. The capital-stock-adjustment-multiplier interaction *is* inherently cumulative. However, a fair proportion of investment is influenced little, if at all, by the relation between capacity and current demand—just how large a proportion depending on the state of business psychology. For this reason the fall in investment due to the interaction of the capital stock adjustment principle and the multiplier is likely to arrive at some sort of subjective floor well before the ultimate floor of zero gross fixed investment is reached.

This will not in itself bring about recovery. But it will establish conditions that facilitate recovery. The recovery may then come about for any of the following causes. (1) Investment and/or consumption is subject to a secular upward drift. (2) Although in most slumps there is not net disinvestment over the economy as a whole, net disinvestment does take place in some sectors, notably in inventories; and it is reasonable to suppose that investment decisions in these sectors will be more sensitive to the relation between capacity and current demand than are investment decisions in those sectors of the economy where the stock of capital is still increasing. (3) Once a floor has been established, shocks are more likely to work in a favourable than in an unfavourable direction. (4) Similarly, once a floor has been established, more significance will come to attach to possible favourable influences, such as interest rate movements, which were too weak to promote recovery while the cumulative contraction was still proceeding strongly. (5) Finally, in so far as the slump was caused or aggravated by disruption in the financial sphere, an improvement will be experienced when the passage of time has re-established more normal conditions there.

Slumps vary greatly in their severity and general character, and there are corresponding differences in the recovery process. Sometimes a combination of unfilled arrears of investment opportunities and buoyant expectations renders almost the whole of fixed investment immune from the recession. The subjective floor of fixed investment is then reached almost at once, and the recession is dominated by inventory behaviour. The fall in income is not great, there is little excess capacity, and a short spell of disinvestment in inventories is soon followed by a recovery in inventory investment and the recession is brought to an end. On other occasions the economy may be so saturated with capital or confidence so badly damaged that the floor is not reached till income is very low. The burden of excess capacity will then be very heavy and the recovery factors enumerated may take a long time to raise income to the point where the excess capacity is eliminated.[1]

The chief reason for supposing that even the worst slump will not last for ever is perhaps that it *need* not last for ever. If entrepreneurs can only screw themselves up to do enough investment, it will eventually justify itself, since the income generated will absorb the excess capacity. The only exception to this would be where the present level of capacity is already excessive in relation not merely to the current level of income but to the highest income that it is physically possible to reach in the present state of technical knowledge. In this case the elimination of excess capacity is for the moment impossible. But with the passage of time even this obstacle will disappear as the maximum attainable income is raised by the advance of technical knowledge.

[1] Cf. R. A. Gordon, 'Investment Behaviour and Business Cycles', *Review of Economics and Statistics*, 1955, pp. 23–34.

CHAPTER XI

INTERNATIONAL ASPECTS

§ 1. International Transmission of Fluctuations: (1) The Balance of Payments on Current Account. In the first two sections of this chapter we shall consider a situation in which only one country, A, is prone to fluctuations on its own account. We shall ask how A's cycle is affected by its international transactions and how the economy of the rest of the world is affected by the fluctuations in A. In § 3 we shall consider some of the consequences in the international sphere of a world cycle in which all countries fluctuate more or less together without any of them being clearly the prime mover in the process. But there is no hard-and-fast division between the two types of situation; fluctuations in one country, as will presently be seen, tend to transmit themselves to others, and the consequences of a world cycle in which one country is the prime mover resemble in many respects the consequences of a world cycle where no single prime mover can be identified. Much of what is said in § 3 is relevant if the cycle emanates from one country as well as if it does not. In § 1–§ 2, on the other hand, attention will be concentrated on the results that follow specifically from one country being the source from which the cycle emanates.[1]

When national income in A rises or falls, part of the change in expenditure will fall on imports rather than on home-produced goods. Expenditure on imports creates income for foreign producers, not home producers. The rise in imports that occurs when A has a boom thus represents a leakage from the circular flow of income within A, analogous to

---

[1] Much of what is said in this chapter about the relations between countries applies also to the relations between regions within a country.

179

saving. From the point of view of the rest of the world the increase in their exports to A represents an injection into the circular flow of incomes, analogous to investment. The movement in A's imports thus serves to reduce the amplitude of fluctuations in A and transmit them to the rest of the world. This is the basic effect of foreign trade on the working of the cycle. The rise in income in the other countries that stems from the rise in their exports to A will be strengthened if, as is probable, a rise in their domestic investment is induced by the prosperity of their export industries and of the consumer goods industries where the export proceeds are spent.[1]

The ratio of a consequential change in a country's imports to a change in its national income is called the marginal propensity to import. This is a concept analogous to the marginal propensity to save, and, like it, will have a value lying between zero and unity. The size of A's marginal propensity to import is what chiefly determines the extent to which its imports move over the cycle and hence the strength of their effect in damping A's fluctuations and transmitting them to the rest of the world. Account must also be taken of the change in the demand for A's *exports* that will result from the induced change in the rest of the world's income; the magnitude of this depends largely on the marginal propensity of the rest of the world to import from A. This backwash will tend to lessen to some degree the damping and transmissive effects of the original increase in A's imports.[2]

---

[1] We are assuming in this section that international monetary arrangements are such that a country's imports and exports are capable of being unequal, the gap being filled in the short period by movements of gold or credit in some form.   See below, pp. 184–5.

[2] This may be worked out more rigorously in terms of the theory of the so-called foreign trade multiplier.   Let us assume a world of two countries, A and B.   We write Y_a for national income, I_a for investment, X_a for exports, s_a for marginal propensity to save, m_a for marginal propensity to import, all in country A; and likewise Y_b for national income, etc., in country B.   Consider now the effect on Y_a and Y_b of an increase in I_a. I_b is assumed constant.   If A were a closed economy, we should have, by the theory of the multiplier, $\Delta Y_a = \Delta I_a / s_a$.   With A an open economy,

The value of the marginal propensity to import depends largely on the structure of a country's economy. It will be smaller for a nearly self-sufficient country than for one that specialises in the production of a comparatively narrow range of goods and relies on foreign trade for the rest of its requirements. This applies particularly if the industries that the country lacks include the industries that produce investment goods, since the demand for investment goods fluctuates more widely over the cycle than the demand for consumer goods. The marginal propensity to import is thus likely to be high in countries specialising in primary production. The marginal propensity to import will moreover not necessarily be constant at all stages of the cycle. If the boom leads to a rise in home prices or other manifestations of short supply from domestic sources, there will be a greater inducement to draw supplies from abroad. The stronger the tendency to inflation, the

---

imports as well as savings are a source of leakage from the circular flow, and exports as well as investment are a source of injection into it. So we have instead

$$\Delta Y_a = \frac{\Delta I_a + \Delta X_a}{s_a + m_a}.$$

Likewise

$$\Delta Y_b = \frac{\Delta X_b}{s_b + m_b}.$$

Now $\Delta X_a = m_b \Delta Y_b$, and $\Delta X_b = m_a \Delta Y_a$. Hence

$$\Delta Y_a = \frac{\Delta I_a}{(s_a + m_a)\left\{1 - \dfrac{m_a m_b}{(s_a + m_a)(s_b + m_b)}\right\}}.$$

Except in the limiting case where $s_b = 0$, this last expression is bound to give a lower value for ΔY_a than it would have had in a closed economy (viz. $\Delta I_a/s_a$); i.e. foreign trade has a stabilising effect on A's income. In the limiting case the backwash on A's exports of the induced increase in income in B entirely cancels out the damping effect exercised by the increase in A's imports, and income in A rises by as much as it would have done if A had been a closed economy. The minimum rise in Y_b is ΔX_b. This minimum value will occur where $s_b + m_b = 1$; all the extra income derived in B from the increase in exports is then saved or spent on imports, and there are no further multiplier effects within B.

higher the marginal propensity to import will therefore be.[1]

The direct effects on the circular flow of income in A and in the rest of the world that result from fluctuations in A's imports are not the only means by which foreign trade may serve to damp down fluctuations in A and transmit them abroad. There is also the monetary channel. The increase in A's imports (including invisible imports) in the boom will tend to give A an adverse overall balance of payments if there are no offsetting factors. Its reserves of gold or foreign exchange will decline. Under the gold standard or other institutional arrangements that tie the quantity of money in a country to its foreign exchange reserves, this will lead to a decline in the domestic money supply in A and a rise in the rate of interest. In the rest of the world the quantity of money will rise and the rate of interest will tend to fall. The flow of gold or its equivalent from A will thus tend through its effect on the rate of interest to damp down the boom in A by discouraging investment, and at the same time will encourage investment in the rest of the world.[2]

Even if monetary arrangements in A and in the other countries are such as to permit the domestic money supply to be held constant in face of disequilibrium in the balance of payments, A's adverse balance of payments on current accounts will still tend to raise the rate of interest in A and

[1] The level of demand within a country may affect its exports as well as its imports. A high level of demand and prices at home will tend to discourage exports and this will normally strengthen the adverse tendency in the balance of trade that results from the rise in imports. An opposite result is possible, however, if the foreign demand for the country's exports is inelastic, so that the rise in the prices of its exports due to the high home demand causes a less than proportionate fall in their volume. This will tend to offset the adverse effect on the balance of payments that results from the rise in imports, and could conceivably outweigh it. This applies in reverse in a slump: normally the value of the country's exports should rise, but if the foreign demand for them is inelastic it may fall instead.

[2] It has sometimes been suggested that the gold standard had a deflationary effect from the point of view of the world as a whole in as much as it was regarded as more important for monetary authorities to ensure that an outflow of gold was matched by a contraction in the money supply than it was for them to ensure that an inflow of gold was matched by an expansion of the money supply.

lower it elsewhere. The reason for this is as follows. In a closed economy the extra demand for finance that results from a rise in investment will, broadly speaking, be met by a corresponding extra supply of finance from saving, since saving equals investment.[1] In an open economy, however, investment equals saving plus imports minus exports.[2] The excess of imports over exports represents saving done by people in other countries. If there is a rise in investment in A, part of the corresponding increase in saving is thus done by people abroad rather than by people in A. Since savers may be presumed to have a preference, other things being equal, for lending their savings at home rather than abroad, the saving done by people in A will normally be made available on A's capital market, but the sum represented by the excess of imports over exports will not. The supply of finance in A will therefore increase by less than the demand for it, and the rate of interest will go up. In the rest of the world, by the same token, the supply of finance will go up without any offsetting increase in the demand for it, since the excess of exports over imports will be matched by an increase in saving, without (in the first instance) any change in investment; the rate of interest will therefore fall.

Because of the possible effects of balance of payments disequilibrium on the supply of credit, the policy pursued by the monetary authorities and the banks is liable to play a particularly important part in the cycle in countries which are heavily dependent on foreign trade. But even if the monetary authorities are willing to adjust the domestic money supply so as to keep the rate of interest constant, they have still got to take some action if foreign exchange reserves are being lost. They cannot let the loss go on indefinitely. It is bound to be a source of embarrassment to them even if they

---

[1] See Chapter VIII, p. 135.

[2] National income looked at from the point of view of source is equal to output of goods for home consumption plus investment plus exports. National income looked at from the point of view of end-use is equal to consumption of home-produced goods plus imports plus saving. Therefore investment plus exports is equal to saving plus imports.

decide to prevent its impact from being a specifically deflationary one. This point will be further considered in Chapter XIV, § 4.

It has now been shown that movements of the balance of payments on current account will be such as to damp down fluctuations in income in the country where they originate, both by their direct effect on the circular flow of incomes and by their impact on the supply of credit. They may be more than a damper. They may bring about a turning point. This is liable to happen if their effect is felt with a lag or if it involves some non-linear relationship.[1] Non-linearity is quite likely to be present both in the extent to which the balance of payments reacts to movements in the level of national income and in the extent to which the level of national income in turn is affected by the state of the balance of payments. The first is because the marginal propensity to import rises as full employment is approached; the second is because the monetary authorities tend to react more strongly to a fall in foreign exchange reserves if the reserves are already at a low level.

All that has been said in this section depends on the assumption that some way can be found of bridging the gap between imports and exports, say by movements of gold or short-term capital. If this is not so, none of the influences on effective demand that have been discussed can materialise. If for example any tendency to disequilibrium in the balance of payments on current account is instantly corrected by movements in exchange rates, a rise in the level of activity in A will turn the terms of trade against it and so lessen somewhat the rise in real income there and raise real income

[1] Cf. Chapter II, §§ 4–5, and also Chapter VIII, pp. 136–8. It is possible to construct a self-contained model of the cycle based on lagged or non-linear consequences of balance of payment movements, just as it is possible to base a model on lagged or non-linear changes in the internal demand for money. The well-known theory of Sir Ralph Hawtrey is a case in point. See the summary of Hawtrey's views and the references to his writings in G. Haberler, *Prosperity and Depression* (1943), pp. 15–28.

in the rest of the world; but effective demand will not thereby be altered directly. Effective demand is, however, likely to be altered indirectly through the inducement to invest, since the latter will be adversely affected by the slowing down in the rate of growth of real income. The shortage of foreign exchange acts as a kind of ceiling restricting growth and hence discouraging investment. Likewise investment abroad will in this case be stimulated by the rise in real income there.

§ 2. **International Transmission of Fluctuations: (2) Capital Movements.** The behaviour of the overall balance of payments over the cycle will not normally be governed exclusively by the behaviour of exports and imports and the invisible items entering into the balance of payments on current account. Changes in the flow of international lending must also be taken into account. If the balance of payments on current account shifts against A because A has a boom, and there is therefore a rise in the rate of interest in A relatively to the rate of interest elsewhere, there will tend to be a flow of capital to A. This will lessen the adverse movement in A's overall balance of payments. In the limiting case where capital is perfectly mobile between countries, the balance of lending will move in such a way as to cancel entirely the movement in the current account balance and restore interest rates in A and elsewhere to equality. Moreover if A's boom raises interest rates in A by increasing the amount of cash needed internally as well as by giving A an adverse balance of payments on current account, the inflow of capital to A needed to bring about equality between interest rates there and interest rates elsewhere will exceed A's adverse current account balance. If capital is perfectly mobile, the overall balance of payments will then actually move in A's favour, and the rate of interest in the rest of the world will rise.

The international mobility of capital is normally less than complete. Capitalists will require some inducement to make them shift their funds from other countries to A, and some disparity between rates of interest in different countries will therefore persist. The disparity will be the greater the smaller is the circle of capitalists who are sufficiently knowledgeable or confident about conditions in A to be willing to acquire assets there. On the other hand the existence of a boom in A is almost bound to make people more optimistic about its economic prospects. The risk premium on A's securities relatively to the securities of other countries will be reduced, and capitalists will become willing to hold more of A's securities at any given rate of interest. This acts as an independent force attracting capital to A when it has a boom. If this force is sufficiently strong, the inflow of capital may more than offset A's adverse balance of payments on current account and may actually cause the rate of interest in A to fall and that in the rest of the world to rise. The effect is then to strengthen the boom in A and cause some contractionary tendencies elsewhere.

Capital movements may thus serve to weaken or remove the monetary effect of A's international transactions in damping its boom and transmitting it to the rest of the world. They stabilise the overall balance of payments (or perhaps even turn it in A's favour) and thereby lessen the stabilising influence on A's income that a balance of payments deficit would produce. They do not however undo the direct effect on income in A and elsewhere that is exerted by the rise in A's imports relatively to its exports. A's fluctuations will to that extent still be transmitted to other countries, even if the monetary effects are entirely neutralised by capital movements.

In certain circumstances domestic monetary conditions may tend to make the rate of interest higher in a slump than in a boom. The most obvious case is if the slump is accompanied by a crisis. If this tendency outweighs the contrary influence on the rate of interest exerted by the movement in the balance of trade, then the net movement of capital into the country will tend to be higher in the slump than in the boom. This will aggravate the disequilibrium in the balance of payments that arises from the behaviour of the balance of payments on current account, since the latter will tend to be favourable in the slump and unfavourable in the boom. Capital movements will act as an additional stabiliser of income at home and an additional channel by which fluctuations are transmitted to other countries.

§ 3. International Consequences of a World Cycle.

If all countries are affected to a greater or less degree by the cycle and it is not possible to identify any one as being the original source of the instability, it does not follow that the balance of world payments will necessarily be unaffected. Structural and other differences between countries are likely to cause some of them to develop favourable balances and others unfavourable ones as the cycle proceeds. Activity will thereby be encouraged in the former and depressed in the latter.

Most obviously, if the cycle tends to have larger amplitude in one country than in the rest of the world, say because that country has a low marginal propensity to save or because its monetary institutions are particularly unstable, then that country will tend to get an adverse balance of current payments in the boom and a favourable one in the slump, even if parallel fluctuations are going on elsewhere. The same result follows in the absence of differences between countries in the amplitude of the cycle if the structure of a country's economy is such that its income-elasticity of demand for imports (i.e. the proportional change in imports resulting from a given proportional change in national income) is higher than the income-elasticity of demand in the rest of the world for imports from it. In such cases the adverse current balance will tend in the usual way to bring about a rise in the rate of interest in the deficit country relatively to the rest of the world. This will induce some flow of capital to the deficit country from abroad. The deficit will thereby be partly filled and its deflationary monetary effects mitigated.

A world cycle is also likely to cause changes in the rate of international capital flow independently of any induced changes that may result from disequilibrium in the balance of payments on current account. It is well established empirically that countries that are habitually net borrowers borrow more heavily in a world boom than in a world slump. The reason for this, to put it in its simplest terms, is that if a sizeable proportion of a country's investment is normally financed by foreign funds, fluctuations in investment will be accompanied by corresponding fluctuations in the inflow of foreign capital. The clearest example is in the case of so-called direct investment, where the foreign capitalists have the controlling interest in the concerns where they place their funds. Thus United States oil companies operating in South America or in the Middle East will be more likely to carry out investment to extend their capacity there in a boom than in a slump, and this has nothing to do with what is happening to the balance of payments on current account as such. Or it may be that in the borrowing country financial institutions simply do not exist for raising the funds needed to pay for large investment projects, so that the sponsors have to sell securities abroad before they can start work. Or the monetary authorities in the borrowing country, foreseeing that an adverse foreign balance and inflation will result if an attempt is made to finance investment internally, take steps to prevent the expansion of bank credit and so create a shortage of domestic finance before any adverse foreign balance has actually materialised. In these cases foreign capital is an indispensable pre-condition of investment.[1]

---

[1] Another reason why the volume of international lending may vary with the cycle is this. If a country's securities have in general a low credit standing and are subject to a high risk premium, there is more scope for *fluctuations* in the risk premium over the cycle than there is with securities that are regarded as nearly free from risk. A country with a low credit standing may therefore find that in the optimistic atmosphere of the boom its securities stand relatively higher in market estimation than they do in the slump—this notwithstanding that the country in question is not necessarily having a more pronounced boom than other countries. Irrational relaxation of investors' standards of caution about foreign bonds occurred at the peaks of several booms in the heyday of international lending. 1872 is perhaps the classic instance.

Countries that are habitual borrowers are in general also likely to be the ones that develop adverse balances of payments on current account during the boom: that is to say, countries with little saving and heavy dependence on imported investment goods and other manufactures. In this way the current account balance and the balance of lending tend to cancel each other out in their cyclical movement, and the borrowing country is able regularly to show larger cyclical fluctuations in its imports than in its exports without necessarily incurring balance of payments difficulties in the boom.[1] Sometimes the capital movements may predominate, so that the borrower gets a favourable overall balance in the boom; at other times the reverse result may hold. This has no doubt been an important factor in the maintenance of overall balance of payments equilibrium in the cycle. But it has not always operated. If instead it is the lender which develops a favourable current account balance during the slump, say because it is undergoing a particularly violent cycle, the tendency for capital flow to be lower in the slump than in the boom will aggravate the balance of payments disequilibrium. A notable example was provided by the experience of the 1930s. The acute depression in the United States gave adverse balances of payments on current account to countries accustomed to sell to her, and these countries suffered at the same time from the drying up of the flow of American capital which had been so high in the 1920s.[2] One reason why the slump of the 1930s had such an exceptionally disruptive effect on international trade was that the supply of dollars on

[1] It is worth noting that if a country is an habitual borrower, its imports may show larger fluctuations over the cycle than its exports, for the reasons stated in the text, notwithstanding that the fluctuations have been transmitted to it in the first instance from abroad.

[2] The minor fluctuations in American activity between 1922 and 1929, which were not shared by most other countries, were in general associated with *opposite* fluctuations in American lending. American investors apparently found foreign bonds relatively less attractive in boom years, especially during the Wall Street boom of 1929. This inverse relation between the state of activity and the level of capital exports was quite reversed in the great depression of the 1930s.

current account and on capital account thus moved in the same direction. In the nineteenth century, by contrast, when the United States was a net borrower, the decline of American imports in the slump tended to be offset from the balance of payments point of view by a diminished sale of American securities to the rest of the world.

One familiar consequence of the cycle that applies more or less irrespective of where it originates is the movement of the terms of trade. For a variety of reasons arising out of the structure of primary production, the prices of primary products are much more flexible and their output much less flexible than is the case with manufactures. Fluctuations in the export proceeds of primary producers are thus largely fluctuations in prices. Importers of primary products get an improvement in their terms of trade in the slump which mitigates to some extent the fall in real income which they suffer at that time.

§ 4. International Synchronisation and Divergence.

It was shown in § 1–§ 2 of this chapter that the general tendency is for fluctuations originating in one country to transmit themselves to others. In the simplest case the timing of fluctuations will be roughly the same in the active country and in the passive ones. If the rise and fall in income that results from the international transactions of the passive countries induces a corresponding rise and fall in their domestic investment, their fluctuations will acquire some independent momentum, and will gain in amplitude; and the exact timing of fluctuations in different countries may then diverge to some extent, since the internal dynamics of investment may cause the turning points in the originally passive countries to come rather sooner or later than the corresponding turning points in the first country.

Likewise if several different countries start with independent cyclical tendencies, the existence of links between them by way of trade and lending will tend to keep their fluctuations roughly in step with one another. The degree of conformity between them will depend on the strength of the links connecting them, on whether their fluctuations happen to start off in step, and on whether underlying conditions are similar. If conditions are very different and the links are weak, wide divergences in timing may conceivably develop.

As a matter of history, the general tendency has been for countries to move roughly together in their fluctuations, especially when the fluctuations have been violent ones. Departures from international conformity have arisen largely because the idiosyncrasies of individual national economies have overridden for the time being the influences between them. But attention must also be given to another sort of divergence that has sometimes manifested itself between countries: that which arises not from independence but from systematic inversion.

The most obvious case where the cyclical experience of two countries is liable to diverge systematically is if the original cause (or part cause) of the boom in one was such as to be directly at the expense of the other. Suppose for example that what starts a boom in one country is an autonomous improvement in its balance of trade, resulting from the strengthening of its competitive position in international trade. This might be due to an increase in its industrial productivity, or the discovery of low-cost mineral resources within it, or a swing in consumer tastes towards the products in which it has a comparative advantage, or a shortage in world markets (resulting from bad harvests in other countries) of a primary product that it exports. In this case the one country's gain is another country's loss, and the level of activity in the two will tend to move inversely. Similar results could arise from a change in the pattern of world lending. Capitalists may experience a swing of sentiment in favour of the securities of one country and away from the securities of another—a swing that has little to do with what is going on in either or at least is excessive in relation to any real changes that may be taking place.

Another possible source of systematic inversion between the cyclical experience of two countries is if a boom as such in country A (as distinct from a particular cause of a boom in A) has certain adverse effects on the level of income in the other country B. Now a rise in income in A, the active country, will as such always have a favourable effect on the balance of payments on current account of B, the passive country; and the resulting stimulus to effective demand in B will as a rule induce a rise in investment in B, thus further raising income there. But in certain circumstances, the rise in income in A may *discourage* investment in B, notwithstanding the improvement in B's balance of payments on current account and its favourable multiplier effects.

A boom in A may discourage investment in B for one or more of the following reasons. (For simplicity we assume a two-country world.)

(1) As was shown in § 2, a boom in A may in some circumstances cause capital to flow into A (or increase an existing flow of capital into A or diminish an existing flow of capital out of A) to an extent that exceeds the deterioration of A's balance of payments on current account. There will then be an improvement in A's overall balance of payments and a corresponding deterioration in the overall balance of payments of B. The rate of interest in B will tend to rise and investment there will be discouraged. In this case the two countries are in effect competing for finance.

(2) A boom in A may cause an increase in the net migration of labour from B to A. This will cause a fall in the rate of population growth in B or perhaps even an actual decline in B's population. Investment in B will thereby be discouraged. In this case the two countries are competing for population.

(3) If B already has full employment, an increase in its exports can be achieved only by a reduction in its consumption or its investment. A boom in A, by raising B's exports, may therefore have an adverse effect on investment in B. In this case the two countries are competing for productive resources generally. Investment and exports in B will likewise

be in competition with each other if some bottleneck exists in the production of a commodity which is both exported and used for home investment, even though there is not general full employment.[1]

If investment in A and investment in B stand in a competitive relation to each other for one or more of these reasons, there will be inversion between the movements of investment in A and B respectively, and there will also be inversion between the movement of investment and that of the balance of payments on current account in B as well as in A.[2] This may or may not be accompanied by inversion between the movements of income in the two countries, according as the adverse effect of A's boom on B's investment is or is not outweighed by its favourable effect on B's balance of payments on current account.

A noteworthy case of inversion between the movements of investment in different countries is provided by the fluctuations in building in Great Britain and the United States (see Chapter VI, § 5). There is reason to suppose that this inversion has not been confined entirely to building but has extended as well to other forms of investment which have followed more or less closely the long waves in building in the two countries. An associated phenomenon is the inversion between the movements of British home investment and

---

[1] Another possible cause of inversion is if the two countries are in competition for a limited supply of internationally mobile 'entrepreneurship'—the energy and initiative required to promote investment. If entrepreneurs are occupied by investment at home, they may have less attention to spare for overseas projects, and vice versa. Yet another possible cause is that (as mentioned above, p. 182, n. 1) a boom in A may conceivably turn the balance of payments on current account in A's favour, if the demand for A's exports is inelastic.

[2] Inversion between investment and the balance of payments on current account calls for special explanation in the case of the passive country B, but it is the normal thing for the active country A. Even in A, however, it will be more pronounced if there is a tendency to inversion between investment in A and investment in B, since in that case B's income will rise less than it would otherwise have done or will actually fall in response to a rise in income in A, and as a result there will be correspondingly less increase (or an actual fall) in A's exports.

the British balance of payments on current account; this was especially marked in the period 1870–1914, but signs of it are also to be found in more recent periods.[1] Each of the three causes named above has been suggested as a possible explanation of these phenomena. At least as far as building is concerned, migration is perhaps the most plausible explanation, but the other causes have probably had some significance as well, especially competition for finance.

It should be noted that despite the elements of inversion referred to, fluctuations in *national income* in Great Britain have not generally stood in an inverse relationship to those in the United States. There are two reasons for this. In the first place, the *tendencies* to inversion mentioned above have by no means always been strong enough to produce actual inversion between the movements of total investment in Britain and of total investment in the United States.[2] In the

[1] See below, Chapter XII, pp. 217–22, and Diagram 10 for data and some further discussion. Cf. also A. K. Cairncross, *Home and Foreign Investment 1870–1913* (1953), especially Chapter VII; Brinley Thomas, *Migration and Economic Growth* (1954), especially Chapter XI; Ragnar Nurkse, 'The Relation between Home Investment and External Balance in the Light of British Experience, 1945–55', *Review of Economics and Statistics*, May 1956, pp. 121–54.

[2] The inversion between investment in Britain and investment abroad has been distinctly less uniform than the inversion between investment in Britain and Britain's balance of payments on current account (capital export). This may be explained as follows. Insofar as movements in British capital export were due to autonomous movements in investment and income abroad, the level of investment abroad and the level of British capital export would regularly move together, and if either of them followed an inverse path to that of British home investment, the other would too. But insofar as movements in British capital export were due to autonomous movements in British home investment (capital export being discouraged because home investment was attractive or because the domestic boom had weakened the current account balance of payments), the level of investment abroad might or might not move in line with British capital export, according to what other influences were currently affecting the level of investment abroad. In this case inversion between British capital export and British home investment might or might not be accompanied by inversion between British home investment and investment abroad. An example of a case where it was not is the period around 1900, when a level of investment in Britain which was high for internal reasons probably served to discourage capital export notwithstanding a tolerably

second place, Britain's balance of payments on current account, movements in which broadly reflect those in investment and income in the United States and other overseas countries, has exercised the dominant effect on fluctuations in her national income more frequently than her home investment has. Hence even when the movements of investment in Britain and in the United States have been inverse to each other, the national incomes of the two countries have more often than not tended to move together.

§ 5. National and International Factors in the Cycle in Practice. To ascertain the relative responsibility for a country's fluctuations of internal factors and of externally transmitted ones is important both for the understanding of the cycle as a historical phenomenon and for the formulation of policy. The most obvious criterion is the relative magnitude and direction of movements in domestic investment and in the balance of payments on current account. But this is not entirely satisfactory, because each of these variables reflects both internal and external influences. On the side of the balance of payments, fluctuations in imports are obviously largely the result rather than the cause of movements in income. It might seem for this reason that fluctuations in exports would be a better measure of external forces than fluctuations in the overall balance of payments on current account. But important movements in the value of imports may sometimes occur for reasons other than changes in income in the importing country and may therefore rightly be regarded as independent external influences; they may be due, for example, to harvest variations or to changes in import

---

high level of investment abroad. (On one or two occasions, moreover, the inversion between British capital export and British home investment appears to have been due to accidental factors unconnected with the level of investment abroad: e.g. around 1880, when the effect of harvest variations on Britain's need for imported wheat affected the strength of the British balance of trade and hence Britain's capacity to undertake capital export.)

prices caused by movements in demand in other countries. Moreover, changes in exports, for their part, may be partly a consequence of changes in national income in the exporting country, rather than an independent external influence, in so far as a rise in that country's national income and imports gives other countries increased income and increased command over foreign exchange, or in so far as the level of national income affects the prices of exports and hence their value. On the other side, domestic investment will be influenced by changes in the fortunes of the export trades and their repercussions elsewhere; and it will also be influenced by the monetary consequences of disturbances in the balance of payments. So while these overall figures are obviously relevant in any attempt to apportion responsibility for a country's fluctuations between internal and external forces, they do not by themselves necessarily settle the issue.

It is generally accepted that the foreign transactions of the United States have not exerted more than a minor influence on the course of fluctuations there, at least since the Civil War. But fluctuations in the United States are important to other countries, because although foreign transactions are a small proportion of the U.S. national income, they are a large item in the balance of payments of many other countries because of the size of the U.S. economy. The predominantly active rather than passive rôle of the United States is confirmed by the fact that her imports conform much more closely than her exports do to the pattern of fluctuations in national income. In the inter-war period American fluctuations dominated the world scene not only because of the size of the U.S. economy, but also because of the violence of the fluctuations themselves. Admittedly the exact American pattern was not everywhere reproduced. For example the experience of Great Britain was markedly different, in that the 1930s were in many respects more prosperous than the 1920s. Moreover the downturn in world prices of primary products began in the mid-1920s, well before the American downturn of 1929. But it can still be said with a good deal of plausibility that in so far as there was a world cycle at that time, its source lay in the United States. (This does not mean, of course, that other countries would not have been capable of generating cycles of their own if left to themselves.)

Before 1914 the sources of instability were more various. Fluctuations in the United States economy appear already to have owed relatively little to outside forces, though partial dependence on foreign capital made the United States more sensitive to conditions in European financial centres than she later became. Other countries felt the impact of American fluctuations, but for most of them it was one influence among several. In Germany, internal forces seem to have been paramount. In Britain, domestic investment and the balance of payments on income account both showed big fluctuations, and their curious and largely inverse movements jointly determined the ups and downs of income. In the earlier part of the nineteenth century, capital export was less important to the British economy, and domestic investment was accordingly the main factor in the situation.[1] In the areas of recent European settlement outside the United States—Australia, New Zealand, South Africa, Canada, South America—heavy dependence on overseas demand for the sale of the staple exports was combined with occasional violent booms and setbacks in domestic investment, this investment being largely financed, of course, by foreign capital. These booms, which had substantial repercussions in Britain and elsewhere, developed a momentum of their own, and their turning points were by no means always due to external factors. On some occasions exports fell little or even went on rising throughout the slump. Frequently the downturn was due to such causes

---

[1] In this period in Britain, however, the increase in imports in the boom often contributed materially to halting it by causing an outflow of gold. It appears that this was due at least as much to overadjustment of supply to demand in the manner of the cobweb cycle (cf. Chapter V, § 3) as to an increase in ultimate demand for imports from consumers. The tendency for overadjustment arose from lags in transport and communications, and with the speeding up of these and the establishment of more stable trading conditions later in the century, this feature of the cycle largely disappeared.

as the collapse of a speculative real estate boom or to the inadequacy of the foreign capital inflow to pay for the rising flood of imports. In such circumstances the downturn was often blamed by the people in the country concerned on the withdrawal of foreign capital. On some occasions this explanation may have been true. The difficulty is, however, to tell whether the withdrawal of capital that undoubtedly tended to occur on such occasions was not the result of the slump rather than its cause.[1] But from the broader point of view, this is possibly not very important. In the fifty or so years before 1914, different parts of the world were linked together by trade and lending in a relationship closer, perhaps, than any that has existed before or since. For some purposes it is appropriate, therefore, to regard the countries concerned as forming parts of a single economy. On some occasions one sector of the world economy was thought to offer the greatest scope for investment, and very likely suffered in consequence the earliest and most severe reversal; on others, another. Where the boom broke first, and whether it broke because confidence failed among business men in the country itself or among lenders in the metropolitan country, ceases, according to this point of view, to be a matter of the first importance for our understanding of the cyclical process.

[1] This difficulty of interpretation applies, for instance, to the Australian depression of the 1890s, the depression in South Africa in 1903-9, and the depressions experienced in a number of Latin American countries in the late 1920s and early 1930s.

CHAPTER XII

PERIODICITY AND THE PROBLEM OF MAJOR AND MINOR CYCLES

THE question to be discussed in this chapter is whether and in what sense the observed historical pattern of movements in business activity warrants the description 'cyclical', which we have so far been using without much discussion of its exact meaning. The main point at issue is the extent to which a regular periodicity can be observed in business fluctuations and if so what it is. The earliest writers on the business cycle, guided by the dates of crises in nineteenth-century Britain, thought in terms of a seven- to ten-year cycle. Later research, relating chiefly to the United States, suggested a quite different periodicity, namely three to four years—the 'forty-month' cycle.[1] A widely held view combines these two and postulates the simultaneous existence of a three- to four-year minor cycle and a seven- to ten-year major cycle superimposed on it. Yet other writers have denied that economic fluctuations have any regular periodicity at all. In order to assess these hypotheses we shall examine the historical experience of the United States and Great Britain, with briefer reference to fluctuations in other countries.

§ 1. Are Business Fluctuations merely Random Disturbances? The wholly sceptical view about the existence of 'cycles' in business activity may be represented by the following quotation from Irving Fisher:

If by the business cycle is meant merely the statistical

---

[1] The seven- to ten-year cycle is sometimes referred to as the 'Juglar' cycle and the forty-month cycle as the 'Kitchin' cycle. These names, suggested by Schumpeter, derive from early authors on the two types of cycle.

fact that business does *fluctuate* above and below its average trend, there is no denying the existence of a cycle—and not only in business but in any statistical series whatsoever! If we draw any smooth curve to represent the general trend of population, the actual population figures must necessarily rise sometimes above and sometimes below this mean trend line. . . . In the same way weather conditions necessarily fluctuate about their own means; so does the luck at Monte Carlo. Must we then speak of 'the population cycle', 'the weather cycle' and 'the Monte Carlo cycle'? I see no more reason to believe in 'the' business cycle. It is simply the fluctuation about its own mean.[1]

If it were true that ups and downs in business activity reflected nothing more than the operation of random disturbances, as Fisher here in effect contends, there would clearly be no need for any special theory of economic fluctuations. But in its extreme form the contention is not tenable. The observed pattern of fluctuations in national income and suchlike variables differs markedly from the pattern that would result from a purely random series such as the numbers obtained in successive throws of a dice. The most obvious difference is that whereas in a truly random series each value shown will be independent of all others and is equally likely to be the same side or the opposite side of the trend line as the one immediately before it, in series like national income a high value will normally be followed by another high value and a low value by another low value, so that the trend line will be crossed at less frequent intervals. More refined mathematical tests of randomness confirm that to describe economic fluctuations as *merely* the result of random shocks is not permissible.

The highest degree of scepticism about the cycle that is at all plausible in the light of the observed statistics is perhaps

[1] Irving Fisher, 'Our Unstable Dollar and the So-called Business Cycle', *Journal of the American Statistical Association*, 1925, pp. 191-2, quoted in Wesley C. Mitchell, *Business Cycles, The Problem and its Setting* (1927), pp. 465-6.

the hypothesis that the level of income, as well as being subject to random disturbances, has a certain inertia, so that in
any given period it is determined partly by the random shocks
experienced in that period and partly by the level of income
in the preceding period. The admission of inertia removes
the more blatant unrealities of the extreme view as advanced
by Fisher. But even so it is doubtful whether the type of
pattern resulting from such a hypothesis is sufficiently regular to be an acceptable account of reality.

A more sophisticated view, which has also sometimes been
taken to deny the existence of a cycle and hence the need for
any theory to explain it, is that advanced by the Russian
economist Slutsky.[1] According to this doctrine, the level of
business activity *is* determined by random shocks; not, however, by the shocks experienced in the current period alone,
but by a weighted average of the shocks experienced in the
current period and in other recent periods. Slutsky showed
that a series derived by such a summation of random shocks
was capable of manifesting fluctuations of a surprisingly
regular appearance, not less regular than those observed in
reality. However this theory does not imply such a rejection
of accepted notions about the business cycle as has sometimes
been supposed. The theory has close affinities to the model
into which so many theories of the business cycle can be
reduced: that the level of income in period t is determined
partly by any currently experienced random shocks which
may occur and partly by the levels of income in periods $t-1$
and $t-2$ (and possibly still earlier periods as well). The only
difference between this and the Slutsky theory is that, according to the latter, current income is affected by past random
shocks as such, whereas according to the former it is affected
by past random shocks only in so far as these affected past
income. There is a genuine distinction here, but it is rather
a fine one, and from the economic point of view the Slutsky

[1] E. Slutsky, 'The Summation of Random Causes as the Source of
Cyclic Processes', *Econometrica*, 1937, pp. 105–46.

assumption seems the less plausible of the two. In any case in order to establish the Slutsky theory it is necessary to show some economic reason why current income should be affected by past shocks as well as by current ones, and it is difficult to do this without resorting to the same sort of concepts—lags, multipliers, accelerators, etc.—as occupy the centre of the stage in ordinary business cycle theory.[1]

It is unfruitful to push too far discussion in terms of what is the greatest importance that it is statistically plausible to assign to random factors in the causation of fluctuations. It is clear statistically that economic fluctuations are not due *solely* to random factors, and it is also clear both from *a priori* reasoning and from our more detailed knowledge of history that certain forces do operate which are in principle capable of causing fluctuations of a systematic character. The question is really whether these forces are sufficiently strong in relation to random influences and sufficiently unified in their effect to produce some degree of regularity in the timing and shape of fluctuations. Before looking at the empirical evidence on this, however, something should be said on the factors likely to affect the periodicity of fluctuations in theory.

§ 2. Factors Affecting the Duration of Fluctuations in Theory.

Consider first the simplest kind of model of the cycle, one which is stated in aggregative terms and does not take account of erratic shocks. This will usually yield fluctuations of regular periodicity; each successive cycle will have the same duration. What the duration is will depend on the exact

[1] The alternative hypotheses discussed so far can be summarised in symbolic terms as follows, where Y denotes income, ϵ random shocks, and the subscripts time-periods:

(i) the purely random hypothesis: $Y_t = f(\epsilon_t)$.
(ii) random shocks plus inertia: $Y_t = f(Y_{t-1}, \epsilon_t)$.
(iii) Slutsky hypothesis: $Y_t = f(\epsilon_t, \epsilon_{t-1}, \epsilon_{t-2}, \ldots, \epsilon_{t-n})$.
(iv) ordinary difference equation model (sometimes referred to as autoregression) combined with current random shocks:
$$Y_t = f(\epsilon_t, Y_{t-1}, Y_{t-2}, \ldots, Y_{t-n}).$$

nature of the model and the size of the parameters.[1] The
sort of considerations involved are the speed and sensitivity
with which entrepreneurs respond to inducements to invest,
the length of the gestation period, the rate at which the stock
of capital falls due for replacement, the size of the marginal
propensity to consume, the size of the normal capital-output
ratio, etc. In at least some models the duration of the cycle
varies less than might be expected in response to changes in
the parameters.[2] To the extent that this is so, it would not be
quite so surprising as might appear at first sight if the average
duration of the cycle in reality were found to be roughly constant over a long period of time, notwithstanding major
changes in the structure of the economy.

Consider next the consequences of disaggregation. Suppose
that instead of treating investment as a single whole, the
model distinguishes two or more classes of investment, which
differ to a greater or less extent in their characteristics. Thus
a distinction may be made between inventory investment and
fixed investment, and within fixed investment between house-
building and the rest. For reasons indicated in earlier chapters, inventory investment, taken by itself, is likely to have
relatively short cycles, and house-building relatively long
ones. What will then be the pattern of fluctuations in total
investment and national income? To work this out rigorously is complicated and difficult, but some of the possibilities
may be seen fairly readily. At one extreme there may still
be a single unified cycle of more or less constant periodicity.
This may happen (a) if the inherent characteristics of the
different classes of investment are not very different or (b) if
one class of investment is quantitatively dominant or (c) if the
influences common to the different classes of investment, in
particular the level of national income, are dominant and

---

[1] For further discussion see J. R. Hicks, *A Contribution to the Theory of
the Trade Cycle* (1950), Chapter IX, and L. A. Metzler, 'Factors governing
the Length of Inventory Cycles', *Review of Economic Statistics*, 1947,
pp. 1–15.
[2] Cf. Hicks, *op. cit.*, p. 112.

outweigh the influences peculiar to each class or (d) if one class of investment establishes dominance because other classes of investment are much more sensitive to it and to the movements in national income it sets up than it is to them. At the other extreme the different classes of investment may pursue their different individual cyclical paths and thereby bring about multiple cycles in total investment and national income. For this to happen each class of investment must be able to move with some degree of independence of what is happening in the rest of the economy—it must be able to rise when other classes of investment and possibly national income are falling, and conversely. In all but the most extreme cases, however, each class of investment must be a bit affected by what is happening in the rest of the economy, and will therefore not follow exactly the same path as it would do if it were the only form of investment.

We have so far been neglecting shocks. In an aggregative model shocks will disturb the periodicity of the cycle to a greater or less extent, but the cycles will still be of a certain average duration, as determined by the structure of the system, i.e. what the duration of the cycle would have been in the absence of them. Shocks will have a similarly disturbing effect in a disaggregative model. In this case, however, there is a further possibility of some interest. One of the differences between classes of investment may lie in the extent to which they are influenced by shocks. One class of investment· may be particularly sensitive to shocks affecting the economy as a whole, or may be particularly subject to shocks of a kind that affect it alone. Hence even if the other differences between different classes of investment are not such as make them diverge very much, there may still be marked differences in the pattern of their fluctuations because of their differing susceptibility to shocks. The differing pattern of fluctuations in different sectors may then give the appearance of multiple cycles in the economy as a whole.

We turn now to the historical data in order to see what degree of regularity they display, how much support they give to the more specific hypotheses referred to at the beginning of the chapter—the forty-month cycle, the seven- to ten-year cycle, or the combination of the two in some system of major and minor waves—and how they relate to the various theoretical possibilities just discussed.[1]

§ 3. The Periodicity of Fluctuations in the United States.

The following table (p. 206) shows the dates in years and months of lower turning points in 'general business activity' in the United States since the Civil War, as established by the National Bureau of Economic Research.[2] The second column shows

[1] Reference may be given at this point to some of the sources from which information may be had on the historical course of fluctuations in different countries. *Generally*, W. C. Mitchell, *Business Cycles, the Problem and its Setting* (1927); J. A. Schumpeter, *Business Cycles* (1939); A. Spiethoff, 'Business Cycles', in *International Economic Papers No. 3*, 1953, pp. 75–171 (first published in German in 1923); J. Åkerman, *Structures et Cycles Economiques* (1955, first published in Swedish in 1944); W. A. Lewis, *Economic Survey 1919–1939* (1949); E. Lundberg (editor), *The Business Cycle in the Post-War World* (1955). *On the United States*, W. B. Smith and A. H. Cole, *Fluctuations in American Business, 1790–1850* (1935); R. Fels, 'American Business Cycles 1865–79', *American Economic Review*, 1951, pp. 325–49; R. Fels, 'The American Business Cycle of 1879–1885', *Journal of Political Economy*, 1952, pp. 60–75; W. C. Mitchell, *Business Cycles* (1913) (on the period 1890–1912); T. Wilson, *Fluctuations in Income and Employment* (1947) (on the inter-war years); R. A. Gordon, *Business Fluctuations* (1952) (on the inter-war years.) *On Great Britain*, A. D. Gayer, W. W. Rostow, and A. J. Schwartz, *The Growth and Fluctuation of the British Economy 1790–1850* (1953); R. C. O. Matthews, *A Study in Trade-Cycle History: Economic Fluctuations in Great Britain 1833–42* (1954); J. R. T. Hughes, 'The Commercial Crisis of 1857', *Oxford Economic Papers*, 1956, pp. 194–222; W. W. Rostow, *British Economy of the Nineteenth Century* (1948); A. K. Cairncross, *Home and Foreign Investment 1870–1913* (1953); D. H. Robertson, *A Study of Industrial Fluctuation* (1913); A. C. Pigou, *Aspects of British Economic History, 1918–25* (1947). *On other countries*, N. G. Butlin, *Private Capital Formation in Australia* (1955); C. G. F. Simkin, *The Instability of a Dependent Economy: Economic Fluctuations in New Zealand 1840–1914* (1951); C. G. W. Schumann, *Structural Changes and Business Cycles in South Africa 1806–1936* (1938); A. K. Cairncross, *op. cit.*, Chapter III (on Canada).

[2] 'General business activity' in the National Bureau's usage is deliberately left rather a vague concept. Substitution of some other yard-stick, such as Gross National Product, would alter the dates of some individual turning points, but it would not have much effect on the average duration of fluctuations; nor would this be much affected by measuring cycles from peak to peak instead of from trough to trough.

Date		Duration		Date		Duration	
Year	Month	Years	Months	Year	Month	Years	Months
1867	12	3	0	1912	1	2	11
1870	12	8	3	1914	12	4	4
1879	3	6	2	1919	4	2	3
1885	5	2	11	1921	7	3	0
1888	4	3	1	1924	7	3	4
1891	5	3	1	1927	11	5	4
1894	6	3	0	1933	3	5	3
1897	6	3	6	1938	6	7	4
1900	12	3	8	1945	10	4	0
1904	8	3	10	1949	10	4	10
1908	6	3	7	1954	8		

the interval in years and months between each such turning point and the next one. Cycles of three or four years' duration have been much the most frequent:

Duration of cycle in years (to nearest year)	2	3	4	5	over 5
Number of cycles	1	8	6	3	3

Of the six cycles of longer than four years, two include wars (World War II and the Korean War) and the others come in two groups of two successive cycles, associated with the two most severe depressions of the period (the 1870s and the 1930s).

As a first conclusion, therefore, it appears that the existence of a three- to four-year or roughly forty-month periodicity in fluctuations is well attested from the American data, except for certain periods of severe depression and war.

The hypothesis of a major seven- to ten-year cycle superimposed on the three- to four-year one can naturally not be tested from the above dates alone, since it depends on the amplitude of fluctuations as well as their timing. We accordingly show in Diagram 8 the course of manufacturing production in the United States since 1860, which may be

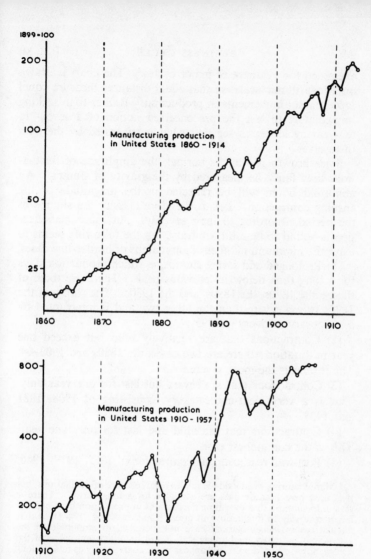

DIAGRAM 8. Manufacturing Production in the United States, 1860–1957 (1899 = 100). *Sources: 1860–1914, E. Frickey,* Production in the United States, 1860–1914 *(1947); 1914–19, National Board of Economic Research; 1919–57, Federal Reserve Board.*

207

examined for evidence of major cycles.[1] The chart is drawn on a logarithmic scale, so that equal distances measure equal *proportional* movements in production. Rather than seeking immediately to test the preconceived notion of a seven- to ten-year cycle, let us see first what is suggested by the data themselves.

Since growth is what is normal, the amplitude of fluctuations may fairly be measured by the gravity of slumps. An abnormal boom will be reflected in the magnitude of the ensuing contraction. Let us therefore classify the slumps of the period according to their severity. Any such classification is bound to be a bit arbitrary, but the following seems to leave the minimum number of anomalous or border-line cases.

(1) Prolonged and severe slumps, in which production stays for a long time below its previous peak. There are three of these: the 1870s, the 1890s, and the 1930s. The slump of the 1890s is less severe than the other two and is interrupted by a temporary recovery in 1895.

(2) Contractions that are relatively mild but exceed one year in duration: there are two cases, the 1880s and 1903–04. The former is the more severe.[2]

(3) Contractions that are severe but last for one year only. This is a very clear-cut category, consisting of 1908, 1921 and 1938.

(4) Contractions that are mild and last for only one year. This is the commonest case.

(5) Post-war readjustment contractions: 1865, 1919, 1946.

[1] Manufacturing production is not an ideal measure of fluctuations, but it is used here because data are available for a long period. There is reason to suppose that over time fluctuations in production have become larger relatively to fluctuations in prices (Chapter X, pp. 174–5), so that fluctuations in *money demand* have not increased in amplitude to the extent that the chart might suggest. It will be noted that some of the contractions recorded on p. 206 appear in the chart merely as retardations of growth and that the dates of turning points in the chart are not always the same as those in the table. This is because the chart relates to manufacturing production and the table to 'general business activity'.

[2] Indeed if account is taken of other evidence, such as price movements. the recession of 1903–04 might be more appropriately included in class (4),

These are clearly a different sort of phenomenon from the others, and will not be discussed further.

It is obvious that slumps of class (1) rank as major and that those of class (4) do not. Whether those of classes (2) and (3), which will hereafter be called middling slumps, should rank as major is debatable.

If the title of major slumps is reserved for those of class (1), the hypothesis that suggests itself is that major slumps tend to occur at roughly twenty-year intervals and that the absence of one in the 1910s was due to the war.[1] Major slumps in general business activity on this reckoning coincide with troughs in the building cycle (see later, p. 212). The hypothesis of a major cycle of roughly twenty-year periodicity, superimposed on minor cycles of much shorter duration, is, incidentally, well supported by the evidence on fluctuations in the United States *before* the Civil War.[2]

If we are willing to rank as major the slumps of classes (2)

---

[1] Although neither 1904 nor 1908 can really rank as a major slump in the sense at present under discussion, some evidence of a longer wave superimposed on the three- to four-year cycles which are so prominent in this period may perhaps be found in the fact that the three peaks 1907, 1910 and 1913 take place at successively lower levels in relation to the line of trend. This is shown clearly in the chart facing p. 338 in E. Frickey, *Economic Fluctuations in the United States* (1942). There is also evidence that unemployment was on the average higher between 1908 and 1915 than between 1900 and 1907. (S. Lebergott, 'Annual Estimates of Unemployment in the United States, 1900–1954', in Universities-National Bureau Committee for Economic Research, *The Measurement and Behavior of Unemployment* (1957).) For an interesting treatment of this period see J. A. Schumpeter, *Business Cycles* (1939), pp. 397–448, especially pp. 424–9.

[2] Fluctuations in this period were dominated by three great booms with peaks in 1818, 1836 and 1855–57. Of the depressions following these three booms, that after 1836 was much the worst. This depression clearly belongs to the same class as those of the 1870s and 1930s. The recessions after 1818 and 1857 caused sharp falls in prices and in statistical series particularly affected by financial and speculative influences, though they seem to have had a less grave effect on the physical volume of trade. In addition to these three long waves, the record shows shorter-period fluctuations more or less like the three- to four-year cycle found in later times. These fluctuations varied in amplitude, but both their booms and their slumps were markedly less violent than those of the three major cycles mentioned.

and (3), as well as those of class (1), we have as successive
major troughs in production 1876, 1885, 1894, 1904, 1908,
1921, 1932, and 1938, with durations of 9, 9, 10, 4, 13 (war),
11, and 6 years respectively.[1] This approaches nearer to a
seven- to ten-year cycle than the result obtained by treating
as major only the slumps of class (1), but the periodicity is
not very good after 1900.

It is difficult to take the matter much further than this by
mere inspection of the chart. The task of description cannot
be entirely separated from that of interpretation, to which
we now turn.

With regard *first* to the interpretation of the three- to four-
year cycle, evidence was quoted in Chapter V, § 5, relating
to the period since 1919, which showed that the chief contribution to these movements in income has been made by inventory investment. The reasons why inventory investment
should be more volatile in the short period than fixed investment were also there discussed. These stem essentially from
the fact that divergences between the actual and the desired
stock of capital both arise and can be corrected more quickly
in the case of inventories than in the case of fixed capital.

It is probable that inventory investment has had short
fluctuations partly because it is inherently prone to cycles of
short duration and partly because it is especially sensitive to
shocks. These two characteristics are not exactly the same
thing, but they will normally go together. To what extent
the inventory cycles of history reflect an endogenous cycle
and to what extent they were initiated by shocks which
affected inventory investment more than other classes of investment is a debatable question.

We do not have data on inventory investment before 1919,
but it seems a likely guess that it contributed largely to the
three- to four-year cycle at that time. Here too the question
arises as to the initiating cause of inventory contractions, and

---

[1] If 1903–04 is put in class (4) rather than class (2), as suggested in footnote 2, p. 208, the anomalously short four-year cycle disappears but an
anomalously long fourteen-year one is introduced instead.

it may be conjectured that they often owed their origins to the stock market convulsions and their reaction on the credit structure which were such a marked feature of the American economy in the quarter-century or so before 1914. So while this type of cycle may fairly be called an inventory cycle if reference is intended to its main manifestation, it is possible that inventory investment has played this part because it is the most sensitive form of investment rather than because it is subject to endogenous cycles.[1]

We turn now to the question of the alleged seven- to ten-year cycle and its relation to the twenty-year building cycle. The most usual approach to this question is to point to the moderately periodic occurrence of major depressions (when these are interpreted in the broader sense to include the middling ones) and say that there exists a seven- to ten-year cycle in fixed investment, with periodic depressions due to the exhaustion of investment opportunities, but that building displays much inertia in face of this cycle and has longer fluctuations of its own, and that the *gravity* of any individual seven to ten-year slump depends very much on whether it coincides with a time of building depression or not.

This approach may be objected to on the grounds that the periodicity referred to is not really very good. More seriously, the objection may be raised that the circumstances surrounding the middling depressions were so diverse that it is difficult to regard them as the manifestation of a regular cyclical tendency. In most cases they were not due to capital saturation, i.e. to the stock of capital being at such a high level in relation to income as to cause a downturn in investment—the basic cause of the downturn according to most

[1] The disappearance of the three- to four-year cycle in the 1870s and 1930s is a curious phenomenon for which no obvious explanation is forthcoming. It used sometimes to be suggested in the 1920s that the mild fluctuations experienced at that time were a healthy sign—'the heart-throb of the American giant'—and the same idea has recently been expressed with reference to the contractions of 1949 and 1954. The absence of the three- to four-year cycle in the two severest depressions suffered by the American economy may perhaps be taken to give this idea some support!

theories designed to explain the cycle as a regular recurrent wave (cf. p. 83). This point will be returned to presently.

For these reasons the suggestion that will tentatively be put forward here is that the twenty-year cycle is the only systematically periodic element in the record of fluctuations in the United States, apart from the short inventory cycle. The tendency to a twenty-year cycle is apparent from the data already quoted, but it stands out even more clearly if moving averages are taken.[1] Since building shows fluctuations of the same timing and does not show any other systematic fluctuations, it is natural to regard the twenty-year cycle in general activity as due to the cycle in building. It looks as though the importance of building and investment closely associated with it is such that the substantial general capital saturation which is the necessary condition of a really severe slump occurs when there is a building slump and not otherwise.

The evidence does not rule out the hypothesis that the long fluctuations in building and in general activity did not stand in the relation of cause and effect but rather were the results of a common cause. Such a common cause could be waves of major innovations; or some process of capital accumulation and digestion of which building was only the most obvious manifestation; or disruptions in monetary and banking institutions, which, from the cyclical point of view, were largely fortuitous and in which any appearance of regular periodicity was accidental. A fair case can in particular be made for an interpretation in terms of the last of these causes. But, on the whole, interpretation of the twenty-year cycle in terms primarily of the building cycle seems the most plausible, so long as it is remembered always that there is a wide range of investment which is intimately associated, both as cause and effect, with the process of rise and fall in building, notably investment in transport. As regards the periodicity of building fluctuations themselves, there are good reasons (see

---

[1] For an extensive collection of relevant data see P. J. O'Leary and W. A. Lewis, 'Secular Swings in Production and Trade, 1870–1913', *Manchester School*, May 1955, pp. 113–52.

Chapter VI) why their duration should be substantial—say not less than fifteen years or so—and why they should not show much responsiveness to short-lived shocks, but the regularity of the twenty-year period that has actually occurred is almost certainly partly fortuitous and owes a significant amount to the influence of wars.

What about fixed investment other than building? It appears that *generally* its fluctuations are pulled into conformity with those of the building cycle, and in contrast to inventory investment, it does not show *regular* independent fluctuations. Possible reasons for this are (a) that the inherent tendency of other fixed investment is to fluctuate in cycles not much shorter than the building cycle or (b) that building and the investment associated with it are quantitatively predominant or (c) that other classes of investment are more readily pulled into conformity with building than building is with them because they are more sensitive to changes in national income. The last of these is perhaps the most likely.

Other classes of fixed investment do not, however, conform perfectly to the pattern of the long cycle in building. In the first place, on certain occasions a distinct divorce has appeared between the timing of capital saturation or its opposite in building and in other classes of fixed investment, and this has been reflected in the pattern of fluctuations in general activity. In the 1880s, for example, when there was much saturation in investment in railroads, a slump of moderate severity developed though building was not specially depressed; and in the period 1905–14 and possibly also in the late 1850s an abundance of investment opportunities elsewhere prevented a really bad slump from happening at a time when building was on the downgrade.

In the second place, other fixed investment is notably more sensitive to shocks than building is. Here we revert to the point made earlier that in most of the middling slumps recorded in the annals the trouble does not seem to have lain chiefly in capital saturation. Extensive capital saturation in the absence of a building depression has been a distinctly unusual phenomenon—only the 1880s provide a clear example. On the other occasions most of the trouble seems to have come from financial disturbances or from an unusually vulnerable state of expectations. Thus we have in 1908 an exceptional financial crisis; in 1921 a belief that war had driven prices up to an unmaintainable level; in 1938 extremely pessimistic expectations engendered by the foregoing depression. A tendency to regular periodic recurrence of such circumstances can hardly be postulated. Some systematic element of a negative sort may be conceded, however, in that the working of the system does not seem to permit two really sharp contractions in fixed investment to occur within an interval of less than five or six years.

To what extent do these conclusions amount to a denial of the existence of 'the cycle' in the United States? They do more or less involve the rejection of the notion of a regular or inherent tendency to fluctuations of 7–10 years' duration. On the other hand they certainly do not involve the rejection of all ideas of regular periodicity. The tendency to a three- to four-year cycle is well established, and is probably to be attributed to the characteristics of inventory investment, which is unable to sustain cumulative movements of long duration. Distinct forces making for periodicity are also apparent in the twenty-year fluctuations in building, and these to a large extent transmit themselves to the economy as a whole.[1] In the

[1] It may be observed that the method adopted above of identifying cycles other than the short inventory cycle by looking for severe slumps implicitly identifies *long* cycles with *severe* cycles. These two concepts are of course not necessarily identical. A long mild wave could in theory be superimposed on shorter sharper ones. In practice, however, the two concepts do normally come to the same thing, because the short waves accommodate themselves to the longer ones: inventory investment and other more volatile forms of investment have one of their relatively frequent slumps at the same time as the infrequent building slump, and so the overall slump is severe. In other words the investment that fluctuates in short waves is pulled into conformity with the investment that fluctuates in long waves, while the reverse does not apply. The period 1900–14 is possibly an exception to this. As was stated above (p. 209, n. 1), a long wave can in a sense be discerned here, but there was no really severe slump. This

ultimate result, however, the pattern is a good deal confused, partly because of erratic factors like wars and institutional derangements of the monetary system, which affect some classes of investment more than others, and partly because from time to time the influences peculiar to individual classes of fixed investment outweigh the influences, such as the level of national income, that are common to them, and as a result these different classes of fixed investment for a while follow substantially different paths.

§ 4. The Periodicity of Fluctuations in Great Britain.   We shall treat the British experience in three separate phases: (a) 1919–38; (b) 1870–1914; (c) before 1870.

(a) In the inter-war period, the British economy underwent two and a half cycles of fairly regular periodicity: peaks in 1920, 1929, and 1938, troughs in 1922 and 1932. But the weight of structural influences was so great, especially in the 1920s, that these fluctuations can hardly be thought of as normal examples of the business cycle, and the circumstances of the two cycles do not strongly suggest a systematic origin of their roughly equal duration. The severe contraction of 1920–22 (more severe than that of 1929–32) was due to the collapse of the old staple export industries, and the partial recovery in the later 1920s, caused by the world boom and the beginnings of expansion in newer lines, had not brought about more than a feeble boom in Britain when the world depression of the 1930s arrived and for a while dragged the British economy with it. The strong recovery from this was dominated by building and the growth of new industries catering for the home market. The three 'booms' of the period were thus all very different: that of 1920 reflected the high prices born of post-war scarcities, and much of the investment then undertaken turned out to be based on grave

---

was no doubt due partly to the advent of the war, but the absence of a severe slump before the war seems to reflect an unusual lack of conformity of the more volatile classes of investment to the pattern displayed by building.

misapprehensions as to the future course of demand; that of 1929 was a rather feeble reflection of the boom in other parts of the world; and that of 1938 was mainly a building boom.

(b) Fluctuations in the British economy between 1870 and 1914 are commonly thought of as the classic case of the business cycle. As may be seen from Diagram 9, fluctuations in the national income in these years followed a remarkably regular pattern, and this is fully confirmed by other evidence on the state of activity, such as the unemployment percentage. Apart from the minor wobbles in the curve around 1877 and 1902, the durations of the cycles measured from trough to trough are 6, 8, 10, 5 years; measured from peak to peak they are 9, 7, 10, 7 years. This is not precisely a seven- to ten-year cycle, but it is as near to it as anyone could reasonably expect. There is not much sign of the three- to four-year type of movement. Home investment and the balance of payments on current account (referred to here as foreign investment[1]), taken as measures of internal and external influences respectively on the level of demand, show when added together substantially the same cycles as national income (see Diagram 9). The occasional divergences between the movements of the two curves in Diagram 9 could easily be due to movements in inventory investment, which is not included in the figures for home investment because of lack of data.

On closer examination, however, this epoch, so far from being one of classic simplicity, emerges as a most complex and obscure one. The aggregate figure of investment has to be broken down into its two components, home and foreign. When this is done, the picture is remarkably transformed

---

[1] Foreign investment—the net acquisition of overseas assets—is a term synonymous with capital export. In the present section it is used loosely as a synonym for the balance of payments on current account, which is what is actually shown in Diagrams 9 and 10. The two differ in that the balance of payments on current account exceeds capital exports by the amount of the net import of gold. In all but a very few years in this period, however, changes in the net import of gold were small compared with changes in capital export.

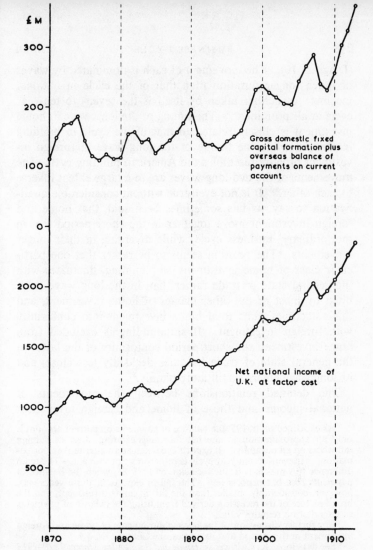

DIAGRAM 9. National Income and Capital Formation in United Kingdom, 1870–1913. (*Sources:* National income, A. R. Prest, 'National Income of the United Kingdom 1870–1946', *Economic Journal*, 1948, pp. 31–62. Gross domestic fixed capital formation and overseas balance of payments on current account, J. B. Jefferys and D. Walters, 'National Income and Expenditure of the United Kingdom, 1870–1952', *Income and Wealth Series V* (1955), pp. 1–40.)

(Diagram 10). The movement of each is dominated by waves of much longer duration than that of the cycle in national income. In neither taken by itself is the seven- to ten-year cycle at all prominent.[1] The timing of the long wave in home investment is closely related to that of the cycle in building in Britain, while the timing of the long wave in foreign investment broadly resembles the American building cycle. The movements of the two long waves are to a large extent inverse to each other.[2] It is not even true without considerable qualification to say, as has sometimes been said, that home and foreign investment move together in the short period (i.e. in the 'ordinary' business cycle) while diverging in their longer movements. The position seems to be rather that one particular class of home investment, shipbuilding, fluctuates with the general state of trade rather than in the long wave exhibited by most of the other classes of home investment, and this sometimes pulls total home investment into conformity with foreign investment. If shipbuilding is excluded from home investment, the short period conformity of the latter to the general state of trade becomes decidedly less close, and its long wave emerges still more plainly.[3]

The detailed relationships between the movements of national income and those of home and foreign investment

[1] As explained on p. 195, the balance of payments on current account is only an approximation to the net income-generating effect of foreign influences on an economy. If exports are taken as an alternative approximation, the seven- to ten-year cycle is rather more prominent. The main difference this makes is in the recession of 1883–86, when the balance of payments rose but exports fell. The fall in exports in those years was, however, considerably smaller than the fall in home investment, and the broad picture of the recession derived from using the balance of payments as the criterion remains valid.

[2] For further discussion of the inverse movements of home and foreign investment in this period and its causes, see Chapter XI, § 4.

[3] See data in A. K. Cairncross, *Home and Foreign Investment 1870–1913* (1953), pp. 168–9. Compare also Cairncross's data on home consumption of 'machinery', *op. cit.*, p. 167. These are not used in his main series on home investment, which is the basis of the data represented in Diagrams 9 and 10 above, but they conform much more closely to the long wave movement than to the shorter movements manifested by shipbuilding.

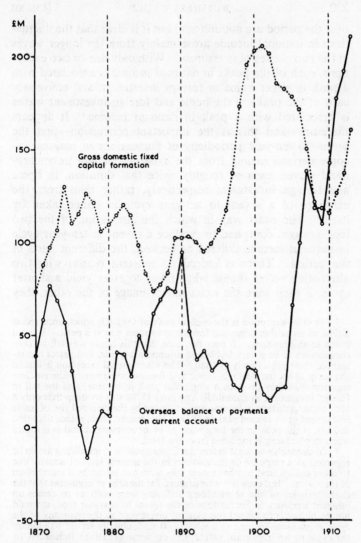

DIAGRAM 10. Home and Overseas Investment in United Kingdom, 1870–1913. (*Source:* Jefferys and Walters, *op. cit.*)

over the period are not uniform; but it is clear that the fluctuations in national income arose mainly from the longer waves in the two classes of investment. With only one or two exceptions, each of the peaks in national income is associated with a peak in either home or foreign investment, and conversely each of the peaks in the home and foreign investment waves is associated with a peak in national income.[1] It appears therefore—and this is the important conclusion—that the seven- to ten-year periodicity of fluctuations in national income derived mainly from the existence of two unsynchronised waves, each of roughly twice that duration, in home and foreign investment respectively, rather than from the existence of a seven- to ten-year cycle in either taken by itself.[2] The exact way in which the alternation of the two longer waves conspired to produce a seven- to ten-year cycle in national income differed as between the different parts of the period. There is indeed no inherent reason why two alternating waves should when taken together yield a shorter cycle; if each were the exact mirror-image of the other, they

[1] The chief exception is the cyclical peak of 1882–83, which occurred at a time when neither home nor foreign investment was at a peak. It owed much to shipbuilding. It may be noted that this boom was felt by contemporaries to be a very feeble and disappointing one, and prices recommenced their fall as early as 1880. The other partial exception is that in the early 1870s the peaks in home and foreign investment come so close together that they produce a single flat peak in income, and the fall in foreign investment in the middle and later 1870s was so steep that only a very minor recovery in income was produced by the renewed rise of home investment to its second peak in 1877. This second peak, rather than that in 1874, is the peak in the long wave of home investment that is revealed when shipbuilding is excluded from the total.

[2] It is debatable to what extent the fluctuations in shipbuilding are to be regarded as a response to fluctuations in the general level of activity due to other causes, and to what extent they were carried on by a momentum of their own. But even if it were granted for the sake of argument that the characteristics of the shipbuilding industry were such as to create an inherent tendency to fluctuations of the seven- to ten-year type, it would not be plausible to regard this class of investment as the mainstay of the cycle in national income as a whole. It undoubtedly served to amplify the cycle to an important extent and on some occasions influenced its timing, but the decisive importance of the long waves in foreign investment and in the rest of home investment at most of the cyclical peaks is manifest.

would cancel out and leave no cycle at all. Their particular pattern in this period was, however, such as to produce the result referred to.

There is much that is obscure in all this, but the behaviour of the home and foreign influences on national income, when considered separately, make it difficult to interpret the observed fluctuations in terms of any simple model of cycles of seven- to ten-year periodicity. It may be tentatively concluded that a seven- to ten-year cycle was not a phenomenon inherent in the working of the economy in this period.

In the United States the timing of major fluctuations in national income has conformed largely to that of the long waves in building, because there has been nu independent counterweight of sufficient importance. Britain too in the period 1870–1914 experienced a long cycle in building and associated categories of home investment. But foreign trade played a far greater part in the British economy than in the American one, and movements in capital export (foreign investment) were of comparable magnitude to those in home investment. They were, moreover, systematically opposed to them, or at the very least not positively related to them, being related rather to the long swings in building and general activity in the United States and other overseas countries to which the capital went. It was from the alternation of the long swings in home and foreign investment that the seven- to ten-year cycle emerged. In the United States, by contrast, there was nothing to challenge the dominance of building and the other classes of investment associated with it, and no clear seven- to ten-year cycle emerged.

(c) Fluctuations of a more or less cyclical character can be traced in the British statistics back to 1790 or perhaps even earlier—in fact almost back to the date commonly thought of as the beginning of the industrial revolution. For the present purpose, however, we may disregard fluctuations before 1820, because although they resembled in many respects the fluctuations of later years, their *timing* was decisively influenced by the course of the wars with France and they cannot therefore throw much light on the question of periodicity.

The generally accepted dates of major cyclical peaks in the British economy between 1820 and 1870 are 1825, 1836, 1845, 1853, and 1865, giving an average duration from peak to peak of exactly ten years. In contrast to the period after 1870, this ten-year cycle was punctuated by numerous shorter and milder fluctuations of the same general type as the American three- to four-year cycle.

This period, at least up till the mid-1850s, does appear on the face of it to offer a more genuine example of seven- to ten-year cycles than any other so far considered, either in Britain or in the United States. Neither a long cycle in capital export nor a long cycle in house-building was present to confuse the picture. Except for a brief period in the 1820s, capital exports was much smaller in relation to the national income than it became, under the influence of overseas railway building, after the mid-1850s, and the importance of capital export in the cycle, though not negligible, was secondary. For some reason that is not wholly clear, the long cycle in house-building was not yet established, or at least did not work in such a way as to transmit itself to the general level of activity.[1] In these circumstances the field was open for fluctuations to be governed chiefly by the behaviour of other classes of domestic investment. When all due allowance is made for fortuitous influences and for the irrational waves of speculative optimism which were a more prominent feature of the cycle in this period than later, it remains plausible to postulate that the dynamics of fixed investment in this period were such as to create some inherent predisposition to fluctuations in the region of ten years' duration. Some such tendency may have persisted later on in the century—witness the

---

[1] For the evidence see A. K. Cairncross and B. Weber, 'Fluctuations in Building in Great Britain, 1785–1849', *Economic History Review*, December 1956, pp. 283–97. There appears to have been a marked decline in house-building in the 1840s, but it was offset by the exceptionally violent railway-building boom of that period.

periodicity of shipbuilding fluctuations referred to above—but it was overlaid by the longer swings in capital export and in house-building and associated classes of home investment.

The shorter fluctuations which punctuated the main cycles before 1850 appear to have been largely inventory cycles associated with foreign trade. Their disappearance later in the century may be attributed to improvements in transport and communications, which greatly reduced the time-lags that had formerly been involved in the conduct of foreign trade.

The conclusions on the periodicity of fluctuations in Great Britain may now be summarised. The observed timing of fluctuations conformed surprisingly well to a roughly seven- to ten-year pattern from early in the nineteenth century until World War II. In this sense the seven- to ten-year cycle was a reality and was experienced as such by labour and capital in Great Britain and also in other countries dependent on the British economy. But it is only with regard to the earlier part of the period that the evidence points at all clearly to this result having arisen out of an inherent seven- to ten-year rhythm in the working of the economy. Between 1870 and 1914 some signs of an inherent rhythm of this sort persisted, notably in the fluctuations of shipbuilding, but the main cause of the seven- to ten-year cycles in income seems to have lain in the alternation of two much longer waves in home and foreign investment respectively, unsynchronised with each other. In the inter-war years of the twentieth century, there was again marked disparity between the behaviour of home investment and the state of the foreign balance, and for much of this period structural disturbances exerted a decisive influence on the level of prosperity.

§ 5. The Periodicity of Fluctuations in Other Countries. All national economies interact with one another to a greater or less extent. The timing of fluctuations in other countries has inevitably been influenced by events in the United States and Great Britain, the two countries that have occupied the leading position in the world economy at different periods. So it is difficult to find further *independent* evidence on the question of periodicity from examining what happened in other countries. The 'imported' element in fluctuations has been especially great in primary producing countries chiefly dependent on foreign trade.

The case of Germany is perhaps the most capable of casting independent light on the problem. There is every appearance that endogenous factors have as a rule been paramount in economic fluctuations in Germany—more so than in Great Britain—and turning points in business activity in Germany have often preceded those in other countries. Between 1870 and 1933 the German economy passed through a series of well-defined major peaks, as measured by industrial production: 1873, 1890, 1906 and (after the interruption of the war) 1927. The existence of a German building cycle before 1914 is well established, and its peaks correspond roughly to those just named. Less prominent peaks in activity occurred in 1883 and around 1900. The contraction of the mid-1880s appears to have arisen mainly from the side of exports. The sequence of events around 1900 was that the unusually violent boom in industrial investment in the 1890s reached its peak about 1898, but the major peak of the building cycle did not come till 1904–06. The only moderately severe recession of the early 1900s reflects these conflicting movements. Such a marked divergence between the movements of building and industrial investment has been unusual in Germany.

The German experience was thus in some ways intermediate between that of the United States and that of Great Britain, as might have been expected from the fact that foreign trade has been more important to Germany than to the United States but not so important as to Britain. Domestic investment on the whole dominated the course of fluctuations in Germany, and the timing of the domestic building cycle was transmitted for the most part to that of fluctuations in general activity. But foreign trade was capable on occasion of producing substantial fluctuations, as it did much more often in Britain but hardly ever in the United States. Moreover on at least one occasion there was a marked divergence in time between the peak in building and that in other classes of investment. As a result the number of sizeable fluctuations in activity that can be discerned in the data exceeds the number of building cycles.

§ 6. **Conclusions.** Of all major countries subject to economic fluctuations, the United States provides the nearest approach to a closed economy, and in that sense its experience may be taken as the 'purest' case-study for the present purpose. Apart from the minor three- to four-year cycle, the existence of which is well established, and which is largely dominated by movements in inventory investment,[1] it is the longer wave associated with the building cycle that is most prominent in the record of fluctuations in the United States. Much the same has been true of Germany. Building, together with the other classes of investment directly connected with it, possesses an inertia which normally prevents it from fluctuating in a shorter cycle, and it pulls other investment into line with it unless the latter has unusually strong reasons for diverging. It is probable that other fixed investment, if left to itself, would be more inclined to fluctuate in shorter waves. Sometimes this tendency has been strong enough to cause a serious divergence between building and other investment. Sometimes, too, the tendency to shorter fluctuations has been able to assert itself because the building cycle itself has been for the moment mild or absent (as it was in Britain up till about 1860). Moreover other investment occasionally reacts to psychological or speculative or fortuitous influences in such a way as to produce sizeable (though usually brief) fluctuations

[1] This short cycle has in modern times been confined chiefly to the United States, though there have been some signs of it in Britain since the war (cf. A. J. Brown, 'Inflation and the British Economy', *Economic Journal*, 1958, pp. 449–63). No entirely convincing explanation for this has been put forward.

out of line with the building cycle. Finally in that period of British history when capital export was most active, the alternation of the long cycle in building and a long cycle in foreign investment (itself connected with the state of activity in the countries to which the investment was being directed) served to bring about seven- to ten-year fluctuations in income in a curious fashion hardly likely to recur in the future.

CHAPTER XIII

THE TREND AND THE CYCLE

FLUCTUATIONS in demand have historically taken place about a rising trend. Reference to trend factors has already been made at a number of points in earlier chapters. It remains now to consider the matter more systematically. The discussion of the theoretical problems of growth in this chapter is intended to relate mainly to advanced or fairly advanced industrial countries, operating under a capitalist system. That is to say, we shall assume, among other things, that there is an active entrepreneurial class, that economic activities are not set in a rigid traditional pattern, that the labour force is reasonably suited to industrial employment, and that shortage of land does not present too serious an obstacle to expansion. The problems of under-developed countries, where some or all of these conditions are not fulfilled, will be referred to only incidentally.

Some economists have regarded the trend and the cycle as intimately related phenomena which it is impossible to treat in separation from each other. Others have held that the two phenomena are independent, or at least could occur independently of each other, the cycle representing a movement of demand relatively to supply and the trend representing a growth in demand and supply *pari passu*. Whichever view is taken, it is indisputable that the occurrence of growth must affect the character of the cycle. Moreover since both fluctuations and growth in demand have in fact taken place, a theory of fluctuations, if it is to be acceptable, must not be such as to preclude a satisfactory explanation of growth, and vice versa.[1]

§ 1. Alternative Models of Long-run Growth in Demand.

The difficulty of devising a theoretical apparatus capable of dealing with both trend and cycle arises largely because theories of the cycle have been mainly concerned with the causes of fluctuations in effective demand, whereas in discussions of growth the demand side has usually been less emphasised than the supply side. A large part of the problem is therefore to evolve an analysis of the demand side of the *growth* process that is consistent with the more familiar type of analysis of *fluctuations* in demand. What causes are responsible for the upward trend in demand over time and how are these causes related to those responsible for fluctuations in demand? A number of alternative approaches to this question will now be considered.

(1) The old-fashioned kind of treatment of economic growth was based implicitly on Say's Law, the doctrine that supply creates its own demand. On this reckoning the growth of demand does not present any separate problem. As far as demand is concerned, the economy is in neutral equilibrium, and any volume of output that can be produced will generate the appropriate amount of demand. Hence if technical progress makes an increase in output possible, there will be no

---

[1] Some leading items in the literature of this subject are R. F. Harrod, *Towards a Dynamic Economics* (1948); J. S. Duesenberry, *Income Saving and the Theory of Consumer Behavior* (1949); J. R. Hicks, *A Contribution to the Theory of the Trade Cycle* (1950); R. M. Goodwin, 'The Problem of Trend and Cycle', *Yorkshire Bulletin of Economic and Social Research*, 1953, pp. 89–97, and 'A Model of Cyclical Growth', in *The Business Cycle in the Postwar World* (1955), edited by E. Lundberg, pp. 203–21; N. Kaldor, 'The Relation of Economic Growth and Cyclical Fluctuations', *Economic Journal*, 1954, pp. 53–71, and 'A Model of Economic Growth', *Economic Journal*, 1957, pp. 591–624; Joan Robinson, *The Accumulation of Capital* (1956), especially Chapters 22 and 27; W. J. Fellner, *Trends and Cycles in Economic Activity* (1956); A. Smithies, 'Economic Fluctuations and Growth', *Econometrica*, 1957, pp. 1–52; and J. S. Duesenberry, *Business Cycles and Economic Growth* (1958).

difficulty on the demand side about achieving it. The assumption of Say's Law is justified if there is a direct link between saving and investment, such that each act of net saving is done specifically in order to finance an equal amount of investment.

Now it is plain that if it is taken without qualification, this assumption offends against the canon laid down above, that a theory of growth must not be such as to preclude a satisfactory explanation of the cycle, since no theory of the cycle can get very far if it assumes that supply is always equal to demand. In order to make it at all plausible, therefore, it would be necessary to maintain that in some way Say's Law holds in the long run but not in the short run. This is in fact one aspect of Schumpeter's theory: in his model entrepreneurs finance investment in the boom by borrowing new money from the banks but repay the banks out of current savings during the recession phase. In this way there is a direct link between the amount of saving and the amount of investment over the cycle as a whole, but not at any particular point within the cycle. But this involves very special assumptions both about the behaviour of entrepreneurs and about the absence of non-entrepreneurial net saving, and it cannot be regarded as a satisfactory general theory. The Keynesian theory of income-determination cannot be quite so summarily relegated merely to the short period. We cannot assume that effective demand, which gives so much trouble in the short period, simply looks after itself in the long period.

(2) A totally different theory that has won some favour in more recent times is based on the accelerator-multiplier interaction of the type discussed in Chapter II. As was there shown, such an interaction can in certain circumstances lead not to fluctuations but to explosive growth. It will do so, for example, in the lagless case discussed in § 3 of Chapter II, and it will also do so with certain values of the parameters in the lagged case. The same applies if a more general investment function of the capital stock adjustment type is used instead of the crude acceleration principle.

The theory proposed is thus that demand grows because the rise in income stimulates investment and this stimulates a further rise in income and so *ad infinitum*. This is a truly demand-oriented theory of growth; the economy is supposed to grow at a rate governed by the operation of demand factors. It implies either that there is always an abundant supply of labour and natural resources to draw on, or else that supply conditions adapt themselves to the state of demand. This is like Say's Law in reverse. While it may be plausible up to a point, it has paradoxical consequences when carried to its logical conclusion. It means that there is no presumption that an increase in population or an increase in productivity due to a technical discovery will as such lead to any increase at all in total output, far less to an increase of corresponding amount. This is rather a surprising doctrine, at least as applied to advanced industrial countries.

If it is admitted that in advanced countries supply conditions, as governed by population growth and technical progress, set a certain ceiling on the rate of growth of output, and that this ceiling is not very high (below 10% per annum, say, in normal circumstances) the theory under consideration can hold only on rather special assumptions. A model of lagged interaction between the multiplier and the capital stock adjustment principle[1] may lead either to explosive growth or to convergence to stationary equilibrium or to fluctuations, according to the values of the parameters. The theory in question requires not merely that the parameters should be such as to lead to growth rather than to one of the

---

[1] *Unlagged* interaction cannot be seriously put forward as a model of sustained growth, because, even apart from any question about the realism of the assumptions required, the growth path that it yields is unstable, in the sense that if some chance disturbance should raise investment in any period above the level indicated as appropriate by the assumptions of the model, the effect on income will be such as to increase rather than diminish the prospective profitability of investment, and the economy will therefore diverge more widely from the previous growth path instead of returning to it. Cf. R. F. Harrod, *op. cit.*, pp. 84–87, and T. C. Schelling, 'Capital Growth and Equilibrium', *American Economic Review*, 1947, pp. 864–67.

other alternatives, but also that the rate of growth involved should not be implausibly high—it should lie between 0 and 10% per annum at the outside. The range of values for the parameters that will give this result is a very narrow one, and it is difficult to believe that it can have held persistently over a long period of time.

A further trouble with this kind of growth model is that some difficulty is experienced in welding on to it a theory of the cycle. If the parameters of the system are such as to lead to explosive growth, they cannot *also* lead to fluctuations, and the cycle therefore has to be explained in terms of speculation, monetary disturbances, and other such factors extraneous to the main process of capital formation.

(3) The third approach to be considered relates the trend much more closely to the cycle. It is based on the 'ratchet' idea referred to in Chapter VII, p. 122. It was there shown that if consumption expenditure is determined partly by current income and partly by the highest income so far attained—the idea being that people tend to regard the past highest income as in some sense normal—then the mere fact that income in one boom has risen higher than it did in a previous boom will prevent income from falling so far in the ensuing slump as it did in the previous slump. A similar argument can be applied to some classes of investment. It was suggested in Chapter X that in a slump entrepreneurs will not as a rule believe that the current low level of income will prevail indefinitely. They will expect a return to something more normal. What they think of as normal will be conditioned by the level of income attained in the last boom. Thus there will be a tendency not only for consumption but also for investment, especially more long-range investment, to fall to a less low level in one slump than it did in the previous one, provided that the most recent boom raised income to a higher level than the previous boom.

In itself this does not constitute a fully-fledged theory of growth, since it does not explain why each boom should carry the economy to a higher level than the previous one.

This gap in the theory can be explained if a certain particular type of cyclical mechanism is assumed. If the inherent tendency of the system is to produce anti-damped cycles and there is a floor which prevents the fluctuations from actually increasing in amplitude, there will be no danger of the system relapsing into stationary equilibrium; and since the floor is rising for the reasons mentioned in the last paragraph, each upswing will start from a higher point than the previous one and will therefore reach a higher point before it turns down, so long as its inherent momentum is no less. The system will thus hoist itself up in a continuing series of cycles.

A variant of this theory is to postulate that the potential instability of the system is restrained not merely by a floor but also by a ceiling in the shape of limited capacity in the investment goods industries. In each boom the capacity of the investment goods industries is enlarged—the exact amount by which it is enlarged depending on the character of the boom and the behaviour of the entrepreneurs in the investment industries—and in the next boom income is therefore able to rise to a higher level before being brought up against the ceiling and turning down. The reasons for the upward trend of income between successive cyclical peaks are then two : (i) each upswing starts from a higher point than the one before; (ii) the bottleneck at the peak is being continually widened. In the simpler version of the theory stated in the last paragraph only the former of these two reasons is operative.[1]

The ratchet theory, either with or without the extra feature referred to in the last paragraph, appears more tenable than either of the two theories so far considered in this chapter. Moreover its chief elements can be combined without inconsistency with the fourth theory that will be discussed below.

---

[1] The continually expanding bottleneck theory would actually be sufficient to yield an upward trend in income between booms even without the operation of a ratchet effect on consumption or investment in the slump; but in that case there would be no upward trend in the level of income reached in successive slumps. The expanding bottleneck effect therefore needs to be combined with the ratchet effect to produce plausible results.

Taken by itself, the ratchet theory is a strictly demand-oriented theory of growth. It is therefore open to the same objection as that raised against the type of model considered under (2) above, that it involves a divorce between the actual rate of growth and the factors operating on the supply side, viz. population growth and technical progress. For this reason the ratchet theory does not in itself appear entirely adequate, even though it incorporates important elements of truth.

§ 2. Growth in Demand due to Population Growth and Technical Progress. We come finally to the theory which appears to have most to recommend it and which will underlie what will be said in the remainder of this chapter. This is that the growth in *possible* production brought about by population growth and technical progress somehow communicates itself to aggregate demand in such a way as to give the latter an upward trend.

That this must happen in some way or other seems self-evident. In order to explain how it happens it is not necessary to go to the lengths of Say's Law and postulate that there is a direct link between saving and investment such as to preclude any possible divergence between overall supply and demand. No departure is necessary from the normal Keynesian treatment of the relation between saving and investment. What is required is to show that population growth and technical progress affect the consumption function and/or the inducement to invest in such a way as to give an upward trend to demand; fluctuations in income due to the causes analysed in earlier chapters can then take place around a rising trend.

Reasons why this should be so have already been indicated in earlier chapters. In the case of consumption, the higher the level of population and productivity, the lower will any given income seem to be in relation to consumers' ideas of what is normal; the greater, therefore, will consumption expenditure be at any level of output (cf. Chapter VII, § 3).

In the case of investment, the higher the level of population and productivity, the greater the amount of labour and natural resources that will be available at a given level of output to co-operate with any new capital that may be created, and consequently the greater the additional output that can be produced by adding to the stock of capital; the greater, therefore, will be the prospective rate of return on investment, given the level of the real national income and the size of the existing capital stock (cf. Chapter IV, § 7). Of these two effects that on investment may perhaps be considered the more fundamental.[1]

The existence of such links between potential supply and effective demand does not imply that actual output is always or indeed ever necessarily equal to the maximum possible. It does not guarantee full employment. The forces described in earlier chapters as responsible for fluctuations in investment and income will continue to operate. But the functions relating consumption and investment expenditure to the level of real income, the stock of capital, etc., will be subject to an upward drift over time, and the fluctuations will therefore take place around a rising trend. The rate of growth described by this trend will be equal to the potential rate of growth permitted by population growth and technical progress—what is commonly referred to as the natural rate of growth[2]—since it is population growth and technical progress

---

[1] With certain types of reaction on the part of consumers, the upward trend in the consumption function may not be a steady movement related to population and productivity growth at all, but may instead be, for example, the discontinuous ratchet effect referred to above. *Some* form of upward trend in the consumption function is, however, a necessary permissive condition of growth in this type of model, even if the active stimulus to growth comes from the investment side. (Likewise if the active stimulus comes from the consumption side, a necessary permissive condition of growth is the rise in the full employment ceiling, which progressively relaxes any restrictions on investment that may be imposed by limited factor availability.)

[2] If population growth is at the rate of x per cent per annum and technical progress increases output per unit of input by y per cent per annum and there are no scarce natural resources, the natural rate of growth is equal to $x+y+xy$ per cent per annum, or $x+y$ per cent per annum as an approximation.

that are responsible for the upward drift in demand. Hence although there is no guarantee of full employment, there is some guarantee against a cumulative increase in unemployment such as would result if the natural rate of growth persistently exceeded the actual rate of growth.

If demand has an upward trend of this sort, income and the capital stock could grow steadily over time at the natural rate of growth, if the capital-stock-adjustment-multiplier interaction were not such as to produce unstable movements in income and if the system were not subject to any other disturbances or shocks. In practice it appears that instability or disturbances of some sort are experienced, and as a result the system fluctuates around its growth path. Periods when income and the capital stock grow at a rate exceeding the natural rate alternate with periods when growth is below the natural rate or there is actual contraction. If the natural rate of growth is high, the upward trend in demand will be strong, and booms will be long and powerful and slumps short and weak. If the natural rate of growth is low, booms will be feebler and slumps more severe. Thus the higher is the natural rate of growth, the higher will be the level of activity and the rate of profit on capital and the rate of capital accumulation averaged over the cycle as a whole.[1]

The upward trend in demand may not work with equal force at all stages of the cycle, even if the advance in population and technical knowledge takes place at an even pace. In particular, the encouragement given to investment by increased factor availability will tend to be less potent at times when there is much unemployment. In the extreme case where increases in factor availability affect investment only at times of full employment and moreover do not directly affect consumption, some modifications of the theory are necessary. Population growth and technical progress are then

---

[1] This approach to the problem of trend and cycle does not by any means preclude the possibility that the natural rate of growth is itself partly a function of the way the economy behaves. This possibility is discussed in § 5 below.

better regarded as removing obstacles to expansion rather than as positively stimulating it. The natural rate of growth will in this case be achieved only if the system is sure of reaching the full employment point at cyclical peaks. So long as this condition is fulfilled, each boom will carry income higher than the previous one did, since in the meanwhile population growth and technical progress will have raised the maximum possible level of production.[1] The condition that the full-employment peak is reached in cyclical booms will be fulfilled if the parameters of the system are such as to produce anti-damped cycles or explosive growth, or if the exuberance of entrepreneurs drives them to go on expanding till some definite check is encountered, notwithstanding some fall in the rate of profit in the meanwhile.

As contrasted with this, the more general theory stated above postulates that an increase in the availability of labour or other factors will encourage investment and/or consumption at any stage of the cycle, so that the potential growth in output will be realised even if the economy never reaches general full employment. The system does not on this assumption need to be prone to anti-damped cycles or explosive tendencies in order for its growth potential to be realised.

If the trend forces do become quite ineffective as a source of encouragement both to investment and to consumption when there is much unemployment, and if moreover cyclical forces do not always carry the economy up to full employment in the boom, growth is not guaranteed, and stagnation with increasing unemployment is a possibility. The economy will then have to wait till a war or some such shock carries it up to a level where the trend forces can again begin to operate. A theory of growth does not need to rule out such contingencies. All that is required of such a theory is to show that there are certain forces *normally* tending to bring

---

[1] This formally resembles the expanding-bottleneck theory that was discussed on p. 232, above. But the difference between the two theories as to what constitutes the ceiling is a far-reaching one.

about growth in demand, not that the growth process is automatic or inevitable in all circumstances.

§ 3. The Equation $G = s/v$ and its Implications.   A tautology
that has attracted a good deal of attention in the theory of
growth is that the proportional rate of growth of output
(denoted by G) is equal to the average saving-income ratio
(s) divided by the marginal capital-output ratio (v): $G = s/v$.
The basis of this tautology is simply that the increase in
output between two periods is equal to the increase in the
stock of capital multiplied by the amount of output obtained
per unit of additional capital.[1]   This suggests the following
problem.   Since s and v may appear to be given by the structure of the system independently of the rate of population
growth or technical progress, how is it possible that changes
in the latter can lead to changes in the actual rate of growth
in the way postulated above?

The chief answer to this question is that though the saving
function may be given by the structure of the system, it does
not follow that s, the average saving-income ratio, is also
given regardless of how the system is behaving.   If population and productivity are growing rapidly and the upward
trend in demand is therefore strong, booms will tend to predominate over slumps.   This will raise the average saving-
income ratio over the cycle as a whole compared with what
it would be if the economy were enjoying on the average a
lower level of activity.   For within the cycle the proportion
of income saved is higher in the boom than in the slump;
consequently the greater the proportion of the cycle that is
spent at a high level of activity, the higher will be the proportion of income saved over the cycle as a whole.   The
reasons why a high level of activity will lead to a high saving-

[1] In symbolic terms, where Y denotes income, K the stock of capital, I
net investment, and S saving, and where G, s, and v have the meanings
stated in the text,

$$G = \frac{\Delta Y}{Y} = \frac{\Delta K}{Y} \cdot \frac{\Delta Y}{\Delta K} = \frac{I}{Y} \cdot \frac{\Delta Y}{\Delta K} = \frac{S}{Y} \bigg/ \frac{\Delta K}{\Delta Y} = \frac{s}{v}.$$

income ratio have already been discussed in Chapter VII. Within each category of income (wages, profits, etc.) the proportion of income saved is higher in the boom than in the slump, and moreover in the boom the distribution of income tends to shift in favour of that class of incomes, namely profits, out of which the marginal propensity to save is highest.[1] Furthermore a country enjoying a boom (or a more powerful boom than is being enjoyed by other countries) will tend to attract capital from abroad and so be enabled to run an adverse balance of payments on current account, thus causing real capital accumulation to proceed at a higher rate proportionally to income than would be permitted by domestic saving alone.

It follows that the equation $G = s/v$ does not uniquely define the rate of growth, for s will adjust itself to the other influences at work. The same is true to some extent of v. In booms the degree of utilisation of capital is higher and the capital-output ratio is lower than it is in slumps. In fact it is this movement in the degree of capital-utilisation, equivalent to a movement along the short-run cost curve, which is largely responsible for cyclical movements in the inducement to invest. Hence if booms preponderate over slumps because the system is growing rapidly, the average level of v will tend

---

[1] The relative importance of the different ways in which the level of activity affects saving is what determines how much effect a change in the natural rate of growth will have on the average degree of unemployment of labour. Among the chief ways stated in Chapter VII through which the level of activity affects the saving-income ratio are (a) the average degree of unemployment, taken as a measure of the extent to which income is deemed to be below 'normal', and (b) the average rate of profit on capital, affecting the proportion of national income accruing to profits and also affecting the proportion of profits saved. If the natural rate of growth rises and the actual long-run rate of growth averaged over the cycle rises correspondingly, the average rate of profit over the cycle must rise by whatever amount is necessary to induce sufficient *investment* to make the capital stock grow at the new natural rate. The greater the extent to which the ratio of *saving* to income responds to this rise in the rate of profit, the less the extent to which the average degree of unemployment will need to fall, in order that between them these two influences should raise the saving-income ratio to the value that the new natural rate of growth requires the investment-income ratio to have.

to be lower than would otherwise be the case. The capital stock will on the average be more fully used, so a given amount of saving will permit a larger increase in output. For this reason too, then, the rate of growth yielded by the equation $G = s/v$ is not a unique one, and the system is capable of adjusting itself to a variety of possible natural rates of growth.

There is however one difficulty. The flexibility of both s and v may be subject to limits. Within each class of income the proportion saved can probably not be permanently raised above a certain level even in the most favourable circumstances, and redistribution of income towards profits can in the limiting case do no more than raise the proportion of income saved in the economy as a whole to the proportion that prevails in the profit sector. Likewise the degree of utilisation of capital will have an upper limit—only a certain amount of output can be got out of a certain stock of machinery however intensively it is used. Hence s is likely to have a maximum value and v a minimum one, and this means that the rate of growth, equal to s/v, will have a maximum value. What happens if this maximum attainable rate of growth is lower than the natural rate of growth as given by population increase and technical progress? This could come about if the natural rate of growth were very high or the propensity to save very low or the normal capital-output ratio very high.

Such a contingency corresponds to the case briefly referred to in connection with the upper turning point (p. 153), where the rise in population and productivity causes the available labour supply to increase faster than the stock of capital even at the top of a boom.[1] If the system is prone to instability there is then no effective ceiling to restrain the upward momentum of the boom. If the system is not prone to instability, the cumulative increase in the excess supply of labour

---

[1] It is equivalent to the case discussed by Harrod (*op. cit.*, pp. 87–89) in which, in his terminology, the natural rate of growth exceeds the warranted rate of growth.

must still lead to a cumulative upward pressure on demand. There will then be no cycles, and the situation will be one of perpetual boom with the inducement to invest getting stronger and stronger. (If any recessions do occur, they will be the result of transitory accidents, not an inherent feature of the system's working.) At the same time the increase in employment will be unable to keep pace with the increase in the labour supply, not because of any deficiency of demand but because of inability to increase the stock of capital at a sufficient pace to give labour the tools to work with. Inflation and excess demand for goods will be accompanied by increasing unemployment of labour.[1]

Such a situation of inflation combined with unemployment would be not unlike that found at the present time in some of the more backward countries of the world, which have a high rate of population growth and are trying to step up productivity quickly towards the level prevailing in more advanced countries. But it has not been characteristic of the historical experience of relatively advanced countries. In the latter, the rate of capital accumulation at the peak of the boom normally seems to have been sufficient not merely to keep up with but to exceed the natural rate of growth. It has exceeded it by a sufficient margin to permit and indeed necessitate an ensuing decline in investment and hence a slump. Taking the cycle as a whole the natural rate of growth has been achieved even though the degree of capital utilisation and the saving-income ratio were not at the highest possible levels all the time.

It is not altogether clear just why it is that in advanced countries the natural rate of growth never appears to have outstripped the maximum possible rate of capital accumulation and so brought about a situation of perpetual boom.

---

[1] It is possible (see above p. 235) that when unemployment has risen above a certain level, a further increase in unemployment will no longer have any stimulating effect on investment or consumption. In this case the situation will differ from that described in the text in that although there will be a cumulative increase in unemployment, it may after a point cease to be accompanied by inflationary tendencies.

The main explanation is probably simply that the flexibility of s and v due to the causes already mentioned has given s/v a large enough range to provide without much difficulty for the rates of population growth and technical progress actually experienced. It is possible, however, that one or both of two other factors may have contributed to keeping the maximum possible rate of capital accumulation above the natural rate of growth: first, variations in the capital-output ratio due to a cause not so far considered; and secondly, induced variations in the natural rate of growth itself. These two possibilities will emerge (see pp. 249 and 251–2) in the course of the next two sections, in which we consider more generally the causes and consequences of changes in the capital-output ratio and the possibility of induced changes in the natural rate of growth.

§ 4. **Changes in the Normal Capital-Output Ratio.** The only source of flexibility in the capital-output ratio that has so far been considered is variation in the degree of utilisation of equipment. But account must also be taken of the fact that a given amount of capital equipment (measured in value terms) can be *designed* to produce more or less output per unit of time at full-capacity working. Account must be taken, in other words, not only of the extent to which the actual capital-output ratio departs from the normal (i.e. changes in the degree of utilisation), but also of changes in the normal capital-output ratio itself, where the normal ratio is understood in terms of Marshallian long-period equilibrium.[1]

Let us assume to start with a given state of technical knowledge. A highly capital-intensive technique of production can then be defined as one which employs much capital per unit of labour. In the given state of technical knowledge there will exist a range of more or less capital-intensive techniques of production, any one of which is technically efficient in the sense that it does not require a higher input of *both*

[1] See above p. 36, n. 2, for a more exact definition.

capital and labour than some other known technique; and capital can be designed appropriate to any of these techniques.

Given the level of employment of labour, the more capital-intensive the technique of production, the higher will be total output. The schedule relating output to the amount of capital employed per man is commonly referred to as the production function. The slope of the production function, i.e. the amount by which the capital-intensity of production needs to be increased in order to produce a given increase in output, may be great or small according to the circumstances. In some circumstances there may be little scope for varying the proportions of labour and capital, and the extra output obtainable from using a more capital-intensive method may be small; in others the reverse may be the case. If the input of labour is fixed and the state of technical knowledge is given, the increase in output due to the use of a more capital-intensive technique must always be less than in proportion to the increase involved in the stock of capital, because of the principle of diminishing returns. The principle of diminishing returns likewise entails that the rate of profit on capital will be lower, the more capital-intensive is the technique of production, assuming demand is such as to lead to the same degree of utilisation of capital. How steeply the rate of profit falls as the degree of capital-intensity rises depends on the slope of the production function.

So far in this section we have been assuming a given state of technical knowledge. Technical progress serves to shift the entire production function in such a way as to reduce the total input of factors required to produce a given output. In the simplest case ('neutral technical progress') it reduces by equal proportions the input of labour and the input of capital measured in terms of labour cost, and does this whatever the initial capital-intensity of production.[1] If technical progress

[1] There are various possible definitions of neutral technical progress. That in the text follows Joan Robinson, *The Accumulation of Capital* (1956), pp. 132–3.

is neutral in this sense and demand rises sufficiently to permit a constant degree of utilisation of capital, a constant capital-intensity of production (defined by some such measure as the ratio of the stock of capital in value terms to output) will be associated with a constant rate of profit as time advances. We assume for the present that technical progress *is* neutral. Then if the capital-intensity of production is constant over time, output will grow at the natural rate of growth, i.e. the rate permitted by population growth and technical progress, provided that there is no change in the average degree of utilisation of resources. If the capital-intensity of production is constant at a high level, output at any point of time will be higher than it would be if the capital-intensity of production were constant at a low level, assuming employment to be the same in both cases.[1] But the *rate of growth* of output over time will not be different in the two cases. The rate of growth of output will differ from the natural rate of growth (assuming no change in the degree of utilisation of resources) only if there is a *change* over time in the capital-intensity of production, i.e. a movement along the production function. If the capital-intensity of production increases over time, the rate of growth of output will exceed the natural rate.

We have so far been assuming that technical progress is neutral in character, i.e. that taken by itself it tends to reduce inputs of labour and capital by the same proportions. If this is not so, the capital-output ratio will tend to change over time in a way different from that so far described. Thus if technical progress has a capital-using (labour-saving) bias, so that it reduces capital input less than it reduces labour input, the capital-output ratio will have a tendency to rise over time. In this case, however, in contrast to the one where the rise in the capital-output ratio is due to a movement along the production function with neutral technical progress, the rate of

---

[1] A condition of low productivity per worker due to a low capital-intensity of production is to be distinguished from one of low productivity due to overall technical backwardness. The former will be accompanied by a high profit rate on capital, but the latter will not necessarily be.

growth of income will not exceed the natural rate, and the rate of profit will not have any tendency to fall.

A high capital-intensity of production means a high normal capital-output ratio and hence a high actual capital-output ratio over the average of the cycle as a whole, if the average degree of utilisation is given. A high capital-output ratio means that a correspondingly high ratio of net investment to income will be needed to make the stock of capital keep pace with any given rate of growth of output. Thus if the natural rate of growth is 3% per annum, and output does in fact grow at this rate over the average of the cycle, the average ratio of net investment to income will need to be $7\frac{1}{2}\%$ if the capital-output ratio is $2\frac{1}{2}$ and 9% if the capital-output ratio is 3. Comparing these two alternative situations and assuming that the consumption function is the same in each, it is plain that over the average of the cycle the level of activity and employment will be higher in the case where the capital-output ratio is 3 than in the case where it is $2\frac{1}{2}$, because the amount of investment will be larger.

The above relates to the comparison of two distinct situations, with differing established capital-output ratios. The process of *transition* from a lower to a higher capital-output ratio will have a further effect, and a substantial one, in raising the level of investment and activity. (This applies equally whether the rise in the capital-output ratio is due to a movement along the production-function associated with a fall in the profit rate or whether it is due to a capital-using bias in technical progress.) The amount of investment required to achieve the necessary once-for-all increase in the capital stock is likely to be large in comparison with that required to keep pace with the ordinary annual increase in output, and is therefore likely to take a considerable time to carry out. Thus in the previous example the transition from a ratio of $2\frac{1}{2}$ to one of 3 will require a once-for-all increase in the capital stock equal to 50% of the annual national income: if national income is 100, the stock of capital will have to rise from 250 to 300.[1] The growth in the stock of capital taking place in these circumstances is sometimes described as falling into two parts: that required to provide for technical progress and population growth, referred to as capital-widening, and that required to effect the movement along the production function, referred to as capital-deepening. The distinction is of course no more than a notional one, since any given act of investment may involve elements of both widening and deepening.

So far in this section we have been concerned with the consequences of changes in the normal capital-output ratio. Let us now consider briefly the causes that may give rise to such changes.

We distinguished above two types of circumstance in which the normal capital-output ratio might change: one was as a result of movement along the production function and the other was as a result of non-neutral technical progress. As far as the latter is concerned, it is apparent that if technical progress has a capital-using bias, booms will tend to get stronger and slumps weaker as time goes on, while if technical progress has a capital-saving bias, the reverse will be true. Inasmuch as purely technical factors are what decides whether technical progress is neutral or capital-saving or capital-using, there is nothing much more to be said in the present context about changes in the normal capital-output ratio due to this cause.[2]

The more difficult and interesting question relates to

[1] Deepening investment may take the form of installing equipment additional to that already in use, or it may take the form of replacing present equipment entirely by other equipment of a more elaborate nature. Much deepening investment will normally be of the latter type. It will therefore tend to be carried out only gradually as the old equipment wears out, unless the advantages of deepening are so great as to justify scrapping the old equipment prematurely. The existence of old equipment that has not yet exhausted its useful life may thus mean that the scope for profitable deepening investment in any particular short-run situation is limited, even though in the long run the additional output obtainable from deepening the capital stock is considerable.

[2] Cf., however, p. 251, n. 1, below.

changes in the normal capital-output ratio due to movements along the production function. In order to elucidate this we have to consider what it is that in any given state of technical knowledge governs entrepreneurs' choice between techniques of differing capital-intensity. The answer to this is not simple, but broadly speaking the choice may be said to depend on the normal, i.e. minimum acceptable, rate of profit on capital. This is easiest to see in the case where firms can borrow as much as they want at a given rate of interest, and this rate of interest therefore determines the minimum acceptable rate of profit on investment. The higher the rate of interest, the more expensive will capital-intensive methods of producing a given output be relatively to less capital-intensive methods.[1] The *level* of the rate of interest will then determine the capital-intensity of production, and the *excess* of the current rate of profit over the rate of interest will determine the strength of the inducement to add to productive capacity of the given capital-intensity. In practice firms cannot usually borrow as much as they want at a fixed rate of interest, and the minimum acceptable rate of return on investment is therefore not so simply determined. The supply curve of external finance to a firm will normally be a rising one, and its own willingness to borrow will be limited by risk considerations. Much investment is financed internally, and internal finance is obviously not in perfectly elastic supply at a given rate of interest. Where the supply of finance is not perfectly elastic,

[1] A low rate of interest will not only encourage the use of a large amount of capital (and a small amount of labour) per unit of output, but will also induce a more rapid rate of replacement of capital. The lower the rate of interest, the less will need to be the margin of advantage of new equipment over old (due to the latter's deterioration or obsolescence) in order to justify replacement. In a sense this is really another aspect of a high capital-intensity of production, since the more rapid the rate of replacement, the higher the ratio of gross investment to income needed to support a given rate of growth of output, even though the capital-output ratio is unaffected. Thus the lower the rate of interest, the newer, as well as the greater in amount, will be the capital equipment that the worker has to co-operate with him. This contributes to the higher productivity per worker associated with the use of a more capital-intensive method of production.

the minimum acceptable rate of return (equal to the rate of return on the marginal investment project) is affected by the opportunities for investment—the firm's demand curve for finance—as well as by the terms on which finance is available. In the extreme case where the supply of finance is perfectly inelastic, so that the amount of investment that can be done is fixed and the firm is resolved to do that amount, the minimum acceptable rate of return is simply the rate of profit that can be obtained at the margin by doing the amount of investment in question; it is this rate which measures the scarcity of capital to the firm and determines the capital-intensity of production.[1]

In view of these complications, and in view also of the unsettled state of economic theory regarding the forces that determine the rate of interest, it is difficult to do more than enumerate a number of possible circumstances in which the minimum acceptable rate of return might alter in such a way as to induce a movement along the production function.

One case, which will be further discussed in Chapter XIV, is where the government engages in a deliberate long-run policy of lowering the rate of interest in order to encourage investment. More generally, one may expect that the minimum acceptable rate of profit will tend to move to some degree in sympathy with the average actual rate of profit. If the natural rate of growth is high and booms therefore preponderate over slumps, so that the average rate of profit over the cycle is high, the rate of interest will have some tendency to be high even if it is determined by purely monetary forces; and if the rate of interest in some way reflects real forces independently of monetary forces, the same will apply even more strongly. Moreover in these circumstances the minimum acceptable rate of profit on investment may well stand unusually high in relation to the gilt-edged rate of interest, because the high average level of investment may make some firms encounter absolute shortages of finance. Similar forces

[1] Cf. T. Scitovsky, *Welfare and Competition* (1952), pp. 203–14, and Joan Robinson, *The Accumulation of Capital* (1956), pp. 101–13.

will be at work tending to keep down the minimum acceptable rate of profit in the case where the natural rate of growth
is low and slumps tend to preponderate.

Similar results may also occur if investment is financed
mainly out of firms' own undistributed profits, so that less
significance attaches to the concept of the rate of interest as
something that has to be paid out by the firm. The minimum
acceptable rate of profit is then largely a psychological phenomenon, and is likely to be influenced by the average rate of
profit experienced in the past. Thus if the average rate of
profit has for a long time been low, firms may accept a low
rate as normal, and the schedule showing the amount of investment done at any given expected rate of profit will then
be correspondingly high. Whether firms' ideas about the
minimum acceptable rate of profit will in fact be adjustable
in this way depends largely on the nature of the ultimate
forces impelling them to do investment, in particular the relative importance of the profit motive on the one hand and the
desire to expand as an end in itself on the other.

If the minimum acceptable rate of profit does respond to
the actual rate of profit and induces corresponding adjustments in the capital-intensity of production, it will serve as a
sort of stabiliser.[1] It will lessen the differences between the

The changes in the capital-intensity of production which we have been
considering in this section have been changes of a long-run character.
Most theoretical models of the cycle disregard the possibility of changes
in the capital-intensity of production within a single cycle, on the grounds
that appreciable changes are unlikely to occur within a short span of time
and that what matters within the cycle is the rise and fall in the inducement
to do investment of a widening character. An exception to this is the
theory of Hayek. (F. A. von Hayek, *Profits, Interest and Investment*
(1939), pp. 3–71). The distinctive feature of this theory is, broadly
speaking, that the rise in the rate of profit in the upswing of the cycle leads
to the use of less capital-intensive methods of production, and that the
reduction in investment resulting from this ultimately outweighs the
inducement to investment of a widening character afforded by the high
profit rate, and so leads to a downturn. This theory is open to the objection that the idea of an increase in the profit rate having a net discouraging effect on investment is very paradoxical. Moreover very
special assumptions would be needed to establish that an increase in the
profit rate encourages investment in the early stages of the upswing and
discourages it in the later stages.

average levels of activity associated with differing natural rates of growth. An economy with a low natural rate of growth will have a high normal capital-output ratio[1] and this will help to keep investment high, and the opposite will apply to an economy with a high natural rate of growth. More particularly, this effect will contribute to preventing the natural rate of growth from exceeding the maximum possible rate of capital accumulation and so leading to a perpetual boom: if the natural rate of growth is very high (or the saving-income ratio is very low), a low capital-intensity of production will enable the available supplies of new capital to be spread thinly and so help to ensure that the rate of growth of the capital stock does not fall short of the natural rate of growth. By lowering v, it will raise the maximum value of s/v.

§ 5. Induced Changes in the Natural Rate of Growth.

So far we have taken the natural rate of growth as a datum. In fact the rates of population growth and technical progress will be partly or even largely influenced by the behaviour of the economy itself, as well as by the institutional, social and other such factors that may fairly be taken as given for present purposes. Any induced change in the natural rate of growth will react back on the behaviour of the economy.

Numbers of different hypotheses have been advanced about the factors affecting the natural rate of growth. One that has been widely held is that technical progress will be slowed down in times of depression, when there is much unemployment and idle capital capacity, and will be speeded up in times of prosperity. There are several grounds for this view.

[1] Even if technical conditions are such that there is no scope at all for altering the capital-intensity of production, responsiveness of the minimum acceptable rate of profit to the actual rate will still serve as some sort of stabiliser, since it will impart some flexibility to the average capital-output ratio over the cycle through its effect on the degree of utilisation consistent with any given rate of capital accumulation. But the greater the scope for varying the normal capital-intensity of production, the smaller the movement in the minimum acceptable rate of profit needed to procure a given change in the average capital-output ratio over the cycle.

In the first place, the presence of unemployed resources will make it easy to expand production without any change in methods, and the impulse to seek out technical improvements will therefore be weak. In the second place, the shortage of jobs will make workers inclined to resist labour-saving innovations and to engage in restrictive make-work practices. In the third place, the scope for experimenting with new methods and finding out which are the most promising will be greater if the level of new investment is high than if it is low. The empirical evidence does not give decisive support to this hypothesis, but it does suggest on the whole that productivity grows faster in prosperous times than in depressed ones.[1] If the level of activity is low, the natural rate of growth is also likely to be prejudiced by the effect on population growth: if there is much unemployment of labour, there will tend to be an adverse effect on marriage rates and fertility rates and also on immigration.

If the effect of the level of activity on the natural rate of growth is as just suggested, it follows that conditions calculated to give a predominance of booms over slumps, such as a high capital-intensity of production or a low propensity to save, will have the additional feature of raising the natural rate of growth and hence the actual rate of growth as well. Likewise if the non-economic factors affecting the natural rate of growth are such as to tend to make it high, their effect will be reinforced by a further induced stimulus to technical progress, since a high natural rate of growth will make for a high average level of activity over the cycle. (This is on the assumption that the natural rate of growth does not exceed the maximum attainable rate of growth. If the saving-income ratio is so low or the natural rate of growth so high that this does happen, the effect on the natural rate of growth,

[1] In the United States differences in the rate of productivity growth appear to have been more marked between the prosperous and depressed phases of the long twenty-year cycle than they have been between the prosperous and depressed phases of fluctuations of shorter duration.

on present assumptions, is equivocal: for there will be on the one hand an acute shortage of capital capacity but on the other hand an increasing amount of unemployment of labour. Population growth will no doubt be discouraged, but it is less clear what will happen to the rate of technical progress. The hypothesis that a *general* shortage of productive factors stimulates technical progress does not indicate how the rate of technical progress will be affected when there are two such opposite tendencies.[1])

A further consequence of this hypothesis is that if a recession develops for reasons other than quantitative capital saturation, e.g. because of monetary causes or a breakdown of speculation or misdirection of investment, technical progress and population growth may be damaged for the duration of the recession; so that even though at the peak of the preceding boom the rate of capital accumulation was not excessive in relation to the natural rate of growth, the reduction in the rate of capital accumulation during the recession does not lead to abnormal arrears of investment or prepare the way for any exceptionally violent boom thereafter. This provides another possible approach to the problem why it is that whatever the natural rate of growth or the propensity to save or the normal capital-output ratio, there always seems to be scope for periodical recessions: reductions in the rate of capital accumulation due to miscellaneous shocks may themselves lower the natural rate of growth.

[1] It is likely that in such circumstances technical progress will be given a capital-saving bias, i.e. the inventions made will be such as to enable the capital-output ratio to be reduced lower than would have been practicable in the previous state of technical knowledge. This will contribute to eliminating the gap between the natural rate and the maximum attainable rate of growth. This is really just an extension of the idea that a condition of capital scarcity will lead to a shift to less capital-using methods of production. In fact the distinction between a shift to a less capital-using technique in a given state of knowledge and an advance in knowledge which makes possible a shift to a less capital-using technique is largely an artificial one, since at any given time study and knowledge about what is technically possible will be largely confined to techniques appropriate to the current degree of scarcity of capital.

A rather different hypothesis is that the impulse to seek out technical improvement varies inversely with the level of the normal or minimum acceptable rate of profit, i.e. that technical progress will tend to be slow in a situation where the normal rate of profit is high, techniques of low capital-intensity are in use, and the productivity of labour is low. This is a good deal more dubious than the hypothesis previously discussed (which incidentally is not inconsistent with it), but a case can be made for it. One ground for it is that those entrepreneurs who own their own capital will, if they are already getting a high return on it, lack any incentive to show initiative. It can also be argued that techniques of low capital-intensity are less susceptible to improvement than those of high capital-intensity. Finally, technical progress involves the scrapping of existing plant, and this will be unwelcome if the rate of interest is high.

If this hypothesis is correct, the tendency for the normal rate of profit to be high when the natural rate of growth is high (see § 4, above) will serve to pull down the natural rate of growth to some degree. The adverse effect on the natural rate of growth of the high normal profit rate will then weaken or offset the favourable effect on the natural rate of growth that may be created (for the reasons stated in the last paragraph but one) by the high average level of activity. (Likewise if the natural rate of growth tends to exceed the maximum attainable rate, the induced rise in the normal profit rate will lower the natural rate of growth and so contribute to eliminating the divergence.)

Yet another hypothesis is that what discourages technical progress is not a high minimum acceptable rate of profit but a high actual rate of profit; the argument being that if the actual level of the profit rate is high, all entrepreneurs, both those who own their capital and those who have borrowed it, will be doing well and will not need to exert themselves. To the extent that the minimum acceptable rate of profit and the actual rate of profit move together, this hypothesis has the same effects as the one just considered. It is, however, not consistent with the first hypothesis discussed in this section; for one aspect of the latter was that a high degree of capital utilisation encourages technical progress, and according to the present hypothesis a high rate of profit, which is one of the chief results of a high degree of capital utilisation, discourages technical progress.

This brief enumeration of hypotheses by no means exhausts the possibilities. What actually happens depends both on how the economy behaves (what determines the normal rate of profit, how flexible the capital-output ratio is, etc.) and on what exactly the natural rate of growth is a function of. There is not yet any settled body of opinion on the latter question. Hence although induced changes in the natural rate of growth may well be of considerable importance, it is not possible in the present state of knowledge to be dogmatic about their exact nature or their extent.

§ **6. Conclusions.**   There is less agreement among economists about the relation between trend and cycle than about most other topics in the theory of the cycle. The hypothesis to which we have given most attention in this chapter is that technical progress and population growth impart a long-run upward trend to the consumption function and/or to the inducement to invest. This upward trend enables fluctuations to take place around an average level which is rising at a rate equal to the natural rate of growth. Variations in the saving-income ratio and in the average degree of utilisation of capital, brought about by variations in the average level of activity, serve as a rule to accommodate the rate of capital accumulation over the cycle as a whole to whatever is required by the natural rate of growth. Attention has also been devoted to influences affecting the normal capital-intensity of production and their impact on the path of growth and fluctuations; these problems of capital theory have been extensively studied by economists, but some doubts may be felt about their practical importance. The reverse is true of the influences affecting the natural rate of growth, especially the influences affecting the rate of technical progress: these are of great practical importance for the understanding of growth, and possibly also for the understanding of fluctuations, but relatively little systematic work has been done on them.

CHAPTER XIV

POLICY FOR THE CONTROL OF THE CYCLE

§ **1. The Aims of Policy.** It is now generally agreed that it is one of the responsibilities of government to prevent the level of economic activity from fluctuating as much as it has done in the past. It is also generally agreed that what is wanted is not merely a stable level of activity but a high one. Disagreement about aims is confined to questions of degree: just how much variation in the level of activity may be tolerated to avoid prejudicing other aims, and just how high a level of activity (in terms, say, of the percentage of the labour force unemployed) should be aimed at.

The purpose of public policy in this sphere is to eliminate the social losses caused by fluctuations. What do these losses amount to? Whether the occurrence of fluctuations affects the long-run rate of growth of output is a debatable question to which we will return in a moment. If we assume for the present that it does not, the social loss due to fluctuations is simply that over the average of the cycle output is lower than it could be: if at the top of the boom there is no unemployment (except unavoidable frictional unemployment) and at the bottom of the slump there is 10% unemployment (again excluding frictional unemployment), then on the average 5% of the labour force is being wasted and real national income is correspondingly lower than it could be. If there is some avoidable unemployment even at the top of the boom, the wastage is still greater. Moreover the hardship caused by the loss of potential real income is made worse by being largely concentrated on a limited class, the unemployed. The ill-effects are not exclusively economic, including, as they are likely to, demoralisation, loss of self-respect, etc. The feeling of insecurity due to the prevalence of unemployment extends to those whose jobs have not actually been affected. The contrast between pre-war and post-war experience has made plain how all-pervading is the psychological difference between a state of full employment and one of widespread unemployment.[1]

It is sometimes suggested as an objection to a policy of maintaining stable full employment that it will have an adverse effect on economic growth. The short-run gain in production due to the elimination of unemployment, it is argued, will be more than offset by loss in the long run. Now it may or may not be true that particular *means* of implementing a full employment policy are liable to hinder growth. But it is difficult to believe that stable full employment as such will have this result. On the contrary it seems more likely to have the opposite effect. The mere attainment of stability, regardless of the level at which activity is stabilised, will eliminate an important source of uncertainty in entrepreneurs' calculations and enable them to plan ahead more efficiently. Moreover, although this cannot be taken as firmly established, the evidence suggests on the whole that a high level of activity is more conducive to productivity growth than a low one.[2]

It is of course possible for the level of effective demand to be too high. Policy must be addressed to the avoidance of inflation as well as of unemployment. If effective demand for goods or for labour persistently exceeds supply, there will be an inflationary rise in prices and the productive efficiency of the economy will probably be impaired. Production will be held up by shortages, and the more efficient firms and industries will be prevented from growing at the expense of

[1] It is worth pointing out that in the past unemployment due to cyclical deficiency of demand has not been confined to advanced industrial countries. This avoidable source of waste has also been experienced from time to time in primarily agricultural countries, including both relatively sparsely populated countries of recent European settlement and those under-developed countries that have in addition a problem of chronic unemployment (or under-employment) due to other causes.

[2] See Chapter XIII, § 5.

the less efficient ones because even the latter will be able to earn good profits. The avoidance of excess demand implies a level of unemployment above zero, since a certain amount of slack in the economy is necessary for its efficient working. (It should, however, be one of the aims of policy to reduce frictions so as to make this minimum necessary amount of slack as small as possible.)

Another objection brought against a full employment policy is that it is bound to involve a chronic rise in the price level which will cause hardship to fixed-income receivers, disrupt the country's external economic relations, and may ultimately undermine confidence in the currency and lead to a runaway inflation. This is a large issue which can only be touched on here. In so far as price-increases are the result of excess demand, there is no obvious reason why they should be inevitable under a régime of full employment. As stated above, the aim of policy is to avoid excess demand as well as to avoid unemployment, and it is only if policy-makers are too exclusively concerned with the avoidance of unemployment that demand-induced price-increases will become endemic. But price-increases may also arise from another source and one against which the avoidance of excess demand provides no guarantee. This kind of inflation occurs when trade unions and other groups, including profit-earners, who because of their monopolistic position are able substantially to dictate their own remuneration, each demand payments which when taken collectively exceed the value of the national product at current prices. A wage- or price-increase in one industry is at the expense of those engaged in other industries and so leads to an increase in wages and prices there as well. In former times the danger of a chronic increase in the price-level occurring for this reason was less, largely because counterbalancing downward pressure on prices was exerted by the development of a buyer's market every time there was a depression. The knowledge that good trade alternated with bad probably also induced those whose bargaining position was strong in the boom not to exploit it to the full, in the expectation that similar forbearance would be shown by the other side when the slump came. The assurance of full employment removes these checks. It does not follow, however, that the danger would necessarily be removed at the present time by permitting a moderate amount of unemployment. Rapid rates of increase in money wages have been experienced since the war in a number of countries where the level of unemployment has been quite high. In so far as an increased tendency to this kind of inflation has been in evidence since the war, full employment has probably not been the only cause; a significant part has probably also been played by the increased strength of organised monopolistic groups, specially trade unions.

If the rate of wage-increase could be shown to be very sensitive to the average level of unemployment, a case could be made for keeping the level of unemployment higher than is needed to provide for frictions by a sufficient margin to maintain price-stability. If, however, it is the case that, given existing wage- and price-fixing institutions, only a really high level of unemployment would serve to keep the rate of wage-increase down to that compatible with price-stability, such a policy will have less to commend it. Account has to be taken not only of the immediate waste involved by unemployment but also of possible prejudicial effects on entrepreneurial confidence and the rate of technical progress. The main hope then lies in persuading those responsible for negotiating wages and fixing prices to show moderation, and thereby avoid a spiral which in the long run benefits no one. Some reform in wage- and price-fixing institutions may also be desirable.

The danger of this kind of inflation presents a serious and difficult problem, but it is not one which study of the business cycle as such is capable of casting much light on, and we shall therefore not discuss it further.

§ 2. Policies for Combating Deflationary or Inflationary Tendencies. The basis of the Keynesian theory of economic policy, which now dominates thinking in this field, is that the government can and should regulate the flow of aggregate spending in such a way as to keep demand at the desired level. It will stimulate spending if there is a tendency to unemployment and it will restrain spending if there is a tendency to inflation. The chief means available to it for regulating the flow of spending may be briefly enumerated as follows:

Private consumption expenditure may be regulated: by varying the level of taxes and subsidies and so altering the amount of purchasing power left in the hands of consumers; by varying the amount of transfer payments made by the government (pensions, unemployment benefits, etc.); by tightening or relaxing controls over the cost and availability of consumer credit; and by measures affecting the proportion of income saved, e.g. discriminatory rates of taxation on distributed and undistributed profits respectively.

Private investment expenditure may be regulated: by varying the rate of taxation on profits and so affecting (a) the availability of internal finance for investment and (b) the inducement to invest in so far as that depends on the prospective net rate of return after tax; by other taxes or subsidies, especially taxes or subsidies on investment or investment goods; by measures affecting the cost and availability of external finance for investment; and by direct controls (licences, etc.).

Government expenditure on goods and services, including both current and capital expenditure, may be regulated by administrative decision.

Of these measures, those that involve variation in tax revenues or government spending will call for budget deficits (or at least lower surpluses) in times of threatened depression and budget surpluses (or at least lower deficits) in times of threatened inflation. Measures affecting one class of expenditure will of course be liable to affect others indirectly in so far as they lead to changes in the national income, and due account will have to be taken of this.

In addition to the Keynesian policies described above,

useful results may also be obtained from certain institutional reforms. Many past slumps have been aggravated by disruption of the banking system and of the structure in indebtedness, leading to a crisis and general loss of confidence. This danger may be lessened by strengthening the financial system in various ways. A number of reforms designed with this end have been made in the United States since the depression of the 1930s, including such measures as federal insurance of bank deposits and mortgage guarantees. Measures of this sort are plainly not capable of curing a depression entirely, even if the potential weak spots in the financial mechanism are correctly foreseen—which may not be easy. But they should at least serve to eliminate one source of cumulative deterioration of conditions in the depression. How high one rates their significance depends on how much responsibility one believes monetary and banking derangements have had for the major slumps of the past.

The choice between different techniques of regulating demand in any given situation will depend partly on their efficacy and partly on the exact aims which the government is pursuing. One important question of aims is which of the three categories of spending the government judges it most desirable to increase (or reduce): consumption, investment, or its own spending. The issues involved in striking a balance between these three will be discussed in § 6 below. Another question of aims is the extent to which the government interprets the policy of maintaining high-level stability as applying to individual sectors of the economy as well as to the economy as a whole. On the one hand it is plain that full employment cannot be guaranteed to individual industries, far less firms, since this would soon involve the government in a programme of subsidising inefficient or declining businesses. On the other hand resources are not perfectly mobile, especially in the short run, so if the government counters a contraction in a particular industry by creating a *general* expansion of demand, some overall decline in employment and production will be inevitable. Some sort of compromise policy will usually be best. Thus if there is a contraction in building because the demand for new houses has been largely met, it would be wasteful to try to go on providing as many jobs as before in the building industry, and it will be right therefore for the government to cause a general expansion of demand elsewhere so as to make it easier for displaced building workers to transfer to new jobs. At the same time this transfer is bound to be slow and incomplete, and it will therefore be reasonable for the government to step up slum clearance projects as well.

Detailed discussion of the relative efficacy of different techniques of controlling demand will not be attempted here, nor shall we discuss the ways of handling budget deficits or surpluses on the monetary side.[1] Our main purpose is merely to consider the *principles* of policy, viewed in relation to the theory of the cycle. Two general points with regard to the question of efficacy may be noted, however.

In the first place, a distinction may be drawn between measures which affect demand directly, such as changes in government expenditure on goods and services or administrative controls over private investment, and those which affect it indirectly by altering the opportunity or inducement to spend, such as changes in taxation or in the availability of credit. The former kind of measure has the advantage over the latter, that its effects are more exactly predictable[2]; but it

---

[1] Reference may be made to American Economic Association, *Readings in Fiscal Policy* (1955); M. F. Millikan (editor), *Income Stabilisation for a Developing Democracy* (1953); Universities—National Bureau Committee for Economic Research, *Policies to Combat Depression* (1956).

[2] Measures that directly influence demand may, however, have indirect repercussions as well, and these have to be taken into account in choosing between different policies and assessing their ultimate consequences. For example if the aim is to stimulate demand by investment in the form of public works, it will be desirable as far as possible to avoid investment in lines that are competitive with private industry and are therefore liable to discourage private investment. In the 1930s it was even suggested that private investment would be discouraged by *any* sort of increase in public investment in the slump, whether competitive with private investment or not, since capitalists would regard the extension of state activity as foreboding socialist revolution.

involves more direct participation by the government in the detailed working of the economy and may be politically objectionable on that score.

In the second place some measures may be better adapted to restraining inflation than to rescuing the economy from a slump. This is most obviously true of direct physical controls over private spending. It is also probably true of monetary policy, since in the slump interest rates are already low and the small further reduction which policy can procure may not have much effect on investment decisions.

§ 3. The Timing of Counter-cyclical Measures.

Many of the measures referred to in the previous section can be brought into operation in either of two ways: as the automatic consequence of a movement in the level of activity, or as the result of discretionary action by the government. Measures that come into force automatically are commonly referred to as built-in stabilisers. The working of income tax provides a leading example of a built-in stabiliser. If there is a fall in national income and employment, the revenue derived from income tax (and from most other taxes as well) will fall, even though the *rates* of tax are not altered. Likewise contributions to unemployment insurance funds will fall and payments of unemployment benefit will rise. A deficit in the government's accounts will therefore be an automatic and mitigating consequence of a fall in national income. An upward tendency in income will likewise be restrained to some extent by the automatic development of a budget surplus. Another example of a built-in stabiliser is an agricultural price support programme, such as has been adopted in the United States, under which the government in effect undertakes to buy agricultural products if their prices fall below a certain level.

A source of protection against fluctuations analogous to a built-in stabiliser may be mentioned here parenthetically. This is the expectation on the part of business men that severe fluctuations will be avoided. If business men are confident that the government can and will prevent a contraction in income from becoming too large or lasting too long, they will persist in their investment plans in face of moderate fluctuations in demand and so will prevent these fluctuations from becoming worse. In this way a full employment policy helps to bring about its own achievement without the government actually having to do anything, an effect sometimes referred to as 'full employment by magic'. A similar result may stem from a conscious policy on the part of business leaders of trying in the national interest to maintain stable investment programmes in face of fluctuations of demand. This idea that business should share with government some of the responsibility for maintaining stability has attracted some attention in recent years, but its potentialities are rather limited unless firms are willing as a matter of deliberate policy to subordinate their own interests to the national interest. A certain amount of the cyclical variability of investment in the past has no doubt reflected mistaken expectations and could be eliminated to the firms' own advantage as well as that of the economy as a whole; but if fluctuations *do* occur, it will often be in the real interests of a firm to do its investment in the boom rather than in the slump, especially if the capital concerned is relatively short-lived.[1]

The great advantage of built-in stabilisers is that they act promptly. They are not subject to the lags that may be involved in discretionary policy due to the need to ascertain the current state of affairs and decide the measures appropriate to it. Some lags in *operation* may be present even with built-in stabilisers, and the more they can be reduced the better. Thus the pay-as-you-earn system of collecting income tax is to be preferred on this ground to the system under which the tax payable in the current year is assessed on the income of the previous year.

[1] The potentialities of deliberate stabilisation of investment by business are discussed in Universities—National Bureau Committee for Economic Research, *Regularisation of Business Investment* (1954).

Built-in stabilisers of one sort or another are an important adjunct of economic policy. They have no doubt contributed materially to the mildness of the contractions experienced in the United States since the war. On the other hand they are inherently incapable of offsetting a contraction in income entirely. Their effect is very similar to that of a reduction in the marginal propensity to consume: they reduce the secondary repercussions of a primary contraction in demand but do not eliminate the primary contraction itself. If the primary contraction is mild, the elimination of secondary repercussions may be an adequate policy. If it is severe, however, some more positive action will be needed.

The chief difficulty with most discretionary policies is that of timing. Delay will be involved in diagnosing the situation and deciding on the right policy, and in addition changes in fiscal or monetary policy usually take time to carry into effect. In most countries rates of income tax cannot conveniently be altered more often than once a year; programmes of government expenditure on goods and services are difficult to increase or curtail abruptly; and interest rate changes and other measures designed to affect private investment will at best have an immediate effect on investment decisions and may not affect actual investment till considerably later. The lags involved are admittedly not equally long for all types of policy. For example restrictions on consumer instalment credit may be imposed or lifted at short notice and with quick effect. But major changes in demand are bound to take time to bring about. Moreover even after policy has succeeded in influencing demand, there may be a further lag before production is affected, because of changes in the level of inventories.

The existence of these lags prevents inflationary or deflationary tendencies from being immediately compensated by government action and so makes it impossible to achieve complete stabilisation of income. It also has a more subtle danger. An inflationary or deflationary tendency, if left to itself, is unlikely to retain the same force for long; it will become stronger or weaker or will reverse itself. Hence by the time fiscal or monetary policies designed to cope with the initial tendency have become effective, the situation will have changed and the policies will no longer be wholly appropriate. They may even be in the wrong direction if the initial tendency has reversed itself in the meanwhile. This is by no means an impossible result. Quite plausible models can be constructed in which a policy of taking steps to raise demand when production falls systematically aggravates fluctuations because of the intervention of lags.[1] This danger applies particularly to government policy designed to offset inventory fluctuations, since the policy measures are liable to be subject to the same lags as produce the fluctuations themselves.

There are various ways of trying to cope with this problem. In the first place, the government, in framing its budget and making other decisions which will have repercussions some way ahead, must endeavour to make the best possible forecast of how events are likely to develop. In the second place, the operation of the instruments of policy should be speeded up as much as possible, and instruments which cannot be made to work promptly should be avoided unless there is no alternative. In the third place, if there is good reason to believe that a current inflationary or deflationary tendency will soon reverse itself and if it is not too severe, it may be best for the government simply to rely on the built-in stabilisers and not make any attempt to counter it by discretionary policy.

The need to look ahead when framing fiscal and monetary policy makes it appropriate to conclude this section with a word about methods of forecasting. Broadly speaking there are three ways in which the task of short-run forecasting may be approached. (1) The government may simply assume that

---

[1] Cf. M. Friedman, 'The Effects of a Full-Employment Policy on Economic Stability', in *Essays in Positive Economics* (1953), pp. 117–32; A. W. Phillips, 'Stabilisation Policy in a Closed Economy', *Economic Journal*, 1954, pp. 290–323, and 'Stabilisation Policy and the Time-form of Lagged Responses', *Economic Journal*, 1957, pp. 265–77.

the present level of activity will continue, or else it may assume that the present rate of change in the level of activity will continue. While these procedures hardly deserve to be dignified by the name of forecasting, it must be admitted that on a number of occasions they would have produced better results than more sophisticated methods actually used. (2) Enquiries may be made from large firms and from a sample of smaller firms and householders as to their expenditure plans for the forthcoming period. This sort of enquiry can yield valuable information, particularly for forms of expenditure that in their nature have to be planned well ahead, such as major investment projects. On the other hand much expenditure is not of this sort, and plans are liable to be altered. Hence this useful source of information is not by itself a sufficient basis for forecasting. (3) Finally—and this is what in one form or another will always actually be done—a reasoned guess may be made in the light of current and recent past experience. Thus the level of investment will be forecast by taking into account the amount of work already under way, the amount known to be projected, and the amount which it seems likely will be projected in view of the current state of profit, degree of utilisation of capacity, opportunities for innovation, availability of finance, etc., in different sectors of the economy. Forecasts of investment must be based on study of individual sectors rather than on aggregates alone, since forecasts based on aggregates are unlikely to give good results even for aggregates; moreover it is desirable for policy-makers to know from what quarter of the economy inflationary or deflationary tendencies are most likely to emanate. Having derived an estimate for investment, the level of consumption that will be associated with it will be forecast on the basis of what is considered to be the shape of the consumption function, due allowance being made for special influences affecting expenditure on consumer durables, etc. Forecasts of this sort may be made either by means of explicit mathematical equations based on the observed behaviour of the economy in previous years, or they may be made on a more informal basis. In either case a very considerable margin of error must be expected in the present state of knowledge. But in planning its budget the government is obliged in any case to make *some* assumptions about how the economy is going to behave, and that being so all the available information should be used to get the best forecast possible.[1]

§ **4. International Aspects.** We shall now consider the special policy problems involved if a contraction in demand threatens a country not in consequence of a decline in its own investment or consumption but because of a contraction in national income in a foreign country with which it trades.

If national income falls in country A, the problem facing the authorities in country B is two-fold. (1) The decline in income in A will cause the sales of B's exports in A to fall. This will cause a reduction in income and employment in B's export industries, and, if not offset, will have secondary multiplier effects on the rest of B's economy. (2) The fall in B's exports will give B an adverse balance of payments. Steps will have to be taken to check this unless B is willing to allow its foreign exchange reserves to run down and has enough reserves for the purpose.

The two-fold nature of the problem calls for a two-fold line of policy. The task of countering the fall in demand in the export industries is not different in principle from the task of countering a fall of demand affecting industries producing for the home market. The various instruments of policy discussed earlier in this chapter—tax reduction, public works, etc.—are appropriate to both cases. These will accordingly be part of the policy for meeting an externally-originating

[1] Of course if the difficulty of forecasting is so great that the government is on balance as likely to be wrong as right in its view as to whether the level of activity in the ensuing period will tend to be above or below the optimum, it will be best not to attempt to take any compensatory measures of the sort that will not come into operation till that period, since by attempting to do so the government would merely be introducing a further arbitrary source of disturbance in the level of activity.

contraction in demand, subject to a qualification to be discussed presently.[1] It is the balance of payments aspect of the situation that poses a prbolem distinct from that involved by a domestic contraction in demand. This problem is bound up with the broader one, what are the best institutions for dealing with balance of payment disequilibria generally. We shall not discuss the broader question here, but only its application in the present context.

The policy prescribed by the old-fashioned theory of the gold standard for dealing with any adverse balance of payment, however originating, was monetary deflation. Since the effects of this are likely to be at least as much on real output as on prices, it is by definition inconsistent with a full employment policy. The alternatives remaining are to go on drawing on reserves or to take some steps to curtail imports without causing internal deflation.

In the present case, where country B's adverse balance is due to deflationary tendencies in A and not to some other cause such as structural maladjustment or inflationary tendencies in B, the first of these alternatives—drawing on reserves—would be much the best if it were possible. B would then be saved the hardship involved by doing without its customary imports from A—which it might be unable to obtain from domestic sources—and A would not suffer the further deflation of demand that would result from a curtailment of its exports to B. But B's ability to pursue this course depends on its having sufficiently large reserves. And

---

[1] If the factors of production are specific to the export industries and the products of those industries are not suitable for sale on the home market, the usual fiscal and other measures designed to stimulate demand may not be very satisfactory, because of the difficulty of finding alternative employments for the workers displaced from the export industries. This is particularly liable to happen in a highly specialised economy heavily dependent on one or two export industries. It is because many primary producing countries are in this position that there is a case for supplementing ordinary instruments of counter-cyclical policy with commodity-reserve or buffer stock schemes which would provide a source of demand for primary products in the event of a slump.

however large its reserves, it will not be able to go on follow-ing this policy indefinitely if A regularly has slumps and if the balance of payments between them only just balances at times when A has a boom.[1]

One suggestion that has been made to overcome these difficulties is that the government of any country A experi-encing a contraction in demand should make available to other countries an amount of its currency equivalent to the fall in the value of its imports compared with a 'normal' year, receiving in return a corresponding amount of the cur-rencies of the other countries. In this way the supply of international currency reserves would in effect be increased whenever the need arose.[2] (A similar effect would be pro-duced if the government of country A in these circumstances were to make loans to foreign countries or were to buy foreign goods on its own account.) This proposal does not really call for any great altruism on the part of A, though it may appear to, since A will benefit by the maintenance of foreign demand for its products. The chief difficulty in prac-tice—apart from the difficulty of getting governments to accept it—would be to distinguish a decline in A's imports due to a decline in aggregate demand in A from a decline in A's imports due to some other cause for which a different type of remedy would be appropriate.

If the reserves available in any form are not sufficient, the country B which is suffering from an adverse balance of pay-ments because of a slump in A will be obliged to take steps to cut down its imports. It may do this by devaluing its

---

[1] One way out of the difficulty in theory would be to set the exchange rate between A and B at such a level that A ran a balance of payments deficit at times when both had full employment. But this would hardly be feasible as a deliberate policy, because of the difficulty of foreseeing and agreeing in times of general boom which country or countries were likely to have recurring slumps.

[2] United Nations Department of Economic Affairs, *National and International Measures for Full Employment* (1949), a report by J. M. Clark, A. Smithies, N. Kaldor, P. Uri, and E. R. Walker.

currency or by imposing tariffs or quantitative restrictions on imports. The choice between these alternative measures raises general issues in the theory of international economic policy which are outside our scope. One aspect may, however, be mentioned as specially relevant in the present context, and that is the question of discrimination. Suppose countries B, C, and D each develop an adverse balance of payments of 10 with country A because A has a slump, A's overall surplus thus being 30. If B, C, and D now each impose nondiscriminatory restrictions designed to reduce their imports by 10 and so restore their balances of payments to equilibrium, these restrictions will affect their imports from one another as well as their imports from A. Hence after the restrictions have been imposed each will find that its exports fall again and that its balance of payments remains in deficit. Further restrictions will therefore have to be imposed and these will have similar repercussions. Equilibrium will not be finally restored until each country has imposed sufficiently severe restrictions on imports generally to reduce its imports *from A* by 10, and this will involve a much larger reduction in its total imports. The reduction in the volume of trade between B, C, and D is an interference with the international division of labour that is not called for by any disequilibrium in their relations with one another, but it is unavoidable if import restrictions are imposed on a non-discriminatory basis. If on the other hand B, C, and D from the first direct their import restrictions solely against imports from A, reduction in their trade with one another will be avoided. Moreover A will not ultimately be any worse off for having been discriminated against, since other countries will in any case have to reduce imports from A by enough to get rid of the disequilibrium in their balances of payments, and the only question is whether or not the rest of their trade will be reduced in the process. This argument for discrimination is what underlies the 'scarce-currency' clause of the Bretton Woods agreement, under which discrimination against a particular currency is permitted in certain circumstances.[1] It may be noted that if countries B, C, and D devalue their currencies instead of imposing restrictions on imports, there is not the same danger of their trade with one another being cut down, since their exchange rates in terms of one another's currencies will have no necessary tendency to alter but only their exchange rates in relation to the currency of country A. The same applies if they operate a system of flexible exchange rates, so that the values of their currencies alter automatically in response to market forces.

Measures serving to reduce imports differ from measures that supply a country with more reserves and so enable it to continue importing at the former rate in the following respect. A reduction in imports will cause a diversion of expenditure towards home-produced goods.[2] This will stimulate demand and so lessen the need for measures of the first kind discussed above—those designed to raise the level of demand in order to compensate for the reduction in earnings in the export industries.   Indeed in the limiting case where restrictive measures reduce imports by an amount equal to the initial fall in exports and the whole of the sum formerly spent on imports is diverted to home-produced goods, no further measures to stimulate demand will be necessary, and income will be maintained at its original level.[3] (There will of course still be the inconvenience of doing without the imports: it is only the demand side of the problem that is provided for.) On the other hand in the case where part or all of the balance of payments deficit resulting from the initial fall in exports is met by drawing on reserves, loans, etc., rather than by a

[1] The argument depends essentially on the assumption of an asymmetry in reaction between deficit and surplus countries: it is assumed that country A which has a surplus will not on that account feel impelled to expand its imports but that the other countries, which have deficits, will feel impelled to contract imports.

[2] Part of the sum formerly spent on imports may, however, be saved, especially in the short period.

[3] This is so only if the restrictions on imports are sufficient *by themselves* to reduce imports by an amount equal to the original fall in exports; it will not do if part of the fall in imports is due to a fall in national income.

reduction in imports, specific steps to restore demand at home will be needed along the lines indicated previously.

So much for the alternatives open to a country which faces a fall in demand originating from abroad. What policies in the international sphere are indicated for the country where the contraction in demand originates? In the past countries have too often tried to cope with a domestic contraction by 'exporting unemployment'. The balance of payments surplus that a country tends to develop through a reduction in its imports when it has a slump helps, while it lasts, to limit the severity of the contraction in demand: part of its impact is felt abroad rather than at home. There is therefore a tendency for a country in this position to go further and try to get a still more favourable balance of payments by restricting imports, subsidising exports, etc. This is a beggar-my-neighbour policy which transfers part of the contraction in demand to foreign countries without reducing its overall extent. It also aggravates disequilibrium in the international balance of payments. In the long run it will not even bring much benefit to the country practising it, since retaliation by other countries is inevitable. The object of maintaining demand for the country's own goods would be achieved without these harmful effects if the country were instead to increase the supply of its currency to the rest of the world by loans or some such means. The other countries would then be saved from the necessity of cutting down their imports and everyone would benefit. This is the most helpful policy for a country suffering from depression to pursue in the international sphere.

But this policy and indeed all those discussed in the present section are really only a second-best. The best policy both in the interests of the country threatened by a recession and in the interests of the rest of the world would undoubtedly be if the country concerned could eliminate the recession by domestic policies of the type discussed earlier in the chapter. In so far as it is successful in doing this, the problems discussed in the present section do not arise.

§ 5. The Stabilisation of Private Investment: (1) The Factors making for Fluctuations. The compensatory policies outlined earlier in this chapter should be sufficient to prevent really severe or prolonged depressions. But, as already indicated, such policies are not without their limitations and deficiencies. Difficulties of timing are bound to prevent the stabilisation of income from being complete and may make the government's intervention actually harmful. Moreover, if stabilisation of aggregate demand has to be obtained by continually adjusting government spending and taxation so as to offset fluctuations in private spending, frictional wastes will be incurred and the most efficient use of productive resources will be hampered.

Interest therefore attaches to the question how large are likely to be the fluctuations in private spending that will require to be offset by government compensatory measures. Other things being equal, it would be better to get rid of or reduce the tendency of private spending to fluctuate rather than to have to offset it by compensatory measures.

The main prerequisite of stabilising private spending is to stabilise private fixed investment. Fluctuations in inventory investment and autonomous fluctuations in consumption, particularly in expenditure on consumer durables, may present some problem, but if past experience is repeated they will not by themselves bring about major changes in the level of aggregate demand.[1] The question to be asked at the present stage is therefore whether the growth of private fixed investment is likely to be punctuated by large fluctuations, and if so what can be done about it.

Nothing that has been said so far in this book should be taken to imply that fluctuations in investment are inevitable in all circumstances. Even in the absence of compensatory

---

[1] Insofar as expenditure on consumer durables is influenced by factors analogous to those influencing fixed investment, what is said below about stabilising fixed investment also applies *mutatis mutandis* to expenditure on consumer durables.

government policy, it is possible to conceive of circumstances in which the interaction of the multiplier and the capital stock adjustment principle leads to convergence to equilibrium, or at worst to very damped cycles, and the various other possible causes of fluctuations are also in abeyance. In that case the economy could in principle follow a path of steady growth, interrupted only by random shocks. Experience suggests, however, that this is not what has normally happened. In order to cast light on whether it is likely to happen in the future, we may recapitulate very briefly what was said in earlier chapters about the main causes of fluctuations in investment and consider to what extent these causes will be removed by compensatory measures designed to stabilise *total* expenditure, and what are the prospects of removing them by other means.

The first point to be made—and one that must be emphasised—is that if fluctuations in national *income* can be prevented or greatly reduced by compensatory measures if and when the need arises, fluctuations in private *investment* —and hence the gap to be filled by compensatory measures— should also be much less than in the past. Whatever other causes have contributed to fluctuations in investment, the rise and fall in national income over the cycle have certainly played a large part. Even when other causes have initiated the contraction in investment, the consequent fall in income has greatly aggravated it. Moreover confidence on the part of business men that the government will not allow contractions in national income to go beyond a certain point will lessen the sensitivity of investment decisions to such changes in national income as do occur.

But stabilisation of national income will not remove all sources of instability in investment. Among factors capable of causing fluctuations in investment independently of movements in national income the following may be enumerated. (1) Random shocks. These include wars and other political disturbances; major inventions; structural changes in the economy; harvest vicissitudes, etc. From the point of view of a single country, fluctuations emanating from abroad may be regarded as coming into this category. (2) Irrational movements of expectations, misdirection of investment due to entrepreneurial miscalculation, and distortion in the timing or direction of investment due to speculation. (3) Disturbances in the supply of money or in the public confidence in the banking system or the structure of indebtedness. (4) Overshooting due to adjustment lags or competitive distortion. (5) Echo-type replacement cycles, reflecting earlier fluctuations or wars. (6) The tendency in some circumstances for investment, particularly innovatory investment, to stimulate more investment and so lead to a cumulative movement until the stimulus is exhausted.

Some of these, though in principle independent of the movement of national income, are likely to be much less important if income is stabilised, e.g. irrational movements in expectations, and disturbances to public confidence in the banking system. Others, however, remain capable of causing substantial ups and downs in investment. The record of the past suggests that house-building may be especially liable to be affected.

Some of these ups and downs serve no socially useful purpose to set against the dislocation and inconvenience they cause. Overshooting due to adjustment lags is an example. If maladjustment due to such causes threatens to become serious, government action to restrain excessive investment or stimulate deficient investment may be desirable. But some of the other factors referred to in the list above reflect genuine variations in the urgency of the need to add to the nation's capital stock. If fluctuations in investment are due to causes of this type, and can be recognised as such, it will not be sensible to make a fetish of stabilising investment, and the best policy may be to allow investment to fluctuate but take compensatory measures to stabilise the national income. The inconvenience caused by dislocation and by the government's likely inability to achieve complete stabilisation of income if investment fluctuates will have to be taken into account in deciding how much fluctuation in investment to permit, but it will not necessarily be the decisive consideration. If, for example, the capital stock has recently been run down because of a war, it will be desirable to have a period of more intensive investment before reverting to normal. Similarly if large investment opportunities are created by an important technical innovation, it will be a pity to defer enjoyment of the benefit of the innovation merely on the ground that if it is exploited immediately investment opportunities will then fall off. How large a departure from a policy of stabilising investment is likely to be called for by such causes depends, like so many issues in the realm of policy, on what view is taken as to the relative importance of different causes of fluctuations of investment in the past.

Recurrent fluctuations in investment due to the interaction of the multiplier and the capital stock adjustment principle will by definition not occur if national income is stabilised by government compensatory policy. The working of the capital stock adjustment principle does, however, involve some important issues as to the *level* at which investment may be stabilised relatively to the national income. These will be discussed in the next section.

§ 6. The Stabilisation of Private Investment: (2) The Investment-Income Ratio. So long as the minimum acceptable rate of profit on capital is constant, investment will be able to grow at a steady rate only if it is of such an amount as to leave the rate of profit on capital constant. If investment is higher than this, diminishing returns will be experienced, output will not rise as fast as the stock of capital, and the inducement to invest will diminish. In the absence of compensatory policy, a slump will then ensue. If income *is* stabilised by compensatory policy, or nearly so, the fall in investment will not be so great, but there will still be some fall, unless income can be made to grow faster than it was doing before.

It is the essence of the capital stock adjustment theory of the cycle that investment at the upper turning point of the typical cycle *is* at such a level as to cause the stock of capital to increase more rapidly than income and hence to bring about a fall in the profit rate. This situation may come about either because the further growth of income becomes obstructed by a shortage of labour or some other ceiling, or it may come about independently of any such obstruction (or independently of any increase in the seriousness of such obstruction) if there are lags in one or other of the functions regulating the system. The Schumpeterian theory of the cycle also implies, though for different reasons, that the boom level of investment is not maintainable.

What determines the level at which investment must be maintained in order to leave the rate of profit constant and not lead to a falling off of the type described? In an ordinary cycle uninfluenced by policy, it will depend on the exact nature of the cycle and what model it conforms to; but if the government's policy is to maintain a high and stable level of activity by the use, where necessary, of compensatory measures, the possibilities can be a good deal narrowed down, because it can be assumed that certain consequences will be brought about by policy itself. It can be assumed that policy will secure full employment, or something near it, and that changes in investment, if they do occur, will be substantially offset by compensatory policy and will not lead to large changes in national income. It follows that the rate at which it is possible for capital to accumulate without altering the rate of profit will be governed by the rates of population growth and technical progress, i.e. by the natural rate of growth. If the rate of growth of the stock of capital is the same as the natural rate of growth, the capital-output ratio and the profit rate will remain constant (assuming neutral technical progress), because the rate of increase of factor availability will just keep pace with the rate of increase of the capital stock. How high the ratio of net investment to income needs to be to bring about the appropriate rate of growth of capital depends on the capital-output ratio. Thus if the rate of increase of national income, as given by the natural rate of growth, is 3% per annum, and the capital-output ratio at the margin is $2\frac{1}{2}$, net investment equal to $7\frac{1}{2}\%$ of national income will be needed to make the stock of capital grow at the same rate as output. The required ratio of *gross* investment to national income will be affected also by the proportion of the capital stock falling due for replacement in any year.

We shall refer to the investment-income ratio that leaves the rate of profit constant as the *maintainable* investment-income ratio.

Broadly speaking the rate of profit on capital has in the past remained roughly constant in the long run both in the United States and Great Britain.[1] It may reasonably be inferred from this that if the ratio of net investment to income had been higher and the rate of growth of the stock of capital had been correspondingly faster, diminishing returns would have set in and the rate of profit would have fallen (unless there had been some other compensating change in the situation such as a faster rate of technical progress). The high ratio of investment to income that prevailed at the peak of booms and the high rate of capital accumulation associated with it could not have been maintained permanently without causing a decline in profit rates, since the actual alternation of high and low investment-income ratios between the boom and the slump merely left the profit rate roughly constant. This conclusion still holds even if it is contended that historically most cyclical downturns have been due to causes other than capital saturation; for whatever their *causes*, slumps have *led* to a decline in the rate of capital accumulation and

[2] Cf. W. Fellner, *Trends and Cycles in Economic Activity* (1956), pp. 246–57, and E. H. Phelps Brown and B. Weber, 'Accumulation, Productivity and Distribution in the British Economy, 1870–1938,' *Economic Journal*, 1953, pp. 263–88.

thereby have prevented capital saturation as a long-run phenomenon.[1]

It follows that if conditions in the future resemble those in the past, the maintainable ratio of investment to income will be lower than that which prevailed in former booms. But this creates a problem: for the level of activity to be aimed at if there is to be full employment will be not lower than in past booms; and the proportion of income *saved* will likewise tend to be not lower than in past booms, and hence will be higher than the maintainable investment-income ratio. To put the point in another way, the level of investment which is indicated by past experience as the maintainable one will not yield full employment. Hence if the aim of policy is to keep the ratio of investment to income stable and at the same time achieve full employment, the government must be prepared as a regular thing to bolster up demand by raising the ratio of consumption plus government spending to national income through budget deficits, redistribution of incomes, or other such means. This necessity can be avoided only if conditions differ in some way from what they have been in the past: that is to say, if either the rate of growth of income or the normal capital-output ratio is higher, so as to permit a higher maintainable investment-output ratio, or else if the proportion of income saved at full employment is lower.[2, 3]

---

[1] If the growth path of income had been smooth instead of being interrupted by slumps, the average level of income would have been higher and the required amount of capital would have been correspondingly higher too. But the *rate of growth* of the required amount of capital would not necessarily have been any higher, since that depends on the rate of growth of income; and it is the rate of growth of capital that would have been higher if the boom ratio of net investment to income had been a permanency.

[2] There are certain *a priori* arguments that may be advanced to suggest that the adoption of a full employment policy will as such tend to alter conditions in one or other of these ways. If so, the need for persistent deficit finance may be reduced or perhaps eliminated. In the first place, the avoidance of depressions might raise the average rate of technical progress and/or population growth. This is not proved, but it seems quite plausible. In the second place, the saving-income ratio at past cyclical peaks may have been higher than the saving-income ratio would be under conditions of continuous assured full employment, in so far as the

If, then, the investment-income ratio is at the maintainable level and stays there, the government may need permanently to bolster up demand in order to give full employment. Granted that it does so and that the capital stock is initially at the appropriate level in relation to income, the situation will in principle be satisfactory and stable. Investment will have no inherent reason to depart from its current ratio to income, since income and the stock of capital will be growing at the same rate; and since *ex hypothesi* there will be full employment or something near it, the overall supply of factors of production should be sufficiently inelastic to restrain any latent tendency to explosive cumulative movements.

It is quite likely, however, that because of entrepreneurial optimism or because of one of the disturbances mentioned in § 5 investment will tend to rise above the maintainable level. The government then has the choice of either trying in the

---

high ratio at past peaks was due to the belief that the level of activity was abnormally high, and in so far also as profits were an abnormally high proportion of income. The validity of this is difficult to judge, and depends on the exact nature of the consumption function. There is no doubt some truth in it—e.g. the very high proportion of corporate profits saved in the boom is probably partly the result of the view that reserves should be built up against a rainier day. On the other hand this is by no means the only reason for high saving—even for high corporate saving—in the boom. In general the saving-income ratio has diverged more sharply from its long-run average in depressions than at the peak of booms, and this rather suggests that it is depressions, not booms, that are regarded as abnormal, and that the elimination of depressions would accordingly serve to raise the long-run average saving-income ratio in the manner required by the argument in the text. (It may also be pointed out that the relatively high level of saving out of disposable income in the United States since the war does not support the notion that a long period of full employment will lead to a lower saving-income ratio than in past booms.)

[3] A rise in the rate of growth of income may not reduce by much the average amount of unemployment that would result in the absence of government intervention, if the attendant rise in the average profit rate has a large effect on the proportion of income saved (cf. Chapter XIII, p. 238, n. 1). Moreover a rise in the growth rate or in the consumption function may have the effect of raising the *normal* rate of profit (cf. Chapter XIII, pp. 247–8), and this again, by lowering the capital-intensity of production, will lessen the extent by which they diminish the average amount of unemployment and hence the need for deficit finance.

interests of stability to restrain investment and keep it down to the maintainable level, or else allowing it to stay at its new high level, cutting down its own expenditure or raising taxation in the meanwhile, and preparing to meet the consequences of investment's ultimately impending decline. (A third alternative will be mentioned in a moment.) What on the analogy of past experience does *not* seem wise is to act on the assumption that a level of private investment high enough to give full employment without bolstering up by the government will prove maintainable.

So far in this section we have been assuming that the normal, i.e. minimum acceptable, rate of profit is constant, and that the capital intensity of production, i.e. the normal capital-output ratio, is therefore also constant. A different kind of policy for stabilising investment from that of keeping it at a level that leaves the profit rate constant is to keep it at a higher level than this, e.g. at a ratio to income equal to that attained at past cyclical peaks, and to prevent the consequent fall in the rate of profit from leading to a fall in investment by engineering a corresponding fall in the minimum acceptable rate of profit, so inducing a movement along the production function in the direction of more capital-intensive methods of production (cf. Chapter XIII, § 4). If in any given state of technical knowledge there were no scope for using more capital-intensive methods, a rate of capital accumulation above the maintainable level would soon lead to a complete collapse of the profit rate, and no practicable reduction in the minimum acceptable profit rate would be able to prevent a fall in investment. If on the other hand movement along the production function is possible, the fall in the profit rate resulting from any given rate of capital accumulation will be less, since the movement along the production function will help to absorb capital, in two ways. In the first place, if we compare a situation with a high normal capital-output ratio with a situation with a low normal capital-output ratio, the ratio of investment to income required to make the capital stock rise in pace with any given rate of output will be higher in the former than in the latter (see above, p. 278); the 'maintainable' investment-income ratio is thus not something that is uniquely given but something that varies with the capital-intensity of production. In the second place, the process of *transition* to a higher capital-intensity of production will require a large once-for-all addition to the stock of capital.

If the investment-income ratio is above the level that is maintainable at the current capital-intensity of production, a rise in the capital-intensity of production is necessary if capital saturation is to be avoided. Because of the large once-for-all addition to the capital stock needed to effect a rise in the capital-output ratio, the rise in the capital-intensity of production need only be a gradual one. But as the capital intensity of production gradually increases, the maintainable investment-income ratio will gradually rise too, and ultimately the point may be reached where the maintainable investment-income ratio is equal to the high investment-income ratio that actually prevails. The movement along the production function will then cease.

The higher the capital-intensity of production, the higher will be the output per man in any given state of technical knowledge, and the lower will be the rate of profit on capital. Hence if the investment-income ratio is kept at a level that makes possible an increase in the capital-intensity of production, output will grow at a rate exceeding the natural rate of growth, and the profit rate will fall. (This process may be subject to a limit, as indicated at the end of the last paragraph, after which the rate of growth of output reverts to the natural rate.) The amount by which the rate of growth of output exceeds the natural rate and the rapidity with which the profit rate falls depends on the slope of the production function. If the production function is steep and there is relatively little scope for the use of more capital-intensive methods of production, the rate of growth of output will not be much faster than the natural rate and the fall in the profit rate will be rapid. The opposite applies if the production function is relatively flat.

The decision how high an average investment-income ratio to aim at involves issues going beyond the realm of stabilisation policy. If the ratio is held above the level that is maintainable at the current capital-intensity of production, it will be possible for output to grow faster (at least for a time) than it would do if the ratio were lower; on the other hand, of course, the higher the investment-income ratio, the smaller the amount of consumption goods available for enjoyment at any level of income. The choice therefore turns on (a) a question of preference, how much weight is attached to future consumption compared with present consumption,[1] and (b) a question of fact, how great an increase in output can be obtained from more capital-intensive methods of production. If it is believed that the rate of technical progress is itself affected by the level of the profit rate or by other variables, along the lines suggested in Chapter XIII, § 5, the nature and extent of these effects will be another factual consideration to take into account in deciding the issue. For example, if a high level of investment as such helps to induce rapid technical progress, the case for a high investment-income ratio will be strengthened.

Although questions of objective are thus raised that go beyond the realm of stabilisation policy, the issue is one that no stabilisation policy can avoid involving. Granted that the government is going to undertake compensatory measures where necessary to stabilise aggregate demand at the full employment level, the choice between alternative compensatory measures cannot fail to affect in one way or another the ratio of investment to income: the government will have to decide whether it is investment or consumption or its own spending that is to be reduced when there is a threat of inflation or increased when there is a threat of depression. Any actions it takes are bound to have some effect on future investment opportunities and on the rate of growth of output.

[1] Similar questions of preference arise in deciding the optimum proportion to national income of those branches of production for which the government is responsible.

The choice between alternative compensatory measures cannot therefore be dictated solely by technical considerations as to their relative convenience and efficacy, but must be influenced also by these other implications.

§ 7. **The Stabilisation of Private Investment: (3) The Problem in Practice.** In practice great difficulties unfortunately attend both the choice between a higher and a lower investment-income ratio, and the decision as to how and to what extent to try to stabilise the investment-income ratio at whatever level is chosen.

This is largely because of the difficulty of assessing the consequences of maintaining investment at any given level in a particular situation. It is by no means easy even to tell at any given time whether investment does or does not exceed the level that is maintainable at the current capital-intensity of production (i.e. is or is not such as to tend to lower the rate of profit), and it is still more difficult to tell how great an increase in output per head will be achieved by more capital-intensive methods of production. The task of interpretation has a qualitative aspect as well as a quantitative one: the investment currently going on may be misdirected and hence liable to produce a steeper fall in the profit rate than would result from the same volume of investment differently directed. What is involved is a problem of forecasting—forecasting the future trend of output and of the profit rate on investment if capital accumulation continues at its present pace. This is more difficult than the forecasting required for the purposes of ordinary compensatory spending policy, since no help can be derived from knowledge of plans already made and moreover it may be necessary to look several years ahead if the full effects of present investment are to be assessed. If the consequences of maintaining investment at its present level are wrongly forecast, intended policy is likely to go awry in both its aspects: unexpected changes in the profit rate will prevent investment from being stabilised, and the choice that has been made between future growth and present consumption will turn out to have been based on faulty factual premises.

There are also difficulties in implementing policy even if the implications of the current level and character of investment are correctly diagnosed. Thus if the agreed aim is to keep the profit rate constant, and the authorities believe that the current level of investment is higher than is consistent with this, because, say, lags in the adjustment process have caused overshooting, what is called for is a reduction in the rate at which the present type of investment is being carried out rather than any change in the character of investment. But a general policy of restraining investment, e.g. by monetary restrictions, is liable to have the undesigned result of inducing some shift towards less capital-intensive methods of production as well. If on the other hand the object of policy is to have a high investment-income ratio and a falling rate of profit, by what means is the required fall in the minimum acceptable rate of profit to be brought about? It is arguable that in the past the minimum acceptable rate of profit has adjusted itself to the actual rate of profit in the long run, but it certainly has not done so in the short run, and it has not done so sufficiently to give an average level of employment near to full employment. Manipulation of the rate of interest by monetary means will therefore presumably be needed, but the minimum acceptable rate of return on investment is affected not only by the pure rate of interest but also by risk, the structure of the capital market, and other such factors which the government cannot easily control. Moreover what is the assurance that a high level of investment will lead to a gradual and orderly decline in the profit rate rather than to a precipitate decline such as has followed investment booms in the past? The latter danger will of course be lessened if national income is stabilised through compensatory measures where necessary. But much turns also on the character and quality of the investment that is being done. It would seem, therefore, that the control over investment will need to show a fair degree of qualitative discrimination. But this will call for closer government control over the detailed working of the economy than may be politically acceptable, and it will certainly require a high degree of skill on the part of the government.

The difficulty of assessing the implications of a given level of investment and the problems this creates for the formulation of policy may be illustrated by the diverse interpretations that have been put on the post-war experience of the United States and other advanced industrial countries. Discussion of these interpretations is of interest also because of its bearing on the question whether post-war experience is to be regarded as no more than an unusually long boom or whether on the other hand circumstances have in some way changed since before the war so that the problem of the cycle no longer exists in the same form.

Broadly speaking the difficulty in advanced industrial countries since the war has been how to prevent excess demand rather than how to prevent defective demand. The experience of the United States has not been untypical in outline of that in many countries. The ratio of gross investment to income has been higher than in the years before the war and has been at a level about corresponding to that of the boom years of the 1920s. Government expenditure, including military expenditure, has also been a high proportion of national income. The ratio of consumption to national income has fallen, largely because of the heavy taxation imposed to finance government spending. In most European countries the ratio of investment to income has also in recent years been high by pre-war standards, though investment took longer to recover after the war than it did in the United States because of the problems of resettlement and the other claims on the national product (notably exports).

Since the rise in government spending in the United States has been financed by taxation rather than by borrowing, it cannot be said that the post-war boom has been directly based on government spending. Admittedly if government spending and taxation had both been reduced by the same amount, not all of the extra disposable income would have been spent and aggregate demand would on that account have tended to be lower. But the broad conclusion stands that the post-war boom in the United States, like previous booms, has been based on a high level of investment. For European countries this conclusion would require rather more qualification. But for all countries the question remains whether the present level of investment is one that can or should be maintained. For the United States and other countries that have been doing investment at a high pace for a number of years, the issue is whether diminishing returns and a slump in fixed investment may be at hand. (If government spending were to decline, the question would of course become more acute.) For some other countries, notably Great Britain, the question most commonly asked has been rather whether the investment-income ratio has not fallen short of that required to make good past arrears and keep pace with current advances in technical knowledge.

Alternative interpretations of the high level of investment that has prevailed in the United States and elsewhere may now be enumerated.

The first interpretation is that the post-war ratio of investment to income is maintainable, in the sense that it will not lead to any fall in the rate of profit on investment notwithstanding that it corresponds to that found at the top of the boom rather than over the average of the cycle before the war.[1] If this is correct, it does not imply exactly that the problem of the cycle has ceased to exist, since random disturbances will still be liable to occur and to need correction, but it does imply that there is no systematic reason why full employment should not be maintained permanently in the future without special government intervention. This line of

[1] This comparison is really with the inter-war period. Before 1914 the long-run average rate of investment to income in the United States was probably not lower than it has been in the period since 1945. It must be remembered, however, that before 1914 the rate of population growth was higher than it is now, because of immigration.

argument postulates that capital will be able to accumulate faster than in the past without suffering diminishing returns, and it therefore implies that there has been some change in the situation compared with before the war. Such a change could be: an increase in the rate of population growth (population has certainly increased faster than it did between the wars); an increase in the rate of technical progress, itself partly due, perhaps, to the assurance of full employment; a rise in the normal capital-output ratio, resulting from a capital-using bias in technical progress; or a shortening in the average length of life of capital.[1]

The second interpretation is that although the permanently maintainable investment-income ratio is no higher or not much higher than in the past, certain once-for-all factors have caused a great shortage of capital, which is still in the process of being made good. The implication of this view is that investment will ultimately fall off (unless the acceptable rate of return is reduced), but that in the meanwhile there are great advantages in allowing a high rate of investment to

[1] The line of argument described in this paragraph is the exact opposite of the 'stagnation thesis', which was advanced by Alvin H. Hansen under the influence of the great depression of the 1930s. (Cf. Alvin H. Hansen, 'Economic Progress and Declining Population Growth', *American Economic Review*, 1939, pp. 1–15.) According to the stagnation thesis, the scope for capital accumulation in the United States has undergone a permanent reduction compared with the great days of expansion before 1914, for two main reasons, (a) the decline in the rate of population growth resulting from the cessation of unrestricted immigration, and (b) the 'closing of the frontier'—the exhaustion of the scope for territorial expansion and opening up of new natural resources within the United States; as a result severe depressions like that of the 1930s may be expected to become the rule rather than the exception, unless compensating action is taken by the government. The high level of prosperity enjoyed in the United States since the war has put the stagnation thesis under a cloud. But if the stagnation thesis was too much coloured by the special circumstances of the 1930s, its opposite—the optimistic view described in the text, sometimes referred to as the 'secular exhilaration thesis'—may likewise prove to have been too much influenced by the special circumstances of the post-war period. It is worth remembering that in the 1920s also the prolonged prosperity enjoyed by the United States led many observers to believe that major fluctuations were a thing of the past.

continue. Some once-for-all factors that may be cited as having caused a shortage of capital are as follows. (i) The low level of investment during the slump of the 1930s and during the war. (ii) A once-for-all increase in population (as distinct from a higher rate of population growth). This applies to certain countries, notably Western Germany, that have absorbed a large number of immigrants. (iii) A once-for-all improvement in the state of technical knowledge. It is sometimes argued (especially with reference to Great Britain) that by the mid-1950's the removal of fear of slump had caused entrepreneurs to cast off the torpor that formerly afflicted them and take notice of the possibilities of improving methods of production. Great scope for replacing obsolescent machinery thus suddenly made itself apparent.

Even if it is held that there has been no increase in the permanently maintainable investment-income ratio and that the arrears of the type mentioned in the previous paragraph have by now been largely worked off, there is still room for further differences of interpretation. On the one hand it may be held that there is great scope for increasing the capital-intensity of production and speeding up replacement, and that therefore much is to be gained from keeping investment high and bringing about a gradual reduction in the rate of profit. Or the opposite view may be taken, that there is little such scope, in which case a rapid reduction in the rate of profit will be expected. Or a rapid reduction in the rate of profit may be expected not so much on the ground that there is no scope for increasing the capital-intensity of production but on the ground that the form actually taken by investment is not such as to take advantage of this scope but consists rather of the creation of a greater quantity of capital capacity similar in type to that already in existence.

All these shades of opinion (as well as others) have been seriously put forward or at least implied by different observers, and the corresponding conclusions drawn that the rate of investment is too high or about right or too low as the case may be. The existence of arrears of investment opportunities in the post-war years would be generally agreed,[1] but whether these have now been filled and whether there has been a permanent rise in the maintainable investment-income ratio and how great is the scope for increasing output by more capital-intensive methods in the present state of technical knowledge are all controversial questions.[2]

§ 8. Conclusions. The task ,of stabilising private investment is bound to be extremely difficult to accomplish, even if governments show greater skill and consistency in the execution of policy than they are in fact likely to. It would be unrealistic not to expect a good deal of fluctuation in private investment to continue. There will certainly be minor fluctuations associated with inventory investment and with innovations and structural changes in particular industries, and the possibility of fluctuations on a larger scale cannot be ruled out. Compensatory measures of the type described in § 2 will therefore still have to be mainly relied on in order to stabilise aggregate demand. These measures have their limitations, but they should suffice to prevent depressions of

[1] There would probably also be general agreement that the rate at which these arrears have been worked off has been kept down by the competing claims on the national product made by government spending. Had it not been for the high level of government spending for military and other purposes, taxation on profits would have been lower and less resort would have been had to physical and monetary controls on investment designed to prevent inflation. Arrears of capital formation would therefore have been made up more quickly, and there would have been more danger of an early exhaustion of investment opportunities. In this way government spending has probably contributed to prolonging the boom, notwithstanding that it has been fully paid for by taxation.

[2] The difficulties of analysis are further indicated by the forecasting dilemma that has been presented by the several contractions in activity that have occurred since the war. In the United States there have been three of these: 1949, 1954, and 1957–58. On each of these occasions fears have been expressed by some observers that the contraction would develop into a major slump. In 1949 and 1954 these fears were not fulfilled, and at the time of writing recovery from the recession of 1957–58 appears to be well under way, in the United States if not in Europe. The difficulty has been to tell whether the contractions are essentially inventory fluctuations or whether they betoken some more deep-seated tendency to capital saturation.

the damaging character experienced in the past. The mere assurance that it is the government's intention to act in this way if necessary should contribute substantially to steadying business expectations and stabilising private investment.

The danger of inflation has for so long been the paramount concern of government domestic economic policy that measures to combat deflationary tendencies (other than mild and short inventory recessions) may seem outmoded. Yet the experience of the past suggests that in the long run either private investment will not be high enough to give consistent full employment, or else alternatively private investment will have to be maintained at a level that involves a secular decline—though not necessarily a rapid decline—in the rate of profit. Past experience could be misleading if there has now been some permanent change, such as an upward shift in the consumption function or an increase in the rate of technical progress. It is possible that such a change has taken place. But it has yet to be proved.

INDEX

INDEX